THE NORMATIVE FOUNDATIONS FOR EU CRIMINAL JUSTICE

Should the European Union regulate criminal justice? This open access book explores the question forensically, establishing whether a compelling normative justification for EU action in the field exists.

It develops an integrated standard based on the perspectives of the effective allocation of regulatory authority between the EU and the Member States, representation-based political theories, and harm-based theories of criminal law. This is a work that will be welcomed not only by EU criminal law scholars, but also by practitioners, judges and policymakers.

Volume 124 in the Series Modern Studies in European Law

Modern Studies in European Law

Recent titles in this series:

The EU as a Global Digital Actor: Institutionalising Global Data Protection, Trade, and Cybersecurity
Elaine Fahey

Exporting the European Convention on Human Rights
Maria-Louiza Deftou

Judicial Authority in EU Internal Market Law: Implications for the Balance of Competences and Powers
Vilija Velyvyte

The Changing European Union: A Critical View on the Role of Law and the Courts
Edited by Tamara Capeta, Iris Goldner Lang and Tamara Perisin

The Structural Transformation of European Private Law: A Critique of Juridical Hermeneutic
Leone Niglia

The Future of EU Constitutionalism
Edited by Matej Avbelj

The Changing Role of Citizens in EU Democratic Governance
Edited by Davor Jancic

The EU and the Baltic Sea Area
Edited by Allan Rosas and Henrik Ringbom

The Evolving Governance of EU Competition Law in a Time of Disruptions: A Constitutional Perspective
Edited by Carlo Maria Colombo, Kathryn Wright and Mariolina Eliantonio

The European Integrated Border Management: Frontex, Human Rights, and International Responsibility
Giulia Raimondo

Private Autonomy in EU Internal Market Law: Parameters of its Protection and Limitation
Rufat Babayev

Free Movement and Welfare Access in the European Union: Re-Balancing Conflicting Interests in Citizenship Jurisprudence
Victoria Hooton

EU Trade and Investment Treaty-Making Post-Lisbon: Moving Beyond Mixity
Gesa Kübek

The Normative Foundations for EU Criminal Justice: Powers, Limits and Justifications
Jacob Öberg

For the complete list of titles in this series see www.bloomsbury.com/uk/series/modern-studies-in-european-law/

The Normative Foundations for EU Criminal Justice

Powers, Limits and Justifications

Jacob Öberg

•HART•
OXFORD • LONDON • NEW YORK • NEW DELHI • SYDNEY

HART PUBLISHING

Bloomsbury Publishing Plc

Kemp House, Chawley Park, Cumnor Hill, Oxford, OX2 9PH, UK

1385 Broadway, New York, NY 10018, USA

29 Earlsfort Terrace, Dublin 2, Ireland

HART PUBLISHING, the Hart/Stag logo, BLOOMSBURY and the Diana logo are trademarks of Bloomsbury Publishing Plc

First published in Great Britain 2024

A catalogue record for this book is available from the British Library.

A catalogue record for this book is available from the Library of Congress.

ISBN: HB: 978-1-50996-233-4
ePDF: 978-1-50996-235-8
ePub: 978-1-50996-234-1

Typeset by Compuscript Ltd, Shannon

ACKNOWLEDGEMENTS

This book is the outcome of a project that began around four years ago on a rewarding postdoctoral fellowship in Lund between 2018–2020 where I worked on the subject of the constitutional foundations for the EU's criminal procedure. Probing into this area I started to think more critically about the normative justifications for the EU's competence in criminal procedure. From this, I embarked on an intellectual journey to develop a more holistic theory or theoretical framework for testing the legitimacy of EU criminal law.

In 2021, I was awarded with a very generous research sabbatical grant from Riksbankens Jubileumsfond which relieved me of all teaching and management duties for 12 months, allowing me to travel abroad to the Netherlands with my whole family and pursue this research project full time. In this connection I would like to mention in particular the support and feedback from Marja-Liisa Oberg, Claudio Fassio, Eleonor Kristofferson, Susanne Strand, Thomas Denk and Ulf Linderfalk, who all offered very important feedback to the drafting of my subsequently successful research application.

I spent an extremely rewarding academic year between September 2022 and July 2023 as a Visting Fellow at the Amsterdam Centre for European Law and Governance where most of the writing and research that would later become this book were completed. I am primarily indebted to Christina Eckes (then Director of the centre) for facilitating my research stay at the UvA and for providing an inspiring environment for developing and presenting my initial ideas. I would also wish to extend a particular acknowledgement to my friend and colleague Jannemieke Ouwerkerk (Leiden University) who contributed significantly to making my research stay in the Netherlands rewarding. In addition to organising a seminar where I could present some ideas for the book, she initiated and co-organised a larger conference at Leiden University with Jeroen den Voorde, myself and Konstantinos Zoumpoulakis on legal interests and public goods which was one of the highlights of my research stay. I would also wish to extend my gratitude to Sjarai Lestrade and Jasper Krommendijk who provided me with a wonderful opportunity to visit Nijmegen and present some of the ideas in the book. In this connection I would also like to mention the friendly discussions on EU criminal law I had at ACELG with Thomas Vandamme, Kati Cseres, Ivana Isailović and Sergey Vasiliev.

I am also particularly grateful to my current employer and in particular Head of Department, Hanne Søndergaard Birkenmose, at University of Southern Denmark who hired me as a full Professor in EU law and also provided me with the opportunity and time needed to finish the book before I took up my duties at my new employer.

Again, for a second time Sinead Moloney and her team at Hart Publishing: Tom Adams and Sasha Jawed deserve a special acknowledgment. Sinead and her team obviously had an important role in turning this manuscript into a book by giving me the time, confidence (by offering a contract for a book that was very far from complete) and necessary editing and linguistic support to complete this project. All involved made the production of the book a very smooth journey.

I am glad to acknowledge that some of the chapters are based on my previous publications: some sections of Chapter 1 were published as 'Normative justifications of EU criminal law: European public goods and transnational interests' (2021) 27 *European Law Journal*, pp 408–425, while parts of Chapter 3 were published as 'Trust in the Law? Mutual Recognition as a Justification to Domestic Criminal Procedure in (2020) 16 *European Constitutional Law Review*, pp 33–62. Furthermore, some parts of Chapter 5 were published as 'The European Public Prosecutor: Quintessential supranational criminal law?' 28 (2021) *Maastricht Journal of European and Comparative Law*, pp 164–181.

I would furthermore like to thank all those who helped me during my post-doctoral fellowship, my research stay in the Netherlands and after, by reviewing my work, providing feedback on presentations, and helping me generally in the pursuit of my academic career. In relation to my work specifically about the EU's competence in substantive criminal law and criminal procedure, comprehensive discussions with Steve Peers, Valsamis Mitsilegas, Annika Suominen, Stephen Coutts, Jörg Monar, Ermioni Xanthoupolou, Gerard Conway, Isabella Mancini, Björn Lundqvist, Pedro Caeiro, Nina Peršak and Estella Baker have helped in developing the argument in Chapter 3 and Chapter 4. In respect of Chapters 5 and 6 on EPPO, Eurojust and Europol, I have greatly benefited from discussions with Christian Kaunert, Ester Herlin-Karnell, Sarah Leonard, Nicholas Franssen, Joana De Deus Pereira, Thomas Elholm, Michael Levi, Hartmut Aden and Helena Farrand Carapicio.

The late Chris Harding deserves a very special acknowledgment. Co-authoring an article on EU criminal law with Chris on the ship of fools and our many intellectually and morally rewarding discussions on the foundations and legitimacy of criminal law has helped in shaping a lot of my thinking around this widely changing EU policy field. All in all, I do miss Chris very much, not only as a scholar but also as a decent, kind and great human being who left us far too early. I think Chris would have enjoyed this book and it is dedicated to him.

For linguistic support I would like particularly to acknowledge the great contributions of David Stott for smooth and forensic language correction and editing of my book. I am also very indebted to my close family; Monica, Göran, Johann, Oscar, Stina, Curt who have stood by me since I started on my academic path fourteen years ago.

Finally, and most importantly, I would like to acknowledge the outstanding contribution of my wife Marja-Liisa, my sons August and Teodor and my daughter Olivia to this project. Marja-Liisa's emotional and heart-warming support was indispensable for the completion of the book. Her key contribution to this project is that she gently reminded me regularly of the fact that I am not only a researcher but also a person and a partner to someone else. Having said that she also gave me the support for writing this book, including assuming responsibility for our common tasks which I admittedly neglected during phases of this project. While we have an academic life in common, the most important thing we share is a family life. Our daughter Olivia was born in February 2022 in the middle of the project, adding to the joy of August and Teodor and the journey with them so far has been indescribably rewarding. I feel very privileged to have such a lovely family. I believe their presence and gradual development into small people and individuals undoubtedly helped me in completing this book by making my life more meaningful. Most importantly, they reminded me that the most significant things in life are happening outside academia. I would like to end these acknowledgements by dedicating this book to Marja-Liisa, August, Teodor, and Olivia. Without them, I would not have written this book.

Jacob Öberg
Odense, 9 February 2024

CONTENTS

TABLE OF CASES

Court of Justice of the European Union

European Court of Human Rights

Case law from national courts

National constitutional courts

TABLE OF LEGISLATION

Treaties

EU Conventions

Directives

Council decisions and acts

Regulations

European Council documents

Council documents

Council legislative negotiation documents

Commission documents

European Parliament documents

Documents from the intergovernmental European Convention

Opinions of national parliaments

Press releases

1

Introduction

I. Context and Justifications for EU Integration of Criminal Law

EU policy-making in criminal law is a matter of significant public concern for EU citizens and the Member States alike. The exercise of EU public powers in the fields of criminal law and law enforcement has tangible and adverse consequences for the liberties and well-being of individuals.[1] Criminal policies and law enforcement are vehicles of social control which seriously restrict their fundamental right to movement and other fundamental freedoms. Furthermore, EU cooperation in the area of criminal law touches upon core functions of statehood including 'core state powers'[2] such as the safeguarding of internal security and law enforcement.[3] In a specific respect, criminal law reflects a value system which is also the source of its legitimacy in a given society.[4] Given all this, it is apparent that criminal law traditionally has belonged to the realm of national competence and been subject to 'intergovernmental'[5] governance.[6]

Nonetheless, developments in this area in the last 30 years suggest that criminal law is no longer on the periphery of European integration. Whilst some have

[1] F Trauner and A Ripoll Servent, 'The Communitarization of the Area of Freedom, Security and Justice: Why Institutional Change does not Translate into Policy Change' (2016) 54 *Journal of Common Market Studies* 1417; N Walker, 'In Search of the Area of Freedom, Security and Justice: A Constitutional Odyssey' in N Walker (ed), *Europe's Area of Freedom, Security, and Justice* (Oxford: Oxford University Press, 2004) 3, 5–7.

[2] P Genschel and M Jachtenfuchs, 'From market integration to core state powers: the Eurozone crisis, the refugee crisis and integration theory' (2018) 56 *Journal of Common Market Studies* 178; P Genschel and M Jachtenfuchs, 'More Integration, Less Federation: The European Integration of Core State Powers' (2016) 23 *Journal of European Public Policy* 42.

[3] L Besselink, 'Sovereignty, Criminal Law and the New European Context' in P Alldridge and C Brants (eds), *Personal Autonomy, the Private Sphere and Criminal Law: A Comparative Study* (Oxford: Hart Publishing, 2001) 93; German Federal Constitutional Court 2009, *Lisbon Judgment*, Case 2 BvE 2/08, 5/08, 2 BvR 1010/08, 1022/08, 1259.

[4] *Lisbon Judgment* (n 3), paras 249, 252–53, 355.

[5] See the seminal work on intergovernmentalism by S Hoffmann, 'Obstinate or Obsolete? The Fate of the Nation State and the Case of Western Europe' (1966) 95 *Daedalus* 862; A Moravcsik, *The Choice for Europe: Social Purpose and State Power from Messina to Maastricht* (Ithaca/New York: Cornell University Press, 1998).

[6] C Fijnaut, 'Police Co-operation and the Area of Freedom, Security and Justice' in N Walker (ed), *Europe's Area of Freedom, Security, and Justice* (Oxford: Oxford University Press, 2004), 242.

claimed that the integration of criminal law as a 'core state power'[7] is indicative of the notion of 'new intergovernmentalism',[8] 'intensive transgovernmentalism'[9] or 'new institutionalism',[10] none of these theories can satisfactorily explain the significant institutional and policy changes that have taken place in the field of criminal law since the Lisbon Treaty. Paradoxically, in the field of criminal law, comprehensive integration driven by the EU institutions has taken place, embracing new substantive areas and actors despite the fact that the policy area embodies high sovereignty and national identity costs for the Member States.[11]

It is conversely proposed that supranational governance is the most apposite characterisation of developments in this field. Drawing on insights from a body of literature in EU law[12] and political science,[13] the key criteria for assessing the depth of supranational integration include the scope, type and nature of EU competences, the mode and formal rules of decision-making, forms of oversight by supranational bodies, the effectiveness of the decisions taken by EU institutions as well as the intensity of the legal measures adopted at EU level. There are particularly two traits of development in this area which should be emphasised as prima facie evidence of a gradual supranationalisation of the field of criminal law. First, it appears clear that the supranational EU institutions have gained stronger powers after the Lisbon Treaty and that, today, decision-making in the area of criminal law as a whole is governed by the ordinary decision-making procedure and qualified majority voting.[14] Moreover, the enforcement

[7] Genschel and Jachtenfuchs 'More Integration, Less Federation' (n 2).

[8] See CJ Bickerton, D Hodson and U Puetter (eds), *The New Intergovernmentalism: States and Supranational Actors in the Post-Maastricht Era* (Oxford: Oxford University Press, 2015).

[9] S Lavenex, 'Justice and Home Affairs: Communitarization with Hesitation' in H Wallace, MA Pollack and AR Young (eds), *Policy-making in the European Union* (Oxford: Oxford University Press, 2010) 457.

[10] Trauner and Ripoll Servant (n 1).

[11] Genschel and Jachtenfuchs, 'More Integration, Less Federation' (n 2); TA Börzel and T Risse, 'From the Euro to the Schengen Crises: European Integration Theories, Politicization, and Identity Politics' (2018) 25 *Journal of European Public Policy* 83; F Schimmelfennig, 'What's the News in "New Intergovernmentalism"? A Critique of Bickerton, Hodson and Puetter' (2015) 53 *Journal of Common Market Studies* 723.

[12] R Dehousse and J Weiler, 'The Legal Dimension' in W Wallace (ed), *The Dynamics of European Integration* (London/New York: Pinter Publishers, 1990) 242; P Pescatore, *Law of Integration* (Leiden: AW Sijthoff, 1974, English translation); Walker (n 1); M Cappelletti, M Seccombe and J Weiler, *Integration Through Law: Europe and the American Federal Experience* (Berlin/New York: De Gruyter, 1986).

[13] A Stone Sweet and W Sandholtz, 'European integration and supranational governance' (1997) 4 *Journal of European Public Policy* 297.

[14] S Peers, 'Mission Accomplished? EU Justice and Home Affairs Law after the Treaty of Lisbon' (2011) 48 *Common Market Law Review* 661; V Mitsilegas, *EU Criminal Law after Lisbon: Rights, Trust and the Transformation of Justice in Europe* (Oxford: Hart Publishing, 2016). Intergovernmental decision-making nonetheless remains by national vetoes for certain sensitive issues in this area, including operational police cooperation (Art 87(3) of the Consolidated Version of the Treaty on the Functioning of the European Union (TFEU) [2010] OJ C 83/47), operation of law enforcement in foreign jurisdictions (Art 89 TFEU) as well as the decision to create the European Public Prosecutor's Office (Art 86 TFEU).

powers which have been delegated to Europol, Eurojust and the European Public Prosecutor's Office (EPPO) are such as are associated with the core areas of State sovereignty: policing powers, law enforcement and prosecution competences.[15] There is also tentative evidence from recent research on integration in the field of criminal law and policing which suggests that decision-making dynamics and general policy developments indicate stronger supranational governance of the area.[16] It thus appears that the development of EU criminal law indicates a broader shift from a rationale of 'cooperation' to one of 'integration' of national criminal justice systems along functional lines[17] coherent with the traditional integration theories.[18]

The transformation of EU criminal law to a more supranational and integrated policy area, however, imposes requirements on higher standards of legitimacy for the EU's legislative activities in the field as compared to an intergovernmental regime and[19] raises questions regarding the rationale underpinning EU criminal law within the context of a multi-level polity.[20] The following section offers first a more descriptive account for three different rationales and drivers of EU criminal law since the Maastricht Treaty by reviewing key legal and political developments in this area. Thereafter it proceeds to sketch out a normative argument for legitimate justifications for EU criminal law based on European public goods[21] and transnational interests.[22]

[15] See *Lisbon Judgment* (n 3) paras 252–53, 355–62; Besselink (n 3) 101–16 for an outline of such a sovereignty discourse.

[16] J Öberg, 'Exit, Voice and Consensus – A Legal and Political Analysis of the Emergency Brake in EU Criminal Policy' (2021) 46 *European Law Review* 506; S Leonard and C Kaunert, 'The Development of Europol's External Relations: Towards Supranationalism?' (2021) 28 *Maastricht Journal of European and Comparative Law* 229.

[17] L Lindberg, *The political dynamics of European economic integration* (Stanford: Stanford University Press, 1963); E Haas, *The uniting of Europe: political, social, and economical forces, 1950–1957* (Stanford: Stanford University Press,1958) for seminal works on functionalism.

[18] See J Monar, 'Eurojust and the European Public Prosecutor Perspective: From Cooperation to Integration in EU Criminal Justice?' (2013) 14 *Perspectives on European Politics and Society* 339, 343–50; J Öberg, 'Guest Editorial: EU Agencies in Transnational Criminal Enforcement: From a Coordinated Approach to an Integrated EU Criminal Justice' (2021) 28 *Maastricht Journal of European and Comparative Law* 155 for this claim.

[19] V Mitsilegas 'European prosecution between cooperation and integration: The European Public Prosecutor's Office and the rule of law' (2021) 28 *Maastricht Journal of European and Comparative Law* 245.

[20] C Harding and J Banach-Gutierrez, 'The emergent EU criminal policy: identifying the species' (2012) 37 *European Law Review* 758.

[21] S Coutts, 'Supranational public wrongs: The limitations and possibilities of European criminal law and a European community' (2017) 54 *Common Market Law Review* 771.

[22] It is labelled by A Somek, 'The Argument From Transnational Effects I: Representing Outsiders Through Freedom of Movement' (2010) 16 *European Law Journal* 315 as 'transnational effects' whilst C Joerges and J Neyer ('From intergovernmental bargaining to deliberative processes: The constitutionalisation of comitology' (1997) 3 *European Law Journal* 273) term it 'deliberative supranationalism'. 'Transnational interests' is used as a term to bridge these accounts to capture the normative basis for EU intervention in these instances.

II. A Descriptive Account of the Existing Legitimating Rationales for EU Criminal Law

A close analysis of the evolution of EU criminal law over the past 30 years suggests that it is possible to infer three principal drivers for law and policy-making in this area: 'security' for EU citizens; ensuring the effectiveness of EU policies and subsequently a 'rights-based approach' to EU criminal policy. It is appropriate to review the journey of EU criminal law[23] through the lens of these rationales commencing with criminal law as an instrumental tool for enforcing EU policy.

The principle of effective, proportionate and dissuasive sanctions for the purpose of enforcement of EU obligations encapsulates the 'effectiveness' rationale for EU action.[24] This statement first appeared in the prominent *Greek Maize* judgment in 1989 where the Court of Justice ruled on the use of criminal law based on Member State obligations under Article 4(3) TEU.[25] The Court held that whilst the choice of penalties remains within the Member States' discretion, they must ensure that infringements of EU law are criminalised under conditions which are similar to those applicable to infringements of national law of a similar nature and that the penalties are effective, proportionate and dissuasive.[26] Effectiveness has subsequently (prior to the Lisbon Treaty) appeared as a justification for EU competence in criminal law in the Court of Justice's seminal rulings in *Environmental Crimes*[27] and *Ship-Source Pollution*[28] where it recognised a self-standing Community criminal law competence on the premise that criminalisation of infringements of EU rules (on environmental protection) would be essential for the 'effective' implementation of that EU policy.[29]

Post-Lisbon, we can ascertain that 'effectiveness' continues to be the primary justification for shaping policy in respect of EU 'regulatory criminal law'.[30] Along

[23] C Harding and J Öberg, 'The journey of EU criminal law on the ship of fools – what are the implications for supranational governance of EU criminal justice agencies?' (2021) 28 *Maastricht Journal of European and Comparative Law* 192.

[24] See M Dougan, 'From the Velvet Glove to the Iron Fist: Criminal Sanctions for the Enforcement of Union Law' in M Cremona (ed), *Compliance and the Enforcement of EU Law* (Oxford: Oxford University Press, 2012) for a comprehensive analysis.

[25] This is the principle of loyalty which requires that 'The Member States shall take any appropriate measures … to ensure fulfilment of the obligations arising out of the Treaties …' (Art 4(3) 2nd para of the Consolidated Version of the Treaty on European Union (TEU) [2010] OJ C 83/13).

[26] Case 68/88 *Commission v Greece* EU:C:1989:281, paras 23–24. See also Case C-240/90 *Germany v Commission* EU:C:1992:408, Opinion of AG Jacobs, para 12.

[27] Case C-176/03 *Commission v Council (Environmental Crimes)* EU:C:2005:542.

[28] Case C-440/05 *Commission v Council (Ship-Source Pollution)* EU:C:2007:625.

[29] Case C-176/03 *Environmental Crimes* (n 27) para 48; Case C-440/05 *Ship-Source Pollution* (n 28) paras 24–25, 28–39.

[30] Directive (EU) 2017/1371 of the European Parliament and of the Council of 5 July 2017 on the fight against fraud to the Union's financial interests by means of criminal law [2017] OJ L 198/29; Directive (EU) 2018/1673 of the European Parliament and of the Council of 23 October 2018 on combating money laundering by criminal law [2018] OJ L 284/22; Directive (EU) 2019/713 of the European Parliament and of the Council of 17 April 2019 on combating fraud and counterfeiting of non-cash

these lines, Article 83(2) TFEU expresses the rationale for EU intervention in criminal law covering all criminal law provisions aimed at achieving the political objectives of the Union: protection of the environment, protection of the financial market and the four freedoms.[31] It contains per definition criminal law measures which are 'essential to ensure the effective implementation of a Union policy in an area which has been subject to harmonisation measures'.[32] The Commission has been driving policy here, striving to demonstrate the added value of criminalisation at EU level and focused primarily on 'functional' criminalisation.[33] In the literature, the added value of EU criminalisation has been criticised. It has been observed that the EU has decided to take a stand against certain conduct in the field of environmental law and market abuse, even if the evidence to support these legislative initiatives was insufficient to sustain the claim that criminal law is essential for the enforcement of these policies.[34] The EU's action in such cases could potentially be explained with reference to the Union's need to communicate a common sense of justice and expressing the Union's common values. The legitimacy of EU action in criminal law on expressive grounds in the absence of a clear Treaty mandate has, however, been challenged.[35]

The emergence of a supranational agency in the field of criminal law, ie the European Public Prosecutor's Office (EPPO), also sprang from the emphasis on the enforcement of existing EU policies and concerns over misappropriation of EU funds. It had been perceived that Member States' past records in protecting EU funds were insufficient and that a European Public Prosecutor could address these shortcomings.[36] The fashioning of such a body was, however, a contested

means of payment and replacing Council Framework Decision 2001/413/JHA [2019] OJ L 123/18; Directive 2014/57/EU of the European Parliament and of the Council of 16 April 2014 on criminal sanctions for market abuse [2014] OJ L 173/79; Directive 2014/62/EU of the European Parliament and of the Council of 15 May 2014 on the protection of the euro and other currencies against counterfeiting by criminal law and replacing Council Framework Decision 2000/383/JHA [2014] OJ L 151/1; Council Doc 10366/23 re Council 'General Approach, Proposal for a Directive of the European Parliament and of the Council on the definition of criminal offences and penalties for the violation of Union restrictive measures'.

[31] See Commission, 'Communication from the Commission to the European Parliament, the Council, the European Economic and Social Committee and the Committee of the Regions – Towards an EU Criminal Policy: Ensuring the effective implementation of EU policies through criminal law' COM (2011) 573 final, 10–11; see M Fletcher, B Gilmour and R Lööf, *EU Criminal Law and Justice* (Cheltenham: Edward Elgar Publishing, 2008) 183.

[32] J Öberg, 'Union Regulatory Criminal Law Competence after Lisbon Treaty' (2011) 19 *European Journal of Crime, Criminal Law and Criminal Justice* 289.

[33] See COM (2011) 573 final (n 31).

[34] J Öberg, *Limits to EU Powers: A Case Study of EU Regulatory Criminal Law* (Oxford: Hart Publishing, 2017) ch 8; I Wieczorek, *The Legitimacy of EU Criminal Law* (Oxford: Hart Publishing, 2020).

[35] See J Iontcheva Turner, 'The Expressive Dimension of EU Criminal Law' (2012) 60 *American Journal of Comparative Law* 555, 557, 564–74; T Elholm, 'Does EU Criminal Cooperation Necessarily Mean Increased Repression?' (2009) 17 *European Journal of Crime, Criminal Law and Criminal Justice* 191, 224–25; Öberg (n 34).

[36] See M Wade, *EuroNEEDs – Evaluating the need for and the needs of a European Criminal Justice System – Preliminary Report* (Freiburg: Max Planck Institute for Foreign and International Criminal Law, 2011) for an extensive analysis of the need for a European Public Prosecutor.

process. The seeds for the EPPO were considered already in the 1990s by work of the academics in the Corpus Iuris Project which had suggested a scheme of measures including a single set of offences applicable throughout the Union and the establishment of a European centralised prosecutor.[37] It is, however, well known that the ambitious vision of the EPPO as an integrated prosecution agency must be singled out as an extremely sensitive issue in political terms.[38] Member States have voiced fierce opposition towards the establishment of such an office, viewing the EPPO as a further encroachment on national sovereignty, and expressed concerns over the far-reaching implications of such an office on the functioning of national criminal justice systems.[39] Despite these objections, the Lisbon Treaty created by means of Article 86 TFEU – following the recommendations of Working Group X – a clear remit to establish a European Public Prosecutor's office. On the basis of this mandate, the Member States finally established – on the basis of enhanced cooperation – the EPPO in 2017. The EPPO is a milestone in European integration as this is the first European agency which has been granted powers to independently prosecute crimes (against the Union's financial interests) in Member State courts. The key rationale for creating the EPPO is 'effectiveness' as it is claimed that the Member States' efforts to date have been inadequate to effectively protect the Union's budget.[40]

The post-Lisbon decisions of the Court of Justice in *Taricco*[41] and *Melloni* also illustrate the Court's concern with effective enforcement of EU rules. In *Taricco* the Court considered the role of time bars to prosecution in the context of a case that involved fraud in relation to VAT. The Court was clear that the time limits applicable under Italian law should not obstruct the prosecution of the EU fraud, giving preference to the principle of effective enforcement.[42] In *Melloni* the Spanish court in charge of executing the arrest warrant considered refusing the surrender of a person on the basis that Spanish constitutional law offered stronger protection against judgments *in absentia* than that available in the executing state (Italy).[43]

[37] See M Delmas Marty and JAE Vervaele, *The Implementation of the Corpus Juris in the Member States – Penal Provisions for the Protection of European Finances* (Antwerpen: Intersentia, 2001).

[38] A Weyembergh and C Brière, 'Towards a European Public Prosecutor', Policy paper for the European Parliament, LIBE Committee, November 2016, 9.

[39] See eg the yellow card issued by national parliaments against the EPPO Proposal: Commission, 'Communication from the Commission to the European Parliament, the Council and the National Parliaments on the review of the proposal for a Council Regulation on the establishment of the European Public Prosecutor's Office with regard to the principle of subsidiarity, in accordance with Protocol No 2' COM (2013) 851 final; see also the divided opinions among the members of the Convention, Secretariat of the European Convention, 'Draft sections of Part Three with comments' (CONV 727/03), 27 May 2003, 33–34.

[40] See Council Regulation (EU) 2017/1939 of 12 October 2017 implementing enhanced cooperation on the establishment of the European Public Prosecutor's Office [2017] OJ L 283/1 (EPPO Regulation); J Öberg, 'The European Public Prosecutor: Quintessential Supranational Criminal Law?' (2021) 28 *Maastricht Journal of European and Comparative Law* 164.

[41] Case C-105/14 *Taricco and Others* EU: C:2015:555.

[42] ibid, paras 36–58.

[43] Council Framework Decision of 13 June 2002 on the European Arrest Warrant and the Surrender Procedures between Member States [2002] OJ L 190/1, Art 5(1).

The Court of Justice rejected the possibility of conferring additional powers on the executing judicial authority, holding that Article 53 of the Charter could not be construed as giving priority to the national (constitutional) standard of protection over the application of provisions of EU law as this would compromise the primacy and effectiveness of EU law.[44]

Moving on to pan-European security as a rationale for EU criminal law, it is apposite to commence with the TREVI cooperation as a precursor to the provisions on police and judicial cooperation in the Maastricht Treaty.[45] TREVI was set up in 1976 by the then 12 EU Member States to counter terrorism and to coordinate policing in the EU. The group's work was based on intergovernmental cooperation on security between the participating states excluding the supranational EU institutions – the Commission and the European Parliament.[46] 'Security'-oriented rationales were also behind the formal inclusion of criminal justice cooperation as a 'compensatory' measure in the EU integration project.[47] The provisions on judicial cooperation in the Maastricht Treaty were a consequential effect of the construction of an internal market and the gradual opening of national borders which facilitated the pursuit of transnational organised crime.[48] Member States considered that this 'collective action' problem could not be addressed by them alone but had to be addressed by common action leading them to establish a general EU judicial cooperation mechanism.[49] Securitised EU criminal law has been driven by intergovernmental actors, where leading roles have been played by the European Council and the JHA Council,[50] and agenda-setting events such as the Tampere,[51] Hague[52] and Stockholm[53] programmes.

Securitised criminalisation has been prevailing with respect to the area of the 'eurocrimes' in pre-Lisbon legislative activities expressly addressing the 'collective action' problem arising from cross-border criminality.[54] Security-oriented

[44] Case C-399/11 *Melloni* EU:C: 2013:107, paras 55–63.

[45] Containing Title VI on the 'Provisions on Police and Judicial Cooperation in Criminal Matters' of the Consolidated Version of the Treaty on European Union [2002] OJ C 325/5.

[46] The name 'Trevi' has been open to many interpretations but is most likely an acronym for 'terrorism, radicalism, extremism and international violence'; T Bunyan, 'Trevi, Europol and the European state', Statewatch (available at www.statewatch.org/media/documents/news/handbook-trevi.pdf); F König and F Trauner, 'From Trevi to Europol: Germany's role in the integration of EU police cooperation' (2021) 43 *Journal of European Integration* 175.

[47] Commission, White Paper to the European Council, *Completing the Internal Market* (Milan, 28–29 June 1985), COM (85) 310 final, paras 11, 29, 53–56.

[48] E Baker, 'Governing Through Crime – the Case of the European Union' (2010) 17 *European Journal of Criminology* 187, 190–92; CONV 426/02, 'Final report of Working Group X "Freedom, Security and Justice"', Brussels, 2 December 2002, 9–10.

[49] Art 29 of the pre-Lisbon version the Treaty on European Union (n 45).

[50] P Craig, *The Lisbon Treaty: Law, Politics and Treaty Reform* (Oxford: Oxford University Press, 2011) 370–73 explains the leading role of Member States in driving forward policy.

[51] Council, 'Presidency Conclusions, Tampere European Council, 15–16 October 1999'.

[52] Council, 'From General Secretariat to Delegations: The Hague Programme: strengthening freedom, security and justice in the European Union' 16054/04 (2004).

[53] Council, 'The Stockholm Programme: An Open and Secure Europe Serving and Protecting Citizens' [2010] OJ C 115/1.

[54] See CONV 426/02 (n 48) 9–10.

rationales are equally relevant in accounting for the incremental rise of EU criminal justice agencies as a response to the threats of organised transnational crime.[55] External shocks such as 9/11, and the terrorist attacks in Madrid in 2004 and in London 2005, contributed to make the EU's security agenda more visible and triggered the creation of two central agencies in EU criminal justice: Europol and Eurojust.[56] The Member States were the leading players in shaping law in this area. The Tampere European Council in 1999 laid the foundations for the creation for the European Judicial Cooperation Unit (Eurojust) as an EU agency. Eurojust was set up formally in 2002 by a JHA Council decision, with the mission of strengthening the fight against serious and organised crime by coordinating cooperation in criminal matters between the competent authorities.[57] Europol was even more a Member State-driven entity, created as an intergovernmental organisation through a convention,[58] placing it outside of the Community legal framework.[59] The Member States were also responsible for amending the Europol Convention and subsequently pushing through the Decision on Europol, which transformed Europol from an intergovernmental organisation into a Union agency.[60] The Member States' leading influence in shaping the activities of Europol and Eurojust is substantiated by a detailed analysis of the powers of those two agencies. Eurojust and Europol have not been envisaged to have any executive powers to take decisions that required national prosecution or police authorities to commence, conduct, coordinate or end criminal investigations.[61]

Security is still also a pertinent consideration after Lisbon in framing EU criminal policy. The EU's institutional framework for addressing the 'eurocrimes' through common action is now enshrined in Article 83(1) TFEU, listing 10 offences[62] for which the EU is entitled to establish minimum rules concerning the

[55] Arts 29 and 30 of the pre-Lisbon version of the Treaty on European Union (n 45).

[56] JD Occhipinti 'Still Moving Toward a European FBI? Re-Examining the Politics of EU Police Cooperation, Intelligence and National Security' (2015) 30 *Intelligence and National Security* 234; J Monar, 'Eurojust and the European Public Prosecutor Perspective' (n 18) 342–43.

[57] See Tampere European Council (n 51) para 46.

[58] Council Act of 26 July 1995 drawing up the Convention based on Article K.3 of the Treaty on European Union, on the establishment of a European Police Office (Europol Convention) [1995] OJ C 316/1.

[59] M Den Boer and N Walker, 'European Policing after 1992' (1993) 31 *Journal of Common Market Studies* 8.

[60] Council Decision of 6 April 2009 establishing the European Police Office (Europol) [2009] OJ L 121/37; M Busuioc and M Groenleer, 'Beyond Design: The Evolution of Europol and Eurojust' (2013) 14 *Perspectives on European Politics and Society* 289.

[61] See eg the Europol Regulation (EU) 2016/794 of the European Parliament and of the Council of 11 May 2016 on the European Union Agency for Law Enforcement Cooperation (Europol) and replacing and repealing Council Decisions 2009/371/JHA, 2009/934/JHA, 2009/935/JHA, 2009/936/JHA and 2009/968/JHA [2016] OJ L 135/53, Art 6; Regulation (EU) 2018/1727 of the European Parliament and of the Council of 14 November 2018 on the European Union Agency for Criminal Justice Cooperation (Eurojust), and replacing and repealing Council Decision 2002/187/JHA [2018] OJ L 295/138, Arts 3 and 4.

[62] 'Terrorism, trafficking in human beings and sexual exploitation of women and children, illicit drug trafficking, illicit arms trafficking, money laundering, corruption, counterfeiting of means of payment, computer crime and organised crime.'

definition of criminal offences and sanctions. In this instance, criminal law has been used in an expressive way to provide a sense of safety to citizens.[63] Security rationales have also been decisive in the development towards an amended Eurojust Decision,[64] the revised Eurojust Regulation of 2018[65] and the new Europol Regulation adopted in 2016.[66] The outcome to date has been a process of commandeering of the national infrastructures of criminal law to serve a repressive agenda of criminal enforcement.[67]

The emphasis on security has been furthermore relevant in the development of EU judicial cooperation and the principle of mutual recognition. Instead of endeavouring to harmonise national domestic criminal law as a first option, Member States agreed at the 1999 Tampere European Council to introduce the principle of mutual recognition as the main driver for EU criminal policy.[68] The novel EU mutual recognition instruments departed distinctively from traditional international judicial cooperation by being envisaged to function on the basis of quasi-automaticity and mutual trust.[69] However, the implementation of the principle of mutual recognition, most notably through the high-profile European Arrest Warrant, led to controversy and placed great strain on the confidence of Member States in each other's criminal justice systems.[70]

In order to address these concerns of distrust, here we turn to the third driver of EU criminal policy – the EU has developed a wider criminal policy embodying protection for individual rights.[71] The Hague Programme in 2004 had already recognised that common minimum procedural standards on defence and victim rights could strengthen mutual trust between the authorities in Member States responsible for executing mutual recognition requests and thus the operation of mutual recognition.[72] In 2004 the European Commission proposed an ambitious Framework Decision covering a broad range of procedural rights in criminal proceedings. Under the pre-Lisbon provisions of Article 31(1)(c) of the Treaty on European Union, there was no explicit competence to harmonise procedural

[63] Turner (n 35).

[64] Council Decision 2009/426/JHA of 16 December 2008 on the strengthening of Eurojust and amending Decision 2002/187/JHA setting up Eurojust with a view to reinforcing the fight against serious crime [2009] OJ L 138/14.

[65] Eurojust Regulation (EU) 2018/1727 (n 61).

[66] Europol Regulation (EU) 2016/794 (n 61).

[67] Elholm (n 35); Harding and Öberg (n 23).

[68] Tampere European Council (n 51) point 33.

[69] Commission, 'Communication from the Commission to the Council and the European Parliament, Mutual Recognition of Final Decisions in Criminal Matters,' COM (2000) 495 final, 2.

[70] V Mitsilegas, 'The Constitutional Implications of Mutual Recognition in Criminal Matters in the EU' (2006) 43 *Common Market Law Review*, 1277; S Alegre and M Leaf, 'Mutual recognition in European judicial cooperation: A step too far too soon? Case study – The European arrest warrant' (2004) 10 *European Law Journal*, 200; S Peers, 'Mutual Recognition and Criminal Law in the European Union: Has the Council Got it Wrong?' (2004) 41 *Common Market Law Review* 5.

[71] See Baker, 'Governing Through Crime' (n 48) 188–96; Mitsilegas, *EU Criminal Law after Lisbon* (n 14) ch 7.

[72] See 'Hague Programme' (n 52) point 3.3.1–3.3.2.

standards. The Commission, nonetheless, proposed a broad reading of the competence, claiming that such standards would be necessary to promote mutual confidence across the EU.[73] Several Member States, however, rejected implicit EU competence in the field of criminal procedure, and in conjunction with the unanimity requirement in the Council this made agreement on the Framework Decision impossible among the Member States.[74]

The entering into force of the Lisbon Treaty (2007) signals a remarkable evolution of EU criminal law from the European Community viewed primarily as an economic organisation to the EU conceived as a serious penal actor.[75] After Lisbon, there is now an explicit competence in Article 82 TFEU and Article 83 TFEU to harmonise national criminal procedure and substantive criminal law. The Lisbon Treaty in addition provides for important institutional reforms. The introduction of qualified majority voting in the Council, co-decision-making powers for the Parliament and full jurisdiction for the Court of Justice in relation to criminal law currently entrenches EU criminal law (formerly embedded in a formal intergovernmental structure) in a supranational decisional framework.[76]

The stronger mandate of the European Parliament in conjunction with more 'active' policy-making has also contributed to a change of policy direction post-Lisbon towards a larger focus on fundamental rights. The European Council laid the foundations for the development of a different rights-based EU policy in the 2009 Stockholm Programme.[77] In contrast to the situation pre-Lisbon, the new Treaty provision in Article 82 TFEU conferred on the EU legislator a clear mandate to embark on legislating on such rights.[78] Furthermore, the Stockholm European Council underlined that law enforcement measures and measures to safeguard individual rights should go hand in hand and mutually reinforce each other.[79] The Roadmap for strengthening procedural rights of suspected or accused persons in criminal proceedings[80] was adopted by the Council the same year. On the basis of the reinforced Treaty mandate, we have also witnessed, post-Lisbon,

[73] Commission, Proposal for a council framework Decision on certain procedural rights in criminal proceedings throughout the European Union, COM (2004) 328 final, recitals 7, 12, 13 and paras 19–30.

[74] House of Lords' European Union Committee, 'Report on Procedural Rights in Criminal Proceedings – Report with Evidence', 1st Report of Session 2004–05, HL Paper 28 (London: The Stationery Office Limited, 2005), 14–17; House of Lords' European Union Committee, *Breaking the Deadlock: What Future for EU Procedural Rights?*, 2nd Report of Session 2006–07, HL Paper 20 (London: The Stationery Office Limited, 2007).

[75] See E Baker, 'The EU as a Penal Actor' in T Daems, S Snacken and D van Zyl Smit (eds), *European Penology?* (Oxford: Hart Publishing, 2013).

[76] See Peers, 'Mission Accomplished' (n 14); Öberg, 'Exit, Voice and Consensus' (n 16).

[77] Stockholm Programme (n 53).

[78] See J Öberg, 'Trust in the Law? Mutual Recognition as a Justification to Domestic Criminal Procedure' (2020) 16 *European Constitutional Law Review* 33.

[79] See 'Stockholm Programme' (n 53) paras 2.1–2.4.

[80] See Council, 'Resolution of the Council of 30 November 2009 on a Roadmap for strengthening procedural rights of suspected or accused persons in criminal proceeding' [2009] OJ C 295/1.

notable legislative activity in this area, entailing the adopting of seven substantive directives setting out comprehensive rights for defendants and victims.[81]

This brief survey shows the complementarity, yet shortcomings of the traditional rationales used as justifications for European integration of criminal law. 'Security' and 'effectiveness' have been the dominant justifications for EU action in criminal law. This is not surprising as these are conventionally the key justifications also for a national legislator when considering the use of criminal law assuming responsibility to protect the central public good of security.[82] However, the excessive use of security and effectiveness-based rationales has led to a repressive EU criminal policy to date which has trumped other important considerations such as justice and freedom[83] (although post-Lisbon this policy has been mediated through a stronger rights-based approach to EU criminal law legislation).[84] In light of this, it is apparent that a comprehensive deepening of the integration of the EU criminal justice system requires a more robust justificatory framework for accepting such major encroachments into the Member States' criminal justice systems.[85]

III. Purpose and Main Argument of the Book

This account goes beyond understanding the explicit and implicit rationales underlying the EU's criminal law-making activities to date and strives to engage

[81] Directive 2010/64/EU of the European Parliament and of the Council of 20 October 2010 on the right to interpretation and translation in criminal proceedings [2010] OJ L 280/1; Directive 2012/13/EU of the European Parliament and of the Council of 22 May 2012 on the right to information in criminal proceedings [2012] OJ L 142/1; Directive 2012/29/EU of the European Parliament and of the Council of 25 October 2012 establishing minimum standards on the rights, support and protection of victims of crime, and replacing Council Framework Decision 2001/220/JHA [2012] OJ L 315/57; Directive 2013/48/EU of the European Parliament and of the Council of 22 October 2013 on the right of access to a lawyer in criminal proceedings and in European arrest warrant proceedings, and on the right to have a third party informed upon deprivation of liberty and to communicate with third persons and with consular authorities while deprived of liberty [2013] OJ L 294/1; Directive (EU) 2016/343 of the European Parliament and of the Council of 9 March 2016 on the strengthening of certain aspects of the presumption of innocence and of the right to be present at the trial in criminal proceedings [2016] OJ L 65/1; Directive (EU) 2016/800 of the European Parliament and of the Council of 11 May 2016 on procedural safeguards for children who are suspects or accused persons in criminal proceedings [2016] OJ L 132/1; Directive (EU) 2016/1919 of the European Parliament and of the Council of 26 October 2016 on legal aid for suspects and accused persons in criminal proceedings and for requested persons in European arrest warrant proceedings [2016] OJ L 297/1.

[82] See eg the contributions of J Monar, 'Reflections on the place of criminal law in the European construction' (2021) 27 *European Law Journal* 356; P Caeiro, 'Constitution and development of the European Union's penal jurisdiction: responsibility, self-reference and attribution' (2021) 27 *European Law Journal* 441.

[83] See Art 67 TFEU.

[84] See eg A Weyembergh and N Franssen, 'From facts and political objectives to legal bases and legal provisions' (2021) 27 *European Law Journal* 368; I Wieczorek, 'The Emerging Role of the EU as a Primary Normative Actor in the Area of Criminal Justice' (2021) 27 *European Law Journal* 378 for this argument.

[85] See Harding and Banach-Gutierrez (n 20); COM 2011 (573) final (n 31).

with ideas of prescriptive and normative justifications for EU criminal law. In this respect 'normative' can refer to a criminal policy which is in line with fundamental rules of EU law and rule of law principles,[86] but the book rather adopts the notion of 'normative' that suggests that EU criminal policy is assessed or evaluated against an external moral standard or another selected yardstick.[87]

For the purpose of this book, it is appropriate to distinguish between theories of legitimacy of criminal law and other moral theories of criminal law on the one hand and general economic, political and legal theories for assessing the normative rationale for EU action on the other. Whilst the first set of theories primarily assesses the moral choice to criminalise per se (at state level), the second type of theoretical approaches consider the rationale for why the European Union should act or have a responsibility to act,[88] rather than the Member States, in the area of criminal law.

The first group of theories are well placed to evaluate within the internal parameters of criminal law to what extent EU criminal law actions are capable of satisfying a pre-established number of moral principles for criminalisation.[89] Within these the most prominent theories include communitarian theories of criminal law,[90] the Rechtsgüter theory[91] and theories of harm.[92] Within those there are also recent contributions in the literature on EU criminal law which address the legitimacy of EU criminalisation on the basis of the idea of protecting legal goods[93] and which examine EU criminal policy in light of the principle of harm.[94] Beyond the criminal law dominion of theories, there are also theoretical approaches that evaluate EU action based on the internal rationale and objectives for the existence of the Union and the functioning of the EU legal order.[95] The latter includes approaches

[86] Weyembergh and Franssen (n 17) employ this notion.

[87] J Hyman, *Action, Knowledge, and Will* (Oxford University Press, 2015); P Väyrynen, 'Normative Explanation And Justification' (2021) 55 *Noûs* 3: https://doi.org/10.1111/nous.12283.

[88] Caeiro (n 32).

[89] AP Simester and A von Hirsch, *Crimes, Harms, and Wrongs: On the Principles of Criminalisation* (Hart Publishing, 2011); RA Duff, 'Theorizing Criminal Law: a 25th Anniversary Essay' (2005) 25 *Oxford Journal of Legal Studies* 353.

[90] RA Duff, *Answering for Crime: Responsibility and Liability in the Criminal Law* (Hart Publishing, 2007); S Coutts, 'Supranational public wrongs: The limitations and possibilities of European criminal law and a European community' (2017) 54 *Common Market Law Review* 771; E Baker, 'Criminal jurisdiction, the public dimension to "effective protection" and the construction of community-citizen relations' (2001) 4 *Cambridge Yearbook of European Legal Studies* 25.

[91] J Ouwerkerk, 'Old wine in a new bottle: Shaping the foundations of EU criminal law through the concept of legal interests (Rechtsgüter)' (2021) 27 *European Law Journal* 426.

[92] J Feinberg, *The Moral Limits of the Criminal Law Volume 1: Harm to Others* (Oxford University Press, 1987); Simester and Von Hirsch (n 26).

[93] Ouwerkerk (n 91); A Eser, 'The Principle of "Harm" in the Concept of Crime – A Comparative Analysis of the Criminally Protected Legal Interests' (1965–1966) 4 *Duquesne University Law Review* 345.

[94] N Pérsak, 'Principles of EU Criminalisation and Their Varied Normative Strength: Harm and Effectiveness' (2021) 27 *European Law Journal* 463.

[95] I Wieczorek, *The Legitimacy of EU Criminal Law* (Oxford: Hart Publishing, 2020); J Öberg, *Limits to EU Powers: A Case Study of EU Regulatory Criminal Law* (Oxford: Hart Publishing, 2017).

based on competitive federalism,[96] political economy,[97] collective action/public goods[98] and fundamental rights perspectives[99] and approaches based on notions of moral responsibility and attribution in comparative international criminal law.[100]

Some of the key work in this field deserves a particular mention. In her book Herlin-Karnell primarily conceptualises the notion of 'security' and the constitutional implications of freedom as a non-domination-oriented view for understanding AFSJ (area of freedom, security and justice) policies.[101] Mitsilegas has analysed critically the justifications used so far in EU criminal policy and proposed to embrace the protection of fundamental rights in the EU's policies.[102] Coutts in turn has reflected upon the link between criminalisation, citizenship and political community, particularly building on a communitarian and citizenship-based perspective of criminal law.[103] Wieczorek has also recently in a monograph used the perspective of legitimacy to analyse whether EU action in criminal law so far is consistent with the EU's own constitutional values and principles.[104]

To date there is an absence of linkage between more national law-centred approaches to criminalisation and general theories explaining the rationales for EU action. This book endeavours to bridge these different sets of theories in order to offer a more comprehensive framework for analysing the justifications for criminalisation at EU level. This enquiry offers, however, a different principled framework focussing in particular on when and why the EU rather than the Member States should regulate criminal justice, hereto lacking in the literature. The account offered below centring on the EU–Member State relationship also reflects central criteria for legitimacy as EU action post-Lisbon needs to be in conformity with the constitutional principles of conferral, proportionality and subsidiarity.[105]

[96] I Wieczorek, 'Two Models for EU as a Regulator in the Internal Market and the EU Area of Criminal Justice: Is a One-Fits-All-Analysis Possible?' (2021) 27 *European Law Journal* 378; J Öberg, 'Normative Justifications of EU Criminal Law: European Public Goods and Transnational Interests' (2021) 27 *European Law Journal* 408.

[97] D Teichman, 'The Market for Criminal Justice: Federalism, Crime Control, and Jurisdictional Competition' (2005) 103 *Michigan Law Review* 1831.

[98] Wieczorek, 'Two Models for EU as a Regulator' (n 96); Öberg, 'Normative Justifications of EU Criminal Law' (n 96) building on theoretical approaches that can be found in C Peinhardt and T Sandler, *Transnational Cooperation: An Issue-Based Approach* (Oxford: Oxford University Press, 2015); FJ Lee, 'Global Institutional Choice' (2010) 85 *New York University Law Review* 328.

[99] L Mancano, 'A Theory of Justice? Securing the Normative Foundations of EU Criminal Law through an Integrated Approach to Independence' (2021) 27 *European Law Journal* 477.

[100] Caeiro (n 21).

[101] E Herlin-Karnell, *The Constitutional Structure of Europe's Area of 'Freedom, Security and Justice' and the Right to Justification* (Oxford: Hart Publishing, 2019).

[102] V Mitsilegas, *EU Criminal Law after Lisbon* (n 14); V Mitsilegas, 'Normative Foundations of European Criminal Law' in R Schütze (ed), *Globalisation and Governance: International Problems, European Solutions* (Cambridge: Cambridge University Press, 2018).

[103] S Coutts, *Citizenship, Crime and Community in the European Union* (Oxford: Hart Publishing, 2019).

[104] Wieczorek, *The Legitimacy of EU Criminal Law* (n 95).

[105] Art 5 TEU. See J Öberg, 'Subsidiarity as a Limit to the Exercise of EU Competences' (2017) 36 *Yearbook of European Law* 391 for an earlier sketch of a subsidiarity framework for assessing the legitimate scope for EU action.

The book develops an integrated normative standard[106] based on the perspectives of the effective allocation of regulatory authority between the EU and the Member States, representation-based political theories, and prominent theories of criminal law ('public goods' and 'the principle of harm'). In contrast to the existing works, the book incorporates the first comprehensive study on the justifications for EU action in criminal justice, providing for a conventional analysis of the legal framework in EU criminal policy conjointly with a contextual examination of the normative rationale for a more 'integrated' EU criminal law. The former entails a carefully structured multi-disciplinary approach consciously drawing on insights from political and legal thought, social theory and economic analysis.[107] The book argues that the key justification for supranational action lies in demonstrating the existence of European public goods,[108] such as the internal market, the transnational protection of the environment and the provision of security for citizens and other important transnational interests deserving of protection by means of criminal law. It should also be shown that the Union is better placed (given its resources, expertise and incentives) than Member States to protect those interests.[109]

IV. Limitations to the Study – 'EU Criminal Law'

Having outlined the rationales behind the key institutional, legal and policy developments in the area of EU criminal law to date and presented the main thesis of the book, we should linger on the subject matter of this enquiry: 'EU criminal law'. The latter concept is a convenient shorthand term rather than a formal descriptor. Thus, in his pioneering work of 2009, Mitsilegas used it as the title for a book,[110] but then described the scope of the subject therein as 'EU action in criminal matters'. There is definitely a great deal of this criminal law activity in the European political and legal space, and it is activity of significance, but its formal shape remains slippery to the grasp. It is not 'criminal law' as in a national system of criminal law in terms of having a familiar looking organisation of categories under discussion such as substantive criminal law and criminal procedure. We are rather addressing a phenomenon where the EU legislator requires Member States to employ

[106] J Hyman, *Action, Knowledge, and Will* (Oxford: Oxford University Press, 2015).

[107] DW Vick, 'Interdisciplinary and the Discipline of Law' (2004) 31 *Journal of Law and Society* 163; I Ward, *A Critical Introduction to European Law* (Cambridge: Cambridge University Press, 2009).

[108] Key notion for European public goods is the specifically public and collective nature of the interest at stake. We refer to interests which are collective assets belonging to members of a group in which the individual shares common social interests: A Duff, *Answering for Crime: Responsibility and Liability in the Criminal Law* (Oxford: Hart Publishing, 2007) 126; Coutts, 'Supranational public wrongs' (n 21) 787–89; AH Gibbs, *Constitutional Life and Europe's Area of Freedom, Security and Justice* (Ashgate, 2011) 48.

[109] See Art 5(3) TEU. See also, interestingly, the concept of legal interests developed by J Ouwerkerk, 'Old wine in a new bottle: Shaping the foundations of EU criminal law through the concept of legal interests (Rechtsgüter)' (2021) *European Law Journal* 426.

[110] V Mitsilegas, *EU Criminal Law* (Oxford: Hart Publishing, 2009).

the national resources of criminal law to serve specific EU policies or agendas.[111] We thus refer to an EU criminal law system in a narrow sense where the Union itself is the sole creator of criminal law norms and where it is dependent on the Member States with regard to their enforcement.[112] We are thus not speaking of a genuinely supranational criminal law by which the citizens of the EU are directly confronted with the sovereign punitive force of the Union as immediately applicable criminal law. Whilst the creation of the European Public Prosecutor's Office suggests signs of an emerging independent supranational criminal law, EU cannot claim to possess a self-contained EU criminal justice system of its own.[113] While there may be some terminological difficulties with the concept of 'EU criminal law', it should be underlined that this concept differs from 'European criminal law'. 'European criminal law' not only concerns the impact of EU law on national criminal laws but also the legal activities of the Council of Europe and other European organisations, flanking the European Union.[114]

Following this discussion, EU criminal law would then include all instances where the EU exercises by its law-making activities a normative influence on either national substantive criminal law/criminal procedure and practices or on judicial cooperation between the Member States. It is a broad field covering a multi-layered patchwork of legislation and case law in which both European and national courts and European and national legislatures play a role. It covers all EU legislative actions, policies/strategic directions (eg Commission Communications, Justice and Home Affairs (JHA) Council documents, and strategic decisions by the European Council),[115] as well as central legislative actors (ie the European Council, the JHA Council, the European Parliament and the Commission) relating to criminal procedure and substantive criminal law on a domestic level, as well as at the EU level.[116]

In formal terms, the EU's law-making powers on criminal law are found in Title V TFEU (Area of the AFSJ) under the headings of 'judicial cooperation in criminal matters' and 'police cooperation' which contain the legislative competences of Articles 82–88 TFEU.[117] These provisions cover distinctive aspects

[111] See Harding and Öberg (n 23) 193–94.

[112] G Corstens and J Pradel, *European Criminal Law* (The Hague: Kluwer Law International, 2002) 2–3; Harding and Banach-Gutierrez (n 20) 759.

[113] See K Ambos, *European Criminal Law* (Cambridge: Cambridge University Press, 2018) 12–16.

[114] C Harding, 'Review of V Mitsilegas, *EU Criminal Law*' (2010) 35 *European Law Review* 301; A Klip, *European Criminal Law* (Intersentia, 2012) 1–2; H Satzger, *European and International Criminal* Law (München/Oxford/Baden-Baden: CH Beck/Hart Publishing/Nomos, 2012) 43–44; Ambos (n 113) ch 3.

[115] See A Weyembergh and I Wieczorek, 'Is There an EU Criminal Policy?' in R Colson and S Field (eds), *EU Criminal Justice and the Challenges of Legal Diversity* (Cambridge: Cambridge University Press, 2016).

[116] See Baker, 'Governing Through Crime' (n 48) 190–92; J Monar, 'Decision-Making in the Area of Freedom, Security and Justice' in A Arnull and D Wincott (eds), *Accountability and Legitimacy in the European Union* (Oxford: Oxford University Press, 2002) 67–70.

[117] See Harding and Banach-Gutierrez (n 20) 761.

of criminal justice ranging from harmonisation of substantive criminal law (Article 83 TFEU), judicial cooperation and harmonisation of domestic criminal procedure (Article 82), rules on police cooperation (Article 87 TFEU) and provisions regulating operational cooperation for Eurojust, the EPPO and Europol (Articles 85, 86 and 88 TFEU). Notwithstanding these divergences they share some common features. They are all concerned with EU policy-making in areas of significant public concern for EU citizens and the Member States alike. The exercise of EU public powers in the fields of criminal law and law enforcement has tangible and very adverse consequences for the liberties and well-being of individuals.[118] Furthermore, Member States' co-operation in this area touches on core functions of statehood,[119] such as the safeguarding of internal security and law enforcement.[120] Due to these very special features of the EU's powers in this area, it is paramount that the exercise of those competencies is founded on strong normative justifications.

V. Structure of the Book

The book is divided into three parts and seven chapters. Part one (Chapters 1–2) is a general part, constructing an analytical framework to be used when reviewing EU law and policies in the field of criminal justice. Part two (Chapters 3–4) considers the scope, justifications and limits for harmonisation of domestic criminal law, whilst part three (Chapters 5–6) discusses the institutional dimension of EU criminal justice on the basis of the analytical framework developed in Chapter 2. The concluding Chapter 7 reflects on the key lessons from the previous analysis in the book.

Chapter 2 develops an analytical argument for assessing under what circumstances the EU should intervene in the area of criminal justice. Legitimacy in EU criminal law is explored drawing from the perspectives of criminal law philosophy, analysing in particular harm-based and public goods theories as justifications for recourse to criminal law.[121] Subsequently, perspectives of political economy,[122] competitive federalism[123] and the economic theories of market failure and collective action problems[124] are examined in order to develop a coherent analysis of the

[118] Trauner and Ripoll Servant (n 1); Walker (n 1) 5–7.

[119] P Genschel and M Jachtenfuchs, 'More Integration, Less Federation' (n 2).

[120] Besselink (n 3); *Lisbon Judgment* (n 3).

[121] AP Simester and A von Hirsch, *Crimes, Harms, and Wrongs: On the Principles of Criminalisation* (Oxford: Hart Publishing, 2011).

[122] D Teichman, 'The Market for Criminal Justice: Federalism, Crime Control, and Jurisdictional Competition' (2005) 103 *Michigan Law Review* 1831.

[123] S Deakin, 'Legal Diversity and Regulatory Competition: Which Model for Europe?' (2006) 12 *European Law Journal* 440.

[124] C Peinhardt and T Sandler, *Transnational Cooperation: An Issue-Based Approach* (Oxford: Oxford University Press, 2015); J Öberg 'Subsidiarity as a Limit' (n 105).

normative underpinnings of EU action in the area. Finally, it considers political and legal theories of representation as important building blocks in the theoretical framework. The key argument advanced in the chapter is that the economic rationale, moral and democratic premises for accepting EU intervention in the area of criminal law must, to ensure the legitimacy of EU policies, be confined to protecting European public goods or clearly defined transnational interests.

On the basis of the framework developed in the first part of the book, the second part analyses the justifications for harmonisation of domestic criminal law. Chapter 3 analyses the justifications for EU legislative activity in substantive criminal law. First, it examines harm-based theoretical accounts as justifications for harmonisation of EU substantive criminal law, examining as case studies the recent proposals for criminalisation of gender-based violence, the EU proposal on criminalisation of hate speech and hate crime. Subsequently, it considers in depth the transnational criterion, supranational public goods and market failures as rationales for harmonisation of substantive criminal law. The chapter finally addresses dysfunctional judicial cooperation and discusses and criticises mutual recognition as a justification for harmonisation of substantive criminal law under Article 83 TFEU.

Chapter 4 examines the justifications for EU action in the field of domestic criminal procedure. It discusses first how the cross-border criterion should be construed within the context of the EU's competence in criminal procedure competencies in Article 82(2) TFEU, arguing for a narrow reading of this provision. It subsequently addresses justifications based on market failures (free movement) and representation-based democratic rationales substantiating harmonisation. As a case study, the chapter offers a critique of the Victims' Rights Directive on the basis of the cross-border criterion challenging the need to regulate rights for local victims. The chapter then addresses in depth dysfunctional judicial cooperation and collective action problems as arguments for harmonisation. The chapter challenges – on a conceptual and empirical basis – the justification for having EU competence in domestic criminal procedure under Article 82(2) TFEU on the basis that it enables mutual recognition. It suggests a role for the EU to intervene in the protection of individual rights in instances where common action would correct the dysfunctional workings of national political processes by giving 'virtual' political rights to foreign victims and defendants.

Part three of the book analyses, on the basis of the general analytical framework in Chapter 2, the justifications for conferring powers to EU criminal justice agencies. Chapter 5 examines the case for a centralised European prosecutor within the context of Eurojust and the European Public Prosecutor's Office. It critically analyses the justifications based on transnational interests and European public goods as arguments in favour of establishing centralised EU prosecutors to protect transnational and supranational interests. On the basis of this theoretical framework, it analyses the scope, limits and nature of the European Public Prosecutor's powers under Article 86 TFEU and the current EPPO Regulation. This includes a critical analysis of the proposal to extend the EPPO's remit for other offences such as terrorism and organised crime under Article 86 TFEU. The final section of the chapter considers critically as an alternative to a centralised prosecutor a model of judicial cooperation based on the structure of Eurojust under Article 85 TFEU and the recent Eurojust Regulation. It is generally proposed that complex transnational criminal activity circumscribes the scope for EU intervention in the area of operational cooperation in criminal justice.

Chapter 6 considers the normative justification for transforming Europol into a fully-fledged supranational agency. It begins with a discussion of the narrative of Europol, its emergence and the earlier developments of law and policy in this area, including the rationale for creating this agency. Subsequently, it considers issues of institutional competence, expertise, incentives and resources as justifications for a more centralised European police agency to address the threat of transnational criminal activity. Based on these theoretical debates, the chapter analyses critically the scope and nature of Europol's powers in light of Article 88 TFEU and the new Europol Regulation. Finally, it considers the justifications for the alternative of maintaining an EU police agency based on the philosophy of cooperation rather than integration of national criminal justice systems.

The concluding Chapter 7 firstly summarises the findings of the book. Subsequently, it strives to place the proposed framework of the book in the broader political and academic debates on EU criminal policy. In particular, it reflects on the need to recalibrate the justifications for further EU integration in criminal justice used so far in EU policy and legislative practice. It finally endeavours to chart a future course of EU criminal policy, reflecting in detail on the benefits and drawbacks for the EU to depart from a traditional instrumental view on EU criminal policy to a more self-standing 'autonomous' model of justifications for this polity.

2

Normative Framework for Assessing the Justifications in EU Criminal Law

I. Introduction

This chapter outlines a normative framework for assessing the justification of EU action in criminal law.

The previous chapter suggested that it is possible to infer three principal drivers for EU criminal law and policy: 'security' for EU citizens; ensuring the effectiveness of EU policies; and subsequently a 'rights-based approach' to EU criminal policy. 'Effectiveness' and other 'functional'[1] considerations have been the primary justifications for EU action in respect of the development of EU regulatory criminal law[2] and the rise of a European Public Prosecutor.[3] In the area of the eurocrimes in Article 83(1) TFEU and in respect of the development of EU criminal justice agencies such as Europol and Eurojust, the justification for EU action has instead been driven by 'security'-orientated rationales.[4] In this instance, criminal law is employed to serve a 'repressive' and 'expressionist' agenda of criminal enforcement. Finally, we also identified a stronger 'fundamental rights'-based approach to EU criminal policy post-Lisbon facilitated by a stronger Treaty mandate to enact legislation on procedural standards and individual rights.[5] All these justifications offer distinctive ways of understanding why the European Union wishes to take action in criminal justice and wherefore the EU level might be a better venue than Member State level for undertaking those actions.

In light of this, the following wishes to take a step back and reflect on what could be and should be proper normative justifications for EU action in criminal justice searching beyond the Treaty-prescribed limits and justifications. The chapter defines 'normative' broadly to encompass not only justifications based on legal

[1] See J Monar, 'Reflections on the place of criminal law in the European construction' (2021) 27 *European Law Journal* 356.

[2] See E Herlin-Karnell, *The Constitutional Dimension of European Criminal Law* (Oxford: Hart Publishing, 2012) chs 2–5.

[3] J Öberg, 'The European Public Prosecutor: Quintessential Supranational Criminal Law?' (2021) 28 *Maastricht Journal of European and Comparative Law* 164.

[4] V Mitsilegas, *EU Criminal Law After Lisbon* (Oxford: Hart Publishing, 2016) ch 3.

[5] See above ch 1, section II.

rules and principles[6] but also rationales which are considered acceptable as reason for action within the fields of moral and political philosophy, political economy and public choice theory and economics.[7] As will be seen from the analysis in this chapter, it appears that the more 'normative' moral, political and public choice justifications for legislative action regularly concur with the more narrow legal rationales for EU intervention as enshrined in the EU Treaties.

In order to address the question of normative foundations for EU criminal law, the following develops a three-pronged lens of analysis to deconstruct what proper reasons exist for EU action in the field of criminal law. First, the legitimacy of EU criminal law is discussed from the perspective of criminal law theory, contrasting harm-based accounts and theories of public goods in criminal law. It also penetrates the constitutional limits for further integration in EU criminal justice such as the 'harm' criterion in Article 83(1) TFEU (II). In the second stage, the focus turns to a comprehensive examination of economic and legal theories of market failures, European public goods, political economy perspectives and competitive federalism to assess the justificatory rationale for EU action in criminal justice (III). In the final stage, the analysis turns to political philosophy and transnational legal theories which may justify EU intervention to protect certain transnational interests.

II. Harm and Public Goods as Justifications for (EU) Action in Substantive Criminal Law

This section first endeavours to anchor the normative justifications for EU intervention in relevant criminal law theory and philosophy. This is a challenging task since the area of criminal law has historically been developed in a national context and with reference to national concepts and justifications. The most obvious divide is between theorising that purports to be essentially descriptive providing an account of what criminal law 'is', and theorising that rather aspires to offer a normative account of what the criminal law ought to be.[8] A normative account of criminal law (and EU criminal law) includes an examination of what interests it should serve, what values it should recognise to have a legitimate claim

[6] See N Franssen and A Weyembergh, 'From facts and political objectives to legal bases and legal provisions'(2021) 27 *European Law Journal* 368; *Webster's New World Dictionary* (New York: Simon & Schuster, 1989, 3rd College edn) 925 for this definition.

[7] See J Hyman, *Action, Knowledge, and Will* (Oxford: Oxford University Press, 2015) for this notion. The normative approach in criminal law philosophy often coincides with a deontological exercise, examining what criminal law ought to be normatively based upon and thus also informing prescriptively about 'what ought to be': see N Peršak, 'Principles of EU criminalisation and their varied normative strength: Harm and effectiveness' (2021) 27 *European Law Journal* 463; J Feinberg, *The Moral Limits of Criminal Law – Harm to Others* (Oxford: Oxford University Press, 1984); A Ashworth, *Principles of Criminal Law* (Oxford: Oxford University Press, 1999); AP Simester and A von Hirsch, *Crimes, Harms, and Wrongs: On the Principles of Criminalisation* (Oxford: Hart Publishing, 2011).

[8] Recognising that it is often difficult to separate the descriptive from the normative perspective; A Duff, 'Theorizing Criminal Law: A 25th Anniversary Essay' (2005) 25 *Oxford Journal of Legal Studies* 353, 354.

to our respect[9] and what principles we can articulate to guide decisions about criminalisation.[10]

We first consider the prominent harm principle as a central theory in deciding on the scope of criminalisation. To appreciate this principle and the contrasting public goods theory, we commence by considering the nature of criminal law. A defining feature of criminal law is its communicative function speaking with a potent moral voice to actors capable of moral deliberation, authoritatively condemning wrongdoers on behalf of the community as a whole.[11] The debate on criminalisation has led to a certain 'strong' concept of what is criminal, which has a widely supported ethical basis in many legal systems.[12] This is the idea that the label of criminal is appositely applied to conduct which clearly 'harms' the core values of a society[13] and that the function of criminal law is to protect those values as an expressive instrument of condemnation of certain conduct. This idea is articulated by the German Federal Constitutional Court in its *Lisbon Judgment*:

> By criminal law, a legal community gives itself a code of conduct that is anchored in its values, and whose violation, according to the shared convictions on law, is regarded as so grievous and unacceptable for social co-existence in the community that it requires punishment.[14]

Herbert Packer noted some 50 years ago that whilst there is no coherent theory of which conduct should be criminalised, he argued that: 'There is a vast range of economic offenses … where the forms of criminal sanction can be and should be dispensed with.'[15] In this intellectual tradition, it is the sense of a serious damage or threat to social coexistence which justifies criminalisation.[16]

[9] HLA Hart, *Law, Liberty and Morality* (Stanford: Stanford University Press, 1963); *Punishment and Responsibility* (Oxford: Oxford University Press, 1968); 'The House of Lords on Attempting the Impossible' (1981) 1 *Oxford Journal of Legal Studies* 149.

[10] Duff, 'Theorizing Criminal Law' (n 8) 365; J Schonsheck, *On Criminalization: An Essay in the Philosophy of the Criminal Law* (Dordrecht: Kluwer, 1994).

[11] N Lacey, 'Contingency, Coherence and Conceptualism: Reflections on the Encounter between "Critique" and "the Philosophy of the Criminal Law"' in RA Duff (ed), *Philosophy and the Criminal Law: Principle and Critique* (Cambridge: Cambridge University Press, 1998) 9; Simester and Von Hirsch (n 7) ch 1.

[12] For a convenient summary of the main lines of arguments, concept and theory, see JJ Child, AP Simester, JR Spencer, F Stark and GJ Virgo, *Simester and Sullivan's Criminal Law: Theory and Doctrine*, 9th rev edn (Oxford: Hart Publishing, 2022) ch 1.

[13] Commonly referred to as 'deontological' to broadly denote an emphasis on the nature of action or conduct. See L Alexander and M Moore, 'Deontological Ethics' in EN Zalta (ed), *The Stanford Encyclopedia of Philosophy* (Winter 2021 edn): https://plato.stanford.edu/archives/win2021/entries/ethics-deontological/.

[14] Judgment of German Federal Constitutional Court of 30 June 2009, *Lisbon Judgment*, Case 2 BvE 2/08, 5/08, 2 BvR 1010/08, 1022/08, 1259/08, 182/09 (2009), para 355.

[15] HL Packer, *The Limits of the Criminal Sanction* (Stanford: Stanford University Press, 1969), 252–53. This argument was similar to the argument of J Langbein, 'Controlling Prosecutorial Discretion in Germany' (1973) 41 *University of Chicago Law Review* 453, who suggested that the German concept of *Ordnungswidrigkeiten* (administrative offence), in decriminalising the morally neutral, enhances the distinctiveness of what is genuinely criminal.

[16] Commission, 'Communication from the Commission to the European Parliament, the Council, the European Economic and Social Committee and the Committee of the Regions – Towards an EU

We therefore turn our attention to the justification for criminalisation according to the harm principle which departs from the idea that citizens have a claim to be free of legal coercion. Whenever a legislator is faced with a choice between imposing a legal duty on citizens, other things equal, they should leave individuals free to make their own choices.[17] Legitimate grounds for coercive state intervention through criminal law are when the conduct can be considered a (public) wrong[18] and when criminalisation would prevent harm to individuals' interests (the harm to others principle).[19]

When we refer to harm we conceive it as the impeding, setting back, or defeating of a person's fundamental interests.[20] The interests we are referring to here are those shared by nearly all members of society, ie the longer-term means or capabilities that one has, and which can be relied upon to sustain or enhance well-being and the quality of a person's life. In this category are the interests in the continuance for a foreseeable interval of one's life, the interests in one's own physical health, the integrity and normal functioning of one's body, the absence of absorbing pain and suffering and a certain amount of freedom from interference. They are the fundamental requisite of a person's well-being and deep-rooted needs whose fulfilment can be both reasonably hoped for and usually influenced by one's own efforts.[21] The harm principle forces an enquiry into the consequences of conduct, the particular effects of that conduct and the way in which it damages the lives, means and capacities of other persons. Typically, the kind of adverse effect that counts as harm occurs through the impairment of some resource over which the harmed person has a legitimate claim.[22]

To illustrate the application of this principle, some straightforward examples are apposite. Wilful homicide, forcible rape and aggravated assault are considered 'serious crimes against the person' everywhere in the civilised world, thus offering paradigmatic instances where the harm feature is a constitutive part of the crime itself. The criminal law should thus proscribe direct intrusions into important individual legally protected interests such as life, liberty, and health. Equally uncontroversial are serious 'crimes against property' (burglary, theft and offences involving fraud and misrepresentation). In the case of these offences, the moral

Criminal Policy: Ensuring the effective implementation of EU policies through criminal law', COM 2011 (573) final, s 2.2.1.

[17] Feinberg (n 7) ch 2.

[18] Simester and Von Hirsch (n 7) 20, 27; M Moore, *Placing Blame: A Theory of Criminal Law* (Oxford: Clarendon Press, 1997).

[19] Packer (n 15) 262. Whelan discusses this principle with respect to criminalisation of EU competition law: P Whelan, 'A Principled Argument for Personal Criminal Sanctions as Punishment under EC Cartel Law' (2007) 4 *Competition Law Review* 7.

[20] See Feinberg (n 7) 34–36; N Peršak, *Criminalising Harmful Conduct: The Harm Principle, its Limits and Continental Counterparts* (New York: Springer, 2007).

[21] Feinberg (n 7) 42; N Rescher, *Welfare: The Social Issue in Philosophical Perspective* (Pittsburgh: University of Pittsburgh Press, 1972) 5–6; Simester and Von Hirsch (n 7) 18, 21.

[22] Simester and Von Hirsch (n 7) 35; Feinberg (n 7) 34–35; J Raz, 'Autonomy, Toleration, and the Harm Principle' in R Gavison (ed), *Issues in Contemporary Legal Philosophy* (Oxford: Clarendon Press, 1987) 313, 327.

force comes from the legitimate acceptance of an underlying property regime and the instrumental value of the offences in facilitating this regime. The latter facilitates the creation of forms of welfare and human flourishing which are rightly conceived of as a public good by providing a predictable set of rules by which we can pursue a good life. The common feature in crimes of these two categories is the direct production of serious harm to individual persons and groups by involving damage to things such as our physical integrity or our property.[23]

There are also other offences which have an unquestionable place in the penal codes in modern liberal democracies which constitute conduct that causes harm to 'the public', the economy/competition[24] or the environment.[25] Typical of crimes in this general category are counterfeiting,[26] smuggling,[27] fraud with public funds[28] and violation of antipollution regulation. Beyond that it might also be argued that a limited category of crimes of 'abstract endangerment' (eg dangerous driving, which threatens such protected interests) can be justified.[29] Tax evasion is rightly a crime, although there is no particular victim, since a perpetrator who illegitimately reduces their tax burden effectively wrongs their fellow citizens as the money to pay for public goods must then be taken from other citizens. Similarly, attacks on the integrity of the currency (eg counterfeiting) matter because they undermine the systems that coordinate a state's economic activity which would deprive people of many opportunities for well-being. Based on this, we can assert that it is legitimate for the state to intervene when it is necessary to prevent conduct that causes harm to important public institutions and practices.[30]

This is not the place to enter into the debate on the critique against the harm principle. It suffices to say that the harm principle in itself cannot set determinate limits on the scope of the criminal law. The harm to others principle must also involve balancing considerations and a proximity principle. Any harm-based account of the criminal law requires us to identify the harm addressed by each crime, and to show that the harm is sufficiently important to outweigh countervailing considerations, which militate against state intervention. The greater the gravity and likelihood of the harm, the stronger the case for criminalisation;

[23] Simester and Von Hirsch (n 7) 21, 43–49.

[24] See above Whelan (n 19).

[25] Directive 2008/99/EC of the European Parliament and of the Council of 19 November 2008 on the protection of the environment through criminal law [2008] OJ L 328/28; J Öberg, 'Criminal Sanctions in the Field of EU Environmental Law' (2011) 2 *New Journal of European Criminal Law* 402.

[26] Directive (EU) 2019/713 of the European Parliament and of the Council of 17 April 2019 on combating fraud and counterfeiting of non-cash means of payment and replacing Council Framework Decision 2001/413/JHA [2019] OJ L 123/18; Directive 2014/62/EU of the European Parliament and of the Council of 15 May 2014 on the protection of the euro and other currencies against counterfeiting by criminal law and replacing Council Framework Decision 2000/383/JHA [2014] OJ L 151/1.

[27] See Art 83(1) TFEU.

[28] See Directive (EU) 2017/1371 of the European Parliament and of the Council of 5 July 2017 on the fight against fraud to the Union's financial interests by means of criminal law [2017] OJ L 198/29.

[29] A von Hirsch, 'Extending the Harm Principle: "Remote" Harms and Fair Imputation' in AP Simester and ATH Smith (eds), *Harm and Culpability* (Oxford: Oxford University Press, 1996) 259.

[30] JS Mill, *On Liberty* (London: JW Parker and Son, 1859), 13–15.

conversely, the more valuable the conduct is, the stronger the case against criminalisation.[31]

One of the more compelling critiques against the harm principle can be derived from the thinking of Anthony Duff and his 'communitarian' theory of criminal law, including the notions of public goods and public wrongs. According to this set of ideas, the criminal law should deal with those kinds of wrong which are matters of public concern, and which therefore require a collective response from the whole community; wrongs which are, by contrast, properly the concern only of the individual victim should be dealt with under the civil law.[32] The key notion here is that the criminal law should protect common or collective goods, meaning that our examination consists of ascertaining to what extent any individual goods should also count as 'common' goods to be protected under the criminal law.[33]

Duff's key objection to the harm principle is that any proponents of this theory must also concede that there is a moral component of the harm principle in that it does not include private harm but only harm which can be considered a public wrong. According to Duff, individuals can only be punished for wrongs that concern the broader community in a sufficiently serious manner to warrant retribution and condemnation.[34] The communitarian approach envisages that individuals and their goods are of less importance than how they and their goods are understood as (the goods of) members of a community.[35] Criminalisation involves what we may call socially proscribed wrongdoing where certain conduct is authoritatively declared wrong by the community. This is a matter on which the community should take a shared view and claim normative authority over its members.[36] We consider, for example, rape to be criminal not simply by virtue of the physical and emotional harm caused to the victim, but also by its blatant disregard for the respect due that person as a morally autonomous individual. It is not a 'private' matter in which the community has no proper interest, but rather a non-negotiable wrong which should be condemned by the community. This has to do in part with the intrinsic seriousness of the harm wrought by rape.[37]

I wish to make two key points to summarise and take this discussion further. First, there is, as we will see below, quite a strong endorsement of the harm

[31] Feinberg (n 7) 216; Simester and Von Hirsch (n 11) 37–40.

[32] G Fletcher, 'Domination in Wrongdoing' (1996) 76 *Boston University Law Review* 347.

[33] SS Marshall and RR Duff, 'Criminalization and sharing wrongs' (1998) 11 *Canadian Journal of Law and Jurisprudence* 7, 7–9; Fletcher (n 32); C Roxin, *StrafrechtAllgemeiner Teil*, 3rd edn (Warszawa: CH Beck, 1997) 10–30.

[34] C Taylor, 'Cross-Purposes: The Liberal-Communitarian Debate' in NL Rosenblum (ed), *Liberalism and the Moral Life* (Cambridge, MA: Harvard University Press, 1989) 159; M Sandel, *Liberalism and the Limits of Justice* (New York: Cambridge University Press, 1982) 150.

[35] Simester and Von Hirsch (n 7) 20–29; RA Duff, *Answering for Crime: Responsibility and Liability in the Criminal Law* (Oxford; Hart Publishing, 2007) 123, 135, 137; Duff, 'Theorizing Criminal Law' (n 8).

[36] Marshall and Duff (n 33) 13–14; RA Duff, 'Law, Language and Community: Some Preconditions of Criminal Liability' (1998) 18 *Oxford Journal of Legal Studies* 189.

[37] Marshall and Duff (n 33) 18.

principle in the official documents of the EU institutions[38] and also the Treaties.[39] Based on this, it seems that EU criminalisation measures, at least, need to satisfy the harm principle and substantiate serious harm of criminal activity before they can be subjected to EU regulation. However, it is argued that the harm principle is not sufficient as a limiting criterion for appreciating when the EU should criminalise certain conduct. From the perspective of the European Union as a legislator, it is also apposite to analyse the question of criminalisation on the basis of the public goods concept. The latter offers a framework to appreciate what interests the EU needs to protect by means of criminal law and is also in line with the general EU law constitutional framework.[40]

III. European Public Goods and Transnational Interests as Justifications for EU Criminal Law

A. Transnational Interests and European Public Goods

Building on the above discussion on the harm principle and public goods as rationales for criminalisation, the following intends to connect those ideas to the broader justifications for EU policy-making and the general rationales for why EU action should be preferred over Member State action.

The logical departure point for this purpose is the transnational argument. The fact that an issue to be regulated is of a cross-border nature is one of the core justifications for EU legislative activities.[41] EU action in this instance is often defended on the basis of 'collective action'[42] theories suggesting that the scope of the problem to be regulated (affecting more than one Member State) and the insufficiency of decentralised decision-making by independent states cannot adequately address the problem because of various kinds of cross-border externalities or spillovers.[43]

[38] Council, 'Council Conclusions on model provisions, guiding the Council's criminal law deliberations', 2979th Justice and Home Affairs Council meeting, Brussels, 30 November 2009; Commission, 'Communication from the Commission to the European Parliament, the Council, the European Economic and Social Committee and the Committee of the Regions, Towards an EU Criminal Policy: Ensuring the effective implementation of EU policies through criminal law', COM(2011) 573 final; European Parliament, 'European Parliament resolution of 22 May 2012 on an EU approach to criminal law', 2010/2310(INI).

[39] See Art 83(1) TFEU.

[40] Art 5 TEU.

[41] Several competences in the AFSJ and Title V are for example limited in this way: see Arts 81(1) TFEU; 81(2)(b) TFEU; 81(3) TFEU; 82(2) TFEU; 83(1) TFEU and 88(1) TFEU.

[42] See M Kumm, 'Constitutionalizing Subsidiarity in Integrated Markets: The Case of Tobacco Regulation in the European Union' (2006) 12 *European Law Journal* 503, 513–15, 519–21 for the concept of 'collective action', based originally on M Olson's seminal book, *The Logic of Collective Action: Public Goods and the Theory of Groups, With a New Preface and Appendix* (Boston: Harvard University Press, 1971).

[43] See FJ Lee, 'Global Institutional Choice' (2010) 85 *New York University Law Review* 328, 330; J Öberg, 'Subsidiarity as a Limit to the Exercise of EU Competences' (2017) 36 *Yearbook of European Law* 391 for a general account of this argument.

The cross-border justification is, judging by legislative practice, a central justification for EU action in criminal law.[44] The Commission's general argument is that harmonisation is needed since certain forms of crime have a transnational dimension and the Member States cannot combat them effectively on their own. The EU legislator has claimed that violations of EU environmental rules, terrorism attacks, attacks against information systems, and infringement of market abuse rules are intrinsically cross-border offences affecting the interests of several Member States.[45] Article 82(2) TFEU – which regulates the EU's competence in criminal procedure – constitutionally entrenches the transnational justification, suggesting that the EU may harmonise specific elements of domestic criminal procedure only 'in criminal matters having a *cross-border dimension*', whereas in respect of substantive criminal law the EU may pursuant to Article 83(1) TFEU harmonise 'areas of particularly serious crime with a *cross-border dimension*'.[46]

Building on the discussion in the previous section on public goods, it is claimed that EU legislative intervention is legitimate when it protects certain 'European' public goods and transnational interests which Member States cannot sufficiently protect.[47] With respect to the general transnational argument, it appears that European public goods is a special category of transnational interests. Based on the insights from the debate on public goods, one of the key elements of (European) public goods is the specifically public nature of the interest at stake which can be conceived as collective assets belonging to members of a group in which the individual shares common social interests. In the definition of European public goods belongs classic public goods that correspond to policy areas that have been assumed by the Union through functionalist spillover effects in its quest to secure output legitimacy.[48] Under these criteria, a clean environment and public security would be considered public goods *par excellence*, but we also have public goods associated with the EU's task of generating prosperity through creating market institutions at Union level: eg the internal market (and the EU financial market[49]),

[44] Environmental Crimes Directive (n 22) recital 2; Directive 2009/123/EC of the European Parliament and of the Council of 21 October 2009 amending Directive 2005/35/EC on ship-source pollution and on the introduction of penalties for infringements [2009] OJ L 280/52, recital 14; Commission, 'Proposal for a Directive of the European Parliament and of the Council on criminal sanctions for insider dealing and market manipulation', COM (2011) 654 final, 3, 5, recital 7; Proposal for a Directive of the European Parliament and of the Council on combating terrorism and replacing Council Framework Decision 2002/475/JHA on combating terrorism, COM(2015) 625 final, 2–12; Commission, 'Proposal for a Directive of the European Parliament and of the Council on attacks against information systems and repealing Council Framework Decision 2005/222/JHA', COM(2010) 517 final, 2–8.

[45] ibid.

[46] 'resulting from the nature or impact of such offences or from a special need to combat them on a common basis': see Art 83(1) TFEU.

[47] See Art 5(3) TEU.

[48] J Monar, 'Reflections on the place of criminal law in the European construction' (2021) 27 *European Law Journal* 356.

[49] The integrated European financial system may require criminal law protection from market dysfunctions as suggested by Directive 2014/57/EU of the European Parliament and of the Council of 16 April 2014 on criminal sanctions for market abuse [2014] OJ L 173/79.

the currency and finally public goods that may originate in Member States and then have external effects on citizens elsewhere (eg fighting cross-border crime within the Union).[50] In the language of economists, European public goods are non-excludable (individuals cannot be excluded from their enjoyment) and non-rivalrous (the use by one individual does not reduce its value by another).[51] These public goods are European in the sense that Member States typically cannot adequately provide them and that they must therefore be provided by the EU acting as a public authority. Furthermore, such goods are available for all EU residents and exclude – in principle – non-EU residents, which is the case for example with respect to the four freedoms, the use of the euro or public services provided by the EU institutions.[52]

The internal market should be defined as a central European public good as it safeguards the interests of the community of EU Member States and citizens alike.[53] The primary justification for EU action to protect the common market can be derived from the general legal basis of Article 114 TFEU. This provision suggests that EU legislation should either: (i) have the object of removing differences between national legislations that hinder freedom of movement (transboundary externalities); or (ii) have the object of removing disparities between national rules which are liable to distort conditions for competition (fair competition).[54] The environment is another example of a European public good which may require centralised supranational action to address externalities and protect this collective asset. The Court of Justice has held that the provision in Article 11 TEU stating that 'Environmental protection requirements must be integrated into the definition and implementation of the Union's policies and activities' emphasises the fundamental nature of that objective.[55] The financial resources of the Union and the common euro is arguably

[50] S Coutts, 'Supranational public wrongs: The limitations and possibilities of European criminal law and a European community' (2017) 54 *Common Market Law Review* 771, 787–89; N MacCormick, 'Law as institutional fact' (1974) 90 *Law Quarterly Review* 102; S Collignon (ed), *The Governance of European Public Goods* (Cham: Palgrave Macmillan, 2017).

[51] Neil Walker offers a broader reading of public goods: N Walker, 'The European Public Good and European Public Goods' (15 October 2020), Edinburgh School of Law Research Paper No 2020/20: https://ssrn.com/abstract=3712265, where he suggests it may be more fruitful with a 'thicker' concept of public goods which also includes goods that produce a value which cannot be adequately characterisable in terms of its worth to any or all of the members of that society considered one by one but which instead make essential reference to what all enjoy together. See also J Waldron, 'Can Communal Goods be Human Rights?' in *Liberal Rights: Collected Papers 1981–1991* (Cambridge: Cambridge University Press, 1993) 339–69, 358; I Loader and N Walker, *Civilizing Security* (Cambridge: Cambridge University Press, 2007) ch 6.

[52] F Zuleeg, 'The rationale for EU action: What are European Public Goods?', paper prepared for the BEPA Workshop on 'The political economy of EU public finances: designing governance for change', 5 February 2009, 6; Collignon (n 50).

[53] E Baker, 'Criminal jurisdiction, the public dimension to "effective protection" and the construction of community-citizen relations' (2001) 4 *Cambridge Yearbook of European Legal Studies* 25; Coutts, 'Supranational public wrongs' (n 51) 787–91.

[54] A Ogus, 'Competition between National Legal Systems: A Contribution of Economic Analysis to Comparative Law' (1999) 48 *International and Comparative Law Quarterly* 405, 416.

[55] Case C-176/03 *Commission v Council (Environmental Crimes)* EU:C:2005:542, paras 42–48; Case C-440/05 *Commission v Council (Ship-Source Pollution)* EU:C:2007:625, Opinion of AG Mazák, para 95.

a special category (which will be discussed further below) of intrinsic supranational public goods which may call for the protection of the criminal law.[56] In those instances, the nature of the interests being central for the functioning and the existence of the Union makes a particularly compelling case for EU intervention.

In order to more clearly articulate when the EU should intervene (by means of criminal law), we consider in detail the internal market as being indisputably the most central European public good.[57] The internal market justification is a wide one which can be employed to justify Union intervention in nearly all national policy fields, including criminal law. The broad reading of the internal market is supported by the use of Article 114 TFEU by the EU legislative institutions whose legislative practice suggests a wide discretion for executing the internal market objectives. Potentially, any differences between the laws of the different Member States can be construed as a distortion to competition or as a barrier to trade justifying resort to Article 114 TFEU.[58]

B. The Internal Market as a European Public Good

One of the key arguments of this book is that the internal market justification cannot be employed indiscriminately. Instead it is suggested that supranational action primarily should be employed to address dysfunctional workings of markets, collective action problems and other externalities arising from the economic and social interdependence between states in the EU.[59] The idea of transnational externalities conditioned the Court's reading of the competence contained in Article 114 TFEU in the prominent *Tobacco Advertising* judgment.[60] The pronouncements of the Court that the Union does not enjoy a general power to regulate the internal market, and that it has to show 'appreciable distortions to competition', suggest that it requires evidence of a transnational market failure to substantiate the need for EU action.[61] One of the key lessons from the *Tobacco Advertising* judgment is that a claim from the EU legislator that a measure removes obstacle

[56] On the protection of the EU budget through criminal law: see PIF Directive (n 28) and Council Regulation (EU) 2017/1939 of 12 October 2017 implementing enhanced cooperation on the establishment of the European Public Prosecutor's Office [2017] OJ L 283/1. On the common currency and criminal law: see Directive 2014/62/EU (n 26).

[57] See Art 3(3) TEU; Art 4(2)(a) TFEU; Protocol (No) 27 on the internal market and competition. This justification is explicitly enshrined as a basis for Union action under Arts 114 TFEU and 115 TFEU.

[58] See Case C-547/14 *Philip Morris Brands and Others* EU:C: 2016:325, paras 107–25, 127–36; Case C-210/03 *Swedish Match* EU:C:2004:802, paras 35–40.

[59] S Weatherill, 'Competence creep and competence control' (2004) 23 *Yearbook of European Law* 1, 33–34.

[60] T Horsley, 'Subsidiarity and the Court of Justice: Missing Pieces in the Subsidiarity Jigsaw?' (2012) 50 *Journal of Common Market Studies* 267, 269–71.

[61] Case C-376/98 *Germany* v *European Parliament and Council (Tobacco Advertising)* EU:C:2000:544, paras 84, 98–99, 106–107.

to trade or distortions to competition cannot merely be satisfied by showing an 'abstract' case that the measure serves internal market purposes.[62]

The need to demonstrate transboundary externalities is not the only constraint to the scope of EU legislative action. There is some tentative support in the case law on the fundamental freedoms which carves out another limit narrowing down the EU's harmonisation powers to remove obstacles that are by their nature susceptible of hindering cross-border movements and trade. The case law on fundamental freedoms is extensive, which necessitates a brief recollection of the main lines.[63] The well-known landmark *Dassonville* judgment defined an obstacle to trade broadly as encompassing all trading rules enacted by Member States which are capable of hindering directly, indirectly, actually or potentially intra-state trade.[64] It was succeeded by the equally prominent *Cassis De Dijon* ruling where the Court enshrined the principle of mutual recognition, holding that Member States can only impose further restrictions on the marketing and import of a product lawfully produced and marketed in another Member State if such restrictions are proportionate and justified by mandatory requirements.[65]

There is nonetheless a potentially important exception in the case law on the fundamental freedoms pertaining to the nature of the obstacle. In the seminal *Keck* judgment, the Court of Justice held that a national prohibition on resale at a loss did not – although it did restrict the volume of sales from other Member States – qualify as an obstacle to trade pursuant to Article 34 TFEU. The Court opined that restrictions on certain selling arrangements could not qualify as restrictions unless those provisions were applied discriminately to traders operating within a state's national territory or in law and in fact affected differently the marketing of domestic products and those from other Member States.[66] The *Keck* judgment was followed up by the decision in *Graf*, where the Court held that a national rule which denied a worker entitlement to compensation on termination of employment if they terminated their contract of employment themselves to take up employment in another Member State, when those provisions granted the worker entitlement to such compensation if the contract ended without the termination being attributable to the worker, was not by nature a hindrance to the free movement of workers.[67] If one assumes for systemic reasons that there is congruence between the law of free movement and the law of EU competences, it thus seems that there are further

[62] See G Davies, 'Democracy and Legitimacy in the Shadow of Purposive Competence' (2015) 21 *European Law Journal*, 2, 7, 17–18.

[63] The literature is vast, see P Koutrakos, N Nic Shuibhne and P Syrpis (eds), *Exceptions from EU Free Movement Law: Derogation, Justification and Proportionality* (Oxford: Hart Publishing, 2016) and C Barnard *The Substantive Law of the EU: The Four Freedoms* (Oxford: Oxford University Press, 2022) for recent comprehensive studies of the case law.

[64] Case 8/74 *Procureur du Roi v Benoît and Gustave Dassonville* EU:C:1974:82, para 5.

[65] Case 120/78 *Rewe-Zentral AG v Bundesmonopolverwaltung für Branntwei* EU:C:1979:42, paras 8–14.

[66] See Case C-267/91 *Keck and Mithouard* EU:C:1993:905, paras 11–18.

[67] See Case C-190/98 *Graf* EU:C:2000:49, paras 23–25.

limits to the internal market justification. The judgments in *Keck* and *Graf* and subsequent case law of the Court[68] confine the exercise of EU jurisdiction by holding that it is not only the likelihood of the risk for obstacles that matters but whether the character of the rule is such as to affect cross-border trade. This means that national divergences which only limit traders' commercial freedom[69] are not such as to constitute obstacles in need of harmonisation. If the nature of the problem has a national dimension without any externalities or affects only theoretically no more than one Member State, the EU's justification in adopting harmonisation measures is questionable.

Another key cross-border justification for EU action relates to 'distortions of competition'. Distortion concerns may arise in certain scenarios, where firms and individuals relocate to jurisdictions with standards that are so low that a moral problem arises. Firms and individuals could then unfairly take advantage of certain states' weak regulation using these states as 'safe havens'.[70] Related to this distortion is the instance where a Member State, in the absence of harmonisation, could enter into a regulatory race in order to attract business and capital to its own jurisdiction on the basis of socially sub-optimal deregulation giving rise to the 'Delaware effect'.[71] When Member States compete under such a scenario, national rules will produce a worse result than harmonised standards. Member States trying to attract business through regulatory laxness will only attract increased business when other Member States do not act in the same way, but if all the other Member States follow, only businesses will gain.[72]

Whilst the distortion of competition argument is recognised as a legitimate rationale for EU harmonisation, there is an abundance of literature challenging the evidence for the premises of the 'race to the bottom' and 'safe haven' scenarios.[73] The key premise here is that the effects of regulation are intrinsically difficult to predict and quantify in empirical terms. Literature on 'competitive federalism'

[68] See Case C-148/10 *DHL* EU:C:2011:654, para 62; Case C-379/92 *Peralta* EU:C:1994:296, paras 23–24.

[69] See, however, Case C-142/05 *Åklagaren v Percy Mickelsson and Joakim Roos* EU:C:2009:336, paras 24–28 for a different narrower approach by the CJEU to obstacles to trade.

[70] See Kumm, 'Constitutionalizing Subsidiarity in Integrated Markets' (n 42) 509–10.

[71] See WL Cary, 'Federalism and Corporate Law: Reflections upon Delaware' (1974) 83 *Yale Law Journal* 663, 668, 701–5; LA Bebchuk, 'Federalism and the Corporation: The Desirable Limits on State Competition in Corporate Law' (1992) 105 *Harvard Law Review* 1435, 1443–44.

[72] See R Van den Bergh, 'The subsidiarity principle in European Community law: some insights from law and economics' (1994) 1 *Maastricht Journal of European and Comparative Law* 337, 345, 355–56.

[73] See eg R Revesz, 'Rehabilitating Interstate Competition: Rethinking the "Race to the Bottom" Rationale for Federal Environmental Regulation' (1992) 67 *New York University Law Review* 1210; WE Oates, 'An Essay on Fiscal Federalism' (1999) 37 *Journal of Economic Literature* 1120, 1134–37; CM Radaelli, 'The Puzzle of Regulatory Competition' (2004) 24 *Journal of Public Policy* 1; D Vogel, 'Trading up and governing across: transnational governance and environmental protection' (1997) 4 *Journal of European Public Policy* 556; L Enriques and M Gatti, 'The Uneasy Case for Top-Down Corporate Law Harmonization in the European Union' (2006) 27 *University of Pennsylvania Journal of International Economic Law* 939; C Peinhardt and T Sandler, *Transnational Cooperation: An Issue-Based Approach* (Oxford: Oxford University Press, 2015); Lee (n 43); S Deakin, 'Legal Diversity and Regulatory Competition: Which Model for Europe?' (2006) 12 *European Law Journal* 440.

and economics suggests that EU legislative action should only take place under certain conditions. In the first instance it must be evinced that national disparities give rise, or risk giving rise, to transnational market failures. Furthermore, EU legislative action must be more effective than Member State action in addressing those failures. Devolution to the federal (EU) level is typically justified for policies involving significant economies of scale and externalities across countries as well as low transaction costs.[74] This could be the case where there the spillover effects from national policies are high, where states do not have the required capacity or expertise (global crime) and where policy-making involves real-time response such as crisis management or decisions on rapidly evolving matters.[75]

Enriques and Gatti have illustrated – on the basis of the example of harmonisation of national company law – why the distortion of competition argument is rarely substantiated in the case of EU harmonisation. With no European 'Delaware' in sight, rules to prevent a 'race to the bottom' are unwarranted. They also observe that EU harmonisation, far from lowering transaction costs, has raised them and can hardly be expected to do otherwise in the future.[76] Whereas Enriques' and Gatti's argument does not reject EU harmonisation *per se*, their findings suggest that claims of the existence of distortions of competition require empirical support. Evidence from regulatory scholarship also suggests that race to the bottom scenarios have overestimated the role played by regulation in market behaviour. Vogel, discussing environmental standards in the US, notes that while state jurisdictions compete with one another to attract investment, they have generally not chosen to do so by maintaining lower environmental standards. On the contrary, many state standards are stricter than federal ones. Research suggests that industrial location is sensitive to factors other than regulations, such as a well-developed industrial base, labour costs, access to markets and other non-regulatory variables.[77]

C. Arguments on Comparative Federalism

From the broader debate on federalism, the key issue on justifications seems to be whether the assertion that a policy area is of a cross-border nature or a regulated issue has such implications sufficient for a federal legislator (like the EU) to act. Lenaerts has for example argued within the context of EU environmental law that it is easy to justify the need for EU action as 'any kind of' of cross-border spillover effects justify Union action.[78] He observes that spillovers in the field

[74] ibid.

[75] See in particular B Coeuré and J Pisani-Ferry, 'The Governance of the European Union's International Economic Relations: How Many Voices?' in A Sapir (ed), *Fragmented Power: Europe and the Global Economy* (Brussels: Bruegel, 2007) 36–42.

[76] See Enriques and Gatti (n 73) 953, 969, 978, 998.

[77] See Radaelli (n 73) 2–3, 5–6, 8; Vogel (n 73) 557–59, 561; Revez (n 73).

[78] In addition to 'competitive spillovers'. K Lenaerts, 'The Principle of Subsidiarity and the Environment in the European Union: Keeping the Balance of Federalism' (1994) 17 *Fordham*

of environmental law arise from the fact that Member States might fear that the imposition of strict environmental standards could discourage industry and put the national economy at a competitive disadvantage relative to other Member States. Such a 'race to the bottom' could be avoided by Union action which is therefore justified to correct distortion of competition. Furthermore, even if Member States may be capable of producing the required outcome, EU action would be more 'efficient' than the individual Member States in achieving the objectives of removing 'spillovers'.[79] Examining Lenaert's argument on the basis of the example of 'spillovers', it is argued to be insufficient to refer to a potential or abstract spillover to make the case for EU harmonisation.[80] There must be concrete evidence that the existence of 'spillovers' gives rise to or is likely to give rise to a 'regulatory race' where states compete with each other by ever more lenient environmental laws.[81] This evidence-based reading of the cross-border justification is in line with Protocol No 2 on the Application of the Principle of Subsidiarity and Proportionality[82] which requires the need for EU action to be substantiated by 'quantitative' and 'qualitative' indicators.[83]

A more circumscribed reading of the cross-border justification is furthermore in line with the broader ideas of federalism. The democratic ethos of federalism is to afford local populations the benefits of self-determination and thereby encourage the survival of cultural identities and foster diversity, experimentation and accountability within the larger multidimensional EU polity.[84] This suggests that important issues should be answered in a legislative process with as direct participation as possible by citizens expressing a preference for governance at the most local level. The preconditions for a well-informed public debate are better at the national level than at the EU level, given the fact that the Union consists of 28 Member States with so many participants, barriers to communication and so many different fora. The legitimacy of EU harmonisation would thus be enhanced if matters without a clear cross-border link were to be decided on a local level.[85]

International Law Journal 846, 880–81, also mentions 'product spillovers', 'pollution spillovers', and 'preservation spillovers' following the classification by RB Stewart, 'Environmental Law in the United States and the European Community: Spillovers, Cooperation, Rivalry, Institutions' (1992) *University of Chicago Legal Forum* 41, 48–49.

[79] See Lenaerts, 'The Principle of Subsidiarity and the Environment in the European Union' (n 78) 879–81.

[80] See Case C-292/92 *Hünermund* [1993] ECR I- 6787, Opinion of AG Tesauro, paras 1, 7–9; See Lenaerts, 'The Principle of Subsidiarity and the Environment in the European Union' (n 78) 865, 895.

[81] See Case C-376/98 *Tobacco Advertising* (n 61) paras 84–86, 106–7.

[82] [2010] OJ C 83/206 ('Protocol No 2'), Art 5; D Wyatt, 'Could a "Yellow Card" for National Parliaments Strengthen Judicial as well as Political Policing of Subsidiarity?' (2006) 2 *Croatian Yearbook of European Law & Policy* 1, 8–9.

[83] See ET Swaine, 'Subsidiarity and Self-Interest: Federalism at the European Court of Justice' (2000) 41 *Harvard International Law Journal* 53.

[84] T Stacy and K Dayton, 'The Underfederalization of Crime' (1997) 6 *Cornell Journal of Law & Public Policy* 247, 278.

[85] See P Asp, 'The Importance of the Principles of Subsidiarity and Coherence in the Development of EU Criminal Law' (2011) 1 *European Criminal Law Review* 44, 46; G Bermann, 'Taking Subsidiarity Seriously' (1994) 94 *Columbia Law Review* 332.

All this suggests a general presumption in favour of the exercise of national policy choices which can be rebutted only if there is a clearly added value of EU action compared to Member State action.[86]

D. Virtual Representation and Transnational Interests

Given all this, it is important to reflect on the argument advanced so far, which is that the most legitimate justification for supranational action is to protect European public goods and transnational interests. The underlying premise for this argument is that national democratic processes are intrinsically predisposed to disregard 'transnational' interests. There is a reasonable suspicion that the legitimacy of governance of Member States may – for 'protectionist' reasons – be flawed in certain situations. Because a single state's democracy represents the collective identities of the citizens of a state, it does not have comprehensive mechanisms to ensure that foreign interests are sufficiently considered within its decision-making processes. Comparative federalism supports this idea. Madison maintained in his prominent Federalist paper no 10 that the central government would better protect minority interests from majoritarian oppression as state interests would be dispersed in the larger national polity.[87] All this suggests that the Union (as a central legislator) is better placed than Member States to protect collective transnational interests in the meaning of European public goods such as the internal market, the transnational protection of the environment and the provision of security for citizens in a transnational society.[88]

If we take the example of the internal market, we refer to the interests of individuals moving within the EU to seek employment, live and reside, work, establish themselves or offer services.[89] Following the argument, special protection for products, services and persons should be conferred in the case where these production factors move into another Member State. Service providers, exporters and persons have much less capacity or possibilities, because of cultural, epistemic and language barriers, to influence other Member States' legislation.[90] Taking the example of individual rights in criminal procedures with a cross-border dimension, there is also a compelling argument to confer 'virtual' political rights to foreigners[91] by

[86] See Swaine (n 83) 53–55, 57–58; Kumm, 'Constitutionalizing Subsidiarity in Integrated Markets' (n 42) 515, 520–21.

[87] Stacy and Dayton (n 84) 287; *The Federalist* Number 10, [22 November] 1787, Founders Online, National Archives: https://founders.archives.gov/documents/Madison/01-10-02-0178, 56–65.

[88] A Somek, 'The Argument From Transnational Effects I: Representing Outsiders Through Freedom of Movement' (2010) 16 *European Law Journal* 315, 323–24; Kumm (n 42); C Joerges and J Neyer, 'From intergovernmental bargaining to deliberative processes: The constitutionalisation of comitology' (1997) 3 *European Law Journal* 273, 294.

[89] Arts 20, 21, 30, 34, 35, 45, 49, 54, 56 TFEU.

[90] Somek (n 88) 335–36; M Maduro, 'Reforming the Market or the State? Article 30 and the European Constitution: Economic Freedom and Political Rights' (1997) 3 *European Law Journal* 75, 76–80.

[91] The theory of 'virtual representation' was postulated by JH Ely in *Democracy and Distrust: A Theory of Judicial Review* (Cambridge: Harvard University Press, 1980) ch 6.

the supranational legislator. On this basis the transnational argument defends EU action to correct the dysfunctional workings of national political processes.[92]

There is also a compelling case for the EU to intervene in protecting the internal market (as a public good) when there are transnational collective action problems arising from the fact that the regulatory choices of competing jurisdictions give rise to different economic costs or opportunities for firms (giving rise to structural bias). Mattias Kumm has made this point clearly by observing that when Member State regulation addresses cross-border economic activities, each state has an incentive to engage in strategic competitive behaviour and privilege mobile economic actors.[93] On this basis the EU should be justified in addressing transnational market failures[94] such as protectionist trade barriers, regulatory costs and inefficiencies arising from multiple regimes, and transboundary externalities arising from negative effects occurring in one state as a result of an activity that is regulated or not regulated in another state.[95]

The notion of European public goods furthermore includes a sub-category of essential supranational interests such as the protection of the EU budget, which should be protected by criminal law as the budget is central for the existence of the Union. The nature of this public good, ie the protection of the budget, entails that criminal justice authorities of Member States are predisposed to deprioritise the protection of the Union's financial interests, making them incapable of effectively enforcing crimes against the EU's financial interests. The European Public Prosecutor's Office is therefore entrusted with the objective of protecting the common interests of the EU budget, which go beyond the territories of individual Member States.[96] On the basis of the same line of reasoning, the EU's power to criminalise fraud and other behaviours targeted against the EU's financial interests[97] could be readily justified on the basis that the EU is better positioned than Member States to protect the public good of the EU budget.

In sum, the key argument here thus suggests the need for the EU to demonstrate the existence of European public goods and other important transnational interests deserving of protection by means of criminal law. This is, however, not

[92] The *Cowan* judgment of the Court of Justice (Case 186/87 *Cowan v Trésor public* EU:C:1989:47) is a very illustrative example of the need to confer additional supranational protection for crime victims in other Member States in order for them to exercise their fundamental freedoms: see J Öberg, 'Subsidiarity and EU Procedural Criminal Law' (2015) 5 *European Criminal Law Review* 19 for further analysis.

[93] See Kumm (n 42) 514–15, 517, 524; Maduro (n 90) 61–63, 74–78 for an illustration of this thesis within the field of free movement.

[94] See Zuleeg (n 52); Collignon (n 50) and Coeuré and J Pisani-Ferry (n 75) for a discussion of market failures and European public goods.

[95] ibid.

[96] J Öberg, 'National Parliaments and Political Control of EU Competences – A Sufficient Safeguard of Federalism?' (2018) 24 *European Public Law* 695; M Wade, *EuroNEEDs – Evaluating the need for and the needs of a European Criminal Justice System – Preliminary Report* (Freiburg: Max Planck Institute for Foreign and International Criminal Law, 2011).

[97] PIF Directive (EU) 2017/1371 (n 28).

sufficient. It should also be demonstrated that these interests by their inherent cross-border dimension or on account of stronger expertise, resources or incentives are more effectively protected at EU level than Member State level. As an example of a European public good *par excellence*, we identified the protection of the EU budget or the common currency where there is a genuine supranational interest to protect those goods.

IV. Conclusions

This chapter has developed a normative framework for assessing EU action in criminal law. The first part discussed legitimacy in EU criminal law which was analysed from the perspectives of criminal law theory and philosophy, examining in particular deontological justifications for recourse to criminal law. It proceeded from the assumption that any more serious discussion on the normative case for EU criminalisation must be based on a criminal law theory of harm or public wrong following Duff and Feinberg's leading intellectual work.[98] It is apparent that EU criminalisation needs to substantiate serious harm of criminal activity before it can be subjected to EU regulation on the basis of the Treaty framework in Article 83(1) TFEU. From the perspective of the general EU constitutional framework, the question of criminalisation cannot, however, only be assessed on the basis of the harm principle but must also integrate an analysis of the public goods framework.

The second section discussed the arguments from competitive federalism, economic and legal theories of market failures, and European public good to assess the justificatory rationale for EU action in criminal justice. Building on Duff's work on public goods in criminal law, it was claimed that the key justification for supranational action in criminal law lies in demonstrating the existence of European public goods such as the internal market, the transnational protection of the environment and the provision of security for citizens, and other important transnational interests deserving of protection by means of criminal law. It should also be shown that the Union is better placed (given its resources, expertise and incentives) than Member States to protect those interests.[99]

Ultimately the argument on European public goods was defended on the basis of the idea of 'transnational interests' as this has been articulated in political philosophy and transnational legal theory. The underlying premise for this argument is that national democratic legislatures do not have comprehensive mechanisms to ensure that foreign interests are sufficiently considered within their decision-making processes. The EU institutions are justified in stepping

[98] See above section II.
[99] See above section III (A)–(B).

in as a 'subsidiary' regulator where central regulation helps to protect European public goods or transnational interests where Member States' actions are structurally deficient in protecting those interests. This particularly involves addressing concrete problems in the form of transnational market failures, transboundary externalities or collective action problems where it is unlikely that Member States, because of perverse incentives and resources, are capable of addressing the problem properly.[100]

[100] See above section III (D).

3

Justification for Harmonisation of Domestic Criminal Procedure

I. Introduction

As discussed in Chapter 1, the EU did not begin to formally cooperate in the field of criminal justice before the Maastricht Treaty. The general EU cooperation mechanism established by means of the third pillar responded primarily to the gradually more pressing collective action problem of serious transnational organised crime which Member States were unable alone to deal with.[1] However, instead of endeavouring to harmonise national domestic criminal procedure, Member States agreed at the 1999 Tampere European Council to introduce the principle of mutual recognition as the main driver for EU criminal policy.[2] However, the implementation of the principle of mutual recognition, notably through the high-profile European Arrest Warrant,[3] led to controversy and placed strain on the confidence of Member States in each other's criminal justice systems. National judges voiced strong human rights and constitutional concerns relating to the operation of the instruments and the Court of Justice's narrow 'legalistic' reading of the Framework Decision on the European Arrest Warrant.[4] Judges faced with a request for extradition were reluctant to return defendants to another state when they believed that their human rights had been violated, for example, by deplorable detention conditions[5] or if the consequent trial would be unfair because of inadequate

[1] Commission, White Paper to the European Council, *Completing the Internal Market* (Milan, 28–29 June 1985), COM (85) 310 final, paras 11, 29, 53–56; S Lavenex and W Wallace, 'Justice and Home Affairs – Towards a European Public Order' in H Wallace and others (eds), *Policy-Making in the European Union* (Oxford: Oxford University Press, 2005).

[2] Council, 'Presidency Conclusions, Tampere European Council, 15–16 October 1999', point 33.

[3] Council Framework Decision of 13 June 2002 on the European Arrest Warrant and the Surrender Procedures between Member States [2002] OJ L 190/1.

[4] Case C-303/05 *Advocaten Voor de Wereld* EU:C:2007:261. This principle has been confirmed in subsequent post-Lisbon case law, most prominently in Case C-399/11 *Melloni* EU:C: 2013:107 and Opinion 2/13, *Accession of the European Union to the European Convention for the Protection of Human Rights and Fundamental Freedoms*, EU:C:2014:2454.

[5] Evidence of deplorable detention conditions has been considered by the CJEU as an exceptional circumstance where the principle of mutual trust can be rebutted: Case C-404/15 and C-659/15 PPU *Aranyosi and Căldăraru* EU:C:2016:198.

respect of defence rights.[6] These concerns, in conjunction with damning scholarly criticism of the absence of EU procedural safeguards,[7] eventually entailed a change of policy direction.

In 2004 the Commission proposed an ambitious Framework Decision covering a wide range of procedural rights in criminal proceedings. Under the pre-Lisbon provisions of Article 31(1)(c) of the Treaty on European Union, there was no explicit competence to harmonise procedural standards. The Commission, however, proposed a broad reading of the competence, claiming that such standards would be necessary to promote mutual confidence across the EU.[8] Several Member States, however, rejected the Commission's reading, and in conjunction with the unanimity requirement in the Council, this made agreement on the Framework Decision impractical among the Member States.[9]

The Lisbon Treaty significantly changed the EU legislator's mandate for legislating in the field of criminal law, and there is now an explicit competence in Article 82(2) TFEU to harmonise national criminal procedure. On the basis of the reinforced Treaty scope, we have also witnessed, post-Lisbon, notable legislative activity in this area, entailing the adoption of seven substantive directives setting out comprehensive rights for defendants and victims.[10] Turning to

[6] See eg German Constitutional Court, Judgment of 30 June 2009, 2 BvE 2/08, para 113 (Lisbon); Polish Constitutional Court, 27 April 2005, Decision P 1/05 (European Arrest Warrant).

[7] See eg S Alegre and M Leaf, 'Mutual Recognition in European Judicial Cooperation: A Step Too Far Too Soon? Case Study – The European Arrest Warrant' (2004) 10 *European Law Journal* 200; S Peers, 'Mutual Recognition and Criminal Law in the European Union: Has the Council Got it Wrong?' (2004) 41 *Common Market Law Review* 5.

[8] Commission, Proposal for a council framework Decision on certain procedural rights in criminal proceedings throughout the European Union, COM (2004) 328 final, recitals 7, 12, 13 and paras 19–30.

[9] House of Lords' European Union Committee, 'Report on Procedural Rights in Criminal Proceedings – Report with Evidence', 1st Report of Session 2004–05, HL Paper 28 (London: Stationery Office Limited, 2005) 14–17; House of Lords' European Union Committee, *Breaking the Deadlock: What Future for EU Procedural Rights?*, 2nd Report of Session 2006–07, HL Paper 20 (London: Stationery Office Limited, 2006).

[10] Directive 2010/64/EU of the European Parliament and of the Council of 20 October 2010 on the right to interpretation and translation in criminal proceedings [2010] OJ L 280/1; Directive 2012/13/EU of the European Parliament and of the Council of 22 May 2012 on the right to information in criminal proceedings [2012] OJ L 142/1; Directive 2012/29/EU of the European Parliament and of the Council of 25 October 2012 establishing minimum standards on the rights, support and protection of victims of crime, and replacing Council Framework Decision 2001/220/JHA [2012] OJ L 315/57; Directive (EU) 2016/343 of the European Parliament and of the Council of 9 March 2016 on the strengthening of certain aspects of the presumption of innocence and of the right to be present at the trial in criminal proceedings [2016] OJ L 65/1; Directive 2013/48/EU of the European Parliament and of the Council of 22 October 2013 on the right of access to a lawyer in criminal proceedings and in European arrest warrant proceedings, and on the right to have a third party informed upon deprivation of liberty and to communicate with third persons and with consular authorities while deprived of liberty [2013] OJ L 294/1; Directive (EU) 2016/1919 of the European Parliament and of the Council of 26 October 2016 on legal aid for suspects and accused persons in criminal proceedings and for requested persons in European arrest warrant proceedings [2016] OJ L 297/1; Directive (EU) 2016/800 of the European

the specific provision, Article 82(2) TFEU suggests that the EU may harmonise specific elements of domestic criminal procedure '*[t]o the extent necessary* to *facilitate mutual recognition* of judgments and judicial decisions and *police and judicial cooperation in criminal matters* having a *cross-border dimension*'.[11] At first sight, this provision seems to provide for a broad EU competence to harmonise domestic criminal procedure. There are, nonetheless, substantive constraints for exercising the competence built into the wording of the provision. One of the central limits is the requirement that harmonisation of procedural standards must 'facilitate' 'mutual recognition' of judgments or decisions and 'judicial cooperation'.[12] Another important limitation is that legislation in the field of criminal procedure must be related to 'criminal matters having a cross-border dimension'.[13] This wording gives support for claiming that the EU's competence to legislate on criminal law is 'conditional' on the need to demonstrate that legislation facilitates the proper operation of mutual recognition (and other forms of judicial cooperation) and relates to proceedings that are of a cross-border nature (or have such implications or dimensions).[14]

This chapter intends to unpack these two key justifications for EU legislative activity in the field of criminal procedure, building on the general framework in Chapter 2 on transnational interests and European public goods. First, the chapter addresses in depth dysfunctional judicial cooperation and collective action problems as arguments for harmonisation. The chapter challenges the justification for having EU competence in domestic criminal procedure on the basis that it enables mutual recognition and judicial cooperation. The chapter subsequently addresses justifications based on market failures (free movement) and representation-based democratic rationales substantiating harmonisation. Within this context, it discusses how the cross-border criterion should be construed within the context of the EU's competence in criminal procedure in Article 82(2) TFEU. As a case study, the chapter offers a critique of the Victims' Rights Directive on the basis of the cross-border criterion. The conclusions summarise the argument and offer some wider reflections on the findings.

Parliament and of the Council of 11 May 2016 on procedural safeguards for children who are suspects or accused persons in criminal proceedings [2016] OJ L 132/1.

[11] As enumerated: (a) mutual admissibility of evidence between member states; (b) the rights of individuals in criminal procedure; (c) the rights of victims of crime; (d) any other specific aspects of criminal procedure which the Council has identified in advance by a decision.

[12] Arts 67(3), 67(4) TFEU provide support for the centrality of mutual recognition in the system of judicial cooperation post-Lisbon.

[13] Art 82(1) TFEU, 1st sentence.

[14] See CONV 426/02, 'Final report of Working Group X "Freedom, Security and Justice"', Brussels, 2 December 2002, 10–12.

II. Dysfunctional Judicial Cooperation and Collective Action Problems – The Mutual Recognition Criterion in Article 82(2) TFEU[15]

A. A Legal Analysis of Article 82(2) TFEU

This section outlines an argument for construing mutual recognition as a constraint to EU legislative activity under Article 82(2) TFEU.

Literal and contextual considerations indicate that the expression 'enabling mutual recognition' is capable of effectively confining EU action on criminal procedure. Article 82(2) TFEU proposes that harmonisation of domestic criminal procedure is only permitted '*to the extent that it is necessary*' to 'facilitate mutual recognition'. In this regard there are two alternative readings of 'necessary' in the ordinary usage of the English language. The narrow understanding suggests that 'necessary' means 'without factor x result y cannot take place'. It does mean something which in the accomplishment of a given object is indispensable. A less stringent interpretation would suggest that 'necessary' entails that the means to enable a certain object must be of greater benefit for some purpose.[16] Nevertheless, 'necessary' should be construed in its context, which is the operation of mutual recognition and its connected terms, 'to the extent' and 'facilitate' mutual recognition.[17] This suggests that it must be established that harmonisation of procedural standards makes a positive contribution to the operation of mutual recognition.

A historically sensitive construction also suggests that the mutual recognition criterion is a significant limit on EU action. Working Group X, which was responsible for the thinking behind the provision, emphasised that the key justification for conferring EU competence in the field of domestic criminal procedure was that such harmonisation would enhance mutual trust among the Member States and thus facilitate the application of the principle of mutual recognition.[18] The underlying principle in the report by Working Group X was the 'accessory' nature

[15] Parts of the following analysis is based on J Öberg, 'Trust in the Law? Mutual Recognition as a Justification to Domestic Criminal Procedure' (2020) 16 *European Constitutional Law Review* 33.

[16] See *Black's Law Dictionary* (St Paul: West Publishing, 1990) 546,1029–30 for the definition of 'necessary'. This reading of Art 82(2) TFEU is supported by several other language versions of the Treaties including: the Swedish, employing the term 'Om det är nödvändigt', the Danish, using the expression 'I den udstrækning det er nødvendigt', the Spanish, employing the term 'En la medida en que sea necesario', the Italian, employing the wording 'Laddove necessario', the French, employing the term 'Dans la mesure où cela est nécessaire' and the Estonian, using the wording 'Määral, mil see on vajalik'.

[17] Art 82(2) TFEU.

[18] CONV 426/02 (n 14) 8–11, 13; European Convention, CONV 727/03, 'Draft sections of Part Three with comments', Brussels, 27 May 2003, 31.

of the proposed harmonisation competence. The Working Group recommended the creation of a legal basis permitting the adoption of common rules of criminal procedure *only* 'to the extent' that such rules were 'needed' to ensure the full application of mutual recognition of judicial decisions.[19]

A narrow reading of the mutual recognition criterion is also faithful to the Member States' aspiration for a clear determination of EU competence in this area. Different attempts in the Convention to extend EU powers under Article 82(2) TFEU to adopt regulations were dismissed as going too far in this contested area.[20] Thus, the EU legislator can only adopt 'minimum rules' and by means of 'directives'. The scope of Article 82 TFEU was further circumscribed in the final drafting rounds of the Convention with an obligation inserted in the text to legislate only in matters having a 'cross-border dimension' showing the 'conditional' nature of the EU's competence.[21] The new institutional setting in the AFSJ with special provisions for criminal law cooperation (providing for an emergency brake[22] and specific decision-making rules[23]) offers further support for the Member States' intention to reassert control over the development of criminal law. The proposed construction of Article 82(2) TFEU is coherent with a 'Member-State friendly' understanding, drawing sharp lines between EU powers and Member States' powers in the field of criminal procedure.[24]

This final points brings us to address the constitutional justification for EU action in this area. A narrow construction of EU competence in domestic criminal procedure is supported by a principled argument which suggests that EU harmonisation must be justified by reference to its potential to address a transnational 'collective action' problem.[25] The collective action problem at issue is the purported absence of 'mutual trust' among state officials in the EU, leading to a suboptimal operation of different judicial cooperation regimes. Harmonisation of criminal procedural standards could consequently be justified to generate sufficient mutual confidence enabling the effective application of the principle of mutual recognition. This understanding of the competence in Article 82 TFEU intrinsically imposes constraints on its exercise. The rationale for having EU competence over domestic criminal procedure is thus that harmonisation measures are capable of

[19] CONV 426/02, (n 14) 8–11.

[20] CONV 727/03 (n 18) 31–32; CONV 821/03, 'Reactions to draft text CONV 802/03 – Analysis', Brussels, 27 June 2003, 88–89.

[21] CONV 821/03 (n 18) 88–89; CONV 727/03 (n 20) 32.

[22] Arts 82(3) and 83(3) TFEU and also J Öberg, 'Exit, Voice and Consensus – A Legal and Political Analysis of the Emergency Brake in EU Criminal Policy' (2021) 46 *European Law Review* 506 for further analysis.

[23] Art 76 TFEU.

[24] See J Öberg, 'The Legal Basis for EU Criminal Law Legislation – A Question of Federalism?' (2018) 43 *European Law Review* 366 for a discussion of how a particular vision of federalism may influence the choice of legal basis for EU criminalisation measures.

[25] M Kumm, 'Constitutionalizing Subsidiarity in Integrated Markets: The Case of Tobacco Regulation in the European Union' (2006) 12 *European Law Journal* 505 provides for a general account of this argument.

addressing the perceived insufficient mutual trust in the Member States' criminal justice systems.[26]

B. Test for Substantiating Compliance with the Mutual Recognition Criterion

On the basis of the reading of the mutual recognition criterion advanced in the previous section, this section discusses the standards that must be satisfied to legislate under Article 82(2) TFEU. Whilst the latter provision does not offer any clear guidance in this regard, it is uncontroversial to suggest that there must be a reasoning in recitals, explanatory memorandums and impact assessments that justifies how an EU harmonisation of a specific procedural right facilitates mutual recognition.[27] The reason-giving requirement in Article 296 TFEU entails that the statement of reasons must disclose the essential factual and legal considerations on which a measure is based and the essential objective pursued by the measure.[28] The reason-giving requirement in Article 296 TFEU seems, however, in light of case law to be of a merely declaratory nature and only requires that reasons, whatever their merits, be offered.[29] It is argued here for a more intense test that requires not only that reasons be given but that these reasons are 'adequate'.[30] In this regard there is a connection between the proposed test and the substantive understanding of the mutual recognition criterion. If we accept the justification of EU competence under Article 82(2) TFEU as based on the need for enabling mutual recognition, the requirement of 'adequate' reasoning entails that there is only one legitimate justification for EU action – ie that harmonisation address specific obstacles to the proper operation of mutual recognition.[31]

It is opportune to illustrate the application of this requirement with a brief case study of EU legislation on procedural rights: the Victims' Rights Directive. Harmonisation of victims' rights has been advanced by the Commission on the basis that the treatment of victims would be a strong indicator of the quality of justice systems in general. Ultimately, it was envisaged that trust-building legislation on victims' rights would benefit the operation of mutual recognition.[32] The

[26] CONV 426/02 (n 17) 9–11; CONV 69/02, 'Justice and Home Affairs – Progress report and general problems', 9, 13.

[27] Art 296 TFEU.

[28] Joined Cases C-154/04 and 155/04 *Alliance for Natural Health and Others* EU:C:2005:449, paras 133–34.

[29] M Shapiro, 'The Giving Reasons Requirement' (1992) *University of Chicago Legal Forum* 179, 182, 198, 215.

[30] Case C-310/04 *Spain v Council* EU:C:2006:521, paras 122–23 for a similar standard from the Court suggesting the need to consider all 'relevant circumstances' when proposing EU legislation.

[31] R Lööf, 'Shooting from the Hip – Proposed Minimum Rights in Criminal Proceedings' (2006) 12 *European Law Journal* 421, 424–30 for a similar point.

[32] Commission, 'Commission Staff Working Paper – Impact Assessment, Accompanying the document, Communication from the Commission to the European Parliament, the Council, the European

idea that harmonisation of defence rights would facilitate the implementation of the principle of mutual recognition has, nevertheless, been subject to criticism, in particular from Mitsilegas. He has observed that the Commission's conventional argument for harmonisation is based on the assumption that it is not compatibility as such that will improve judicial cooperation but the mutual trust it creates that will enhance such cooperation. This train of thought is, nevertheless, not convincing according to Mitsilegas. Because approximation first must create mutual trust, and then only in the second stage facilitates judicial cooperation, it is too indirect to work as a ground for harmonisation.[33]

There is even more force in Mitsilegas' criticism when examining the case for EU action on victims' rights. Article 82(2) TFEU requires a direct connection between a specific harmonisation measure and its effect for the operation of mutual recognition[34] by highlighting harmonisation that is only allowed 'to the extent necessary to facilitate mutual recognition'. The Commission has, however, failed to appreciate this relationship between harmonisation and the operation of mutual recognition. The European Arrest Warrant (EAW) and other MR instruments are intended to function as vehicles in the cross-border enforcement of serious criminality. As these instruments have very adverse consequences for the defendant in the proceedings, there may be a need for common EU procedural standards to ensure the legitimate operation of the regime. Conversely, there is no rational basis for claiming that harmonisation of victims' rights is needed to ensure the operation of mutual recognition.[35] The victim is not and never will be subject to criminal law obligations arising from the operation of mutual recognition.[36] Given all this, it appears that the reasoning does not meet the test advanced of 'adequate' reasoning.

The requirement of an 'adequate' justification is, however, not very difficult to satisfy in practice and hence unlikely to keep 'competence creep' at bay.[37] If the adoption of standards for defendants in criminal proceedings could be justified as 'theoretically' having a positive impact on 'mutual trust', which then may 'facilitate' the operation of mutual recognition, then nearly all rules of criminal procedure would be candidates for EU harmonisation which would entail an illegitimate extension of EU competence.[38] To address these concerns, the chapter

economic and social Committee and the Committee of the Regions, Proposal for a Directive of the European Parliament and of the Council establishing minimum standards on the rights, support and protection of victims of crime, Proposal for a Regulation of the European Parliament and of the Council on mutual recognition of protection measures in civil matters', SEC (2011) 580 final, 5–6, 18–20.

[33] See V Mitsilegas, 'The Constitutional Implications of Mutual Recognition in Criminal Matters in the EU' (2006) 43 *Common Market Law Review* 1277, 1305–7; Case C-300/89 *Commission v Council* EU:C:1991:244, para 10.

[34] See above section II (A) for this point.

[35] See above n 32 for the Commission's substantive reasoning on mutual trust and victims' rights.

[36] House of Lords' European Union Committee, *The European Union's Policy on Criminal Procedure*, 30th Report of Session 2010–12 (London: Stationery Office, 2012), HL Paper 288, paras 45–55.

[37] Mitsilegas (n 33) 1307.

[38] V Mitsilegas, 'The Limits of Mutual Trust in Europe's Area of Freedom, Security and Justice: From Automatic Inter-State Cooperation to the Slow Emergence of the Individual' (2012) 31 *Yearbook of*

argues for a more rigorous test of legality, suggesting that it must be demonstrated with 'relevant' evidence that a specific EU harmonisation measure enhances the operation of mutual recognition.[39] A rhetorical assertion from the Union legislator that divergent national rules on criminal procedure potentially may give rise to problems of mutual recognition is thus not sufficient to justify resort to Article 82(2) TFEU.[40] It should be demonstrated with a sold factual basis[41] that the divergence of formal standards (for example in terms of the right to be present at one's own trial[42]) for a specific right is what makes judges refuse to execute a concrete MR measure.

The evidence also needs to be of a certain quality to pass the test. The Court's case law on rebuttal of the presumption of mutual trust in the AFSJ is instructive in appreciating what type of evidence can be employed to prove the link between harmonisation and mutual recognition. The rulings in *Aranyosi* and *LM* indicate that the evidence which constitutes grounds for postponing or refusing the execution of an MR instrument must provide substantial grounds for believing that the individual, following surrender, would face a 'real risk' that their fundamental rights would be breached. The executing court must be in possession of objective, reliable and specific evidence showing systemic or general deficiencies concerning the adherence to basic fundamental rights standards in the issuing state. The Court has particularly highlighted evidence from the case law of the European Court of Human Rights and reports and other documents produced by bodies such as the Council of Europe, NGOs or the UN as well as by EU institutions as trustworthy sources for this purpose.[43]

In addition to the sources mentioned by the Court, there are several other qualitative indicators available for satisfying the mutual recognition criterion.[44] Such qualitative evidence could, for example, constitute interview studies with judges and prosecutors responsible for the execution of MR instruments, questionnaires to individuals and Member States,[45] as well as comparative studies on legal diversity and

European Law 319, 363–71 has suggested an alternative justification for EU action by arguing that harmonised defence rights are necessary to address the effects of the operation of mutual recognition on the individual. This approach would, however, also offer space for significant competence creep; see House of Lords' Report on *Procedural Rights in Criminal Proceedings* (n 11) 14–17.

[39] Following the interpretation of mutual recognition as a constraint on EU action in section II above.

[40] Case C-376/98 *Federal Republic of Germany v European Parliament and Council of the European Union (Tobacco Advertising)* EU:C:2000:544, paras 83–84, 98–99, 106–7.

[41] Joined Cases C-584/10 P, C-593/10 P and C-595/10 P *Commission and Others v Kadi* EU:C:2013:518, paras 119–20.

[42] Presumption of Innocence Directive (n 10) Arts 8 and 9.

[43] *Aranyosi and Căldăraru* (n 7) paras 80–89, 96, 103; Case C-216/18 PPU *Minister for Justice and Equality* ('*LM*') EU:C:2018:586, paras 59–67, 68, 73; and more recently C-354/20 PPU *Openbaar Ministerie (Indépendance de l'autorité judiciaire d'émission)* EU:C:2020:1033, paras 51–69.

[44] See Commission 'Impact Assessment Guidelines', SEC (2009) 92, 37–40 for definitions of quantitative and qualitative indicators.

[45] Interviews and country questionnaires were for example used in the report of T Wahl and others, *Criminal Procedural Laws across the European Union – A Comparative Analysis of Selected Main Differences and the Impact They Have over the Development of EU Legislation, Annex I, Country Report* (August 2018) 62–63, 73–74, 120–36 for substantiating divergences on procedural criminal law issues.

other scientific studies outlining the nature of specific mutual recognition concerns.[46] It is arguable, however, that the prime evidence for substantiating that harmonisation facilitates the operation of mutual recognition is case law from national courts on the execution of MR instruments.[47] The case law referred to in the Presumption of Innocence Directive Impact Assessment contains instances of 'relevant' evidence, which suggests implicitly that the key concern for national courts, when considering whether to refuse an arrest warrant, related to divergent procedural standards in the issuing state.[48]

In terms of the standard of proof for demonstrating that a specific harmonisation measure satisfies the mutual recognition criterion, the issue is more complex. It is apparent that harmonisation does not need to have a clear quantifiable impact on the building of mutual trust for justifying reliance on Article 82(2) TFEU.[49] Hence, the linkage between harmonisation and mutual recognition does not need to be substantiated with such comprehensive evidence as that required for postponing the execution of an EAW.[50] It is not, however, unreasonable to argue that the EU legislator should substantiate that a specific harmonisation measure leads to positive consequences for the principle of mutual recognition. The proposed standard is that the EU legislator should make it 'likely' that the absence or too feeble protection of certain defence rights in one or more Member States would make judges refuse to execute MR instruments.[51] Theoretical obstacles to the operation of mutual recognition are not sufficient, but the evidence needs to substantiate that national divergences of procedural standards entail a 'real' risk for such refusals by Member States' judicial authorities.[52]

C. A Case Study of the Presumption of Innocence Directive

It is appropriate for the argument here to take a closer look into one central piece of EU legislation adopted under Article 82(2) TFEU – the Presumption of Innocence Directive – to illustrate how mutual recognition can act as a constraint on EU action. In this case, the Commission's key justification for harmonising rights on the presumption of innocence is a claimed absence of mutual trust,

[46] Commission, 'Commission Staff Working Document, Impact Assessment, Accompanying the document, Proposal for measures on the strengthening of certain aspects of the presumption of innocence and of the right to be present at trial in criminal proceeding', SWD (2013) 478 final, point 3.2 includes a list of such studies and reports.

[47] For an overview of case law and country reports, see the general report *Criminal Procedural Laws across the European Union* (n 45).

[48] SWD (2013) 478 (n 46) annex IX.

[49] CONV 69/02, (n 26) 8–9.

[50] *Aranyosi and Căldăraru* (n 7) paras 89, 93–94; *LM* (n 43) paras 60–61; *Openbaar Ministerie* (n 43) paras 54–54, 58–61.

[51] *Tobacco Advertising* (n 40) para 86.

[52] See *Aranyosi and Căldăraru* (n 7) paras 89, 93–94; *LM* (n 43) paras 60-61, for the expression 'real' risk.

which hinders the functioning of the principle of mutual recognition. The case for EU harmonisation of standards on presumption of innocence is that it will increase national judicial authorities' confidence in other Member States' justice systems, which will facilitate the latter's execution of foreign judicial decisions in criminal matters.[53] The Commission further suggests that the public perception that fundamental rights are not respected in every instance has a very detrimental effect on mutual trust and the operation of mutual recognition.[54] Whilst the principles of presumption of innocence set out in the European Convention on Human Rights (ECHR) are generally enshrined in the Member States' legislation, and all of them are parties to the Convention, there is according to the Commission abundant evidence of inconsistent application of those standards by the Member States.[55]

The issue here is what constitutes 'relevant' evidence for the purposes of the mutual recognition criterion. As contended above, Article 82(2) TFEU requires that a direct nexus be demonstrated between harmonisation and the promotion of mutual recognition.[56] It is, however, argued here that the Presumption of Innocence Directive fails to establish this link. The evidence in the impact assessment to this directive is convincing in demonstrating a 'problem' (ie that Member States encroach upon common rights standards) and proving that the EAW system does not work effectively in certain instances (as a result of challenges which lead to costs and delays due to complex investigations into the criminal justice systems of other Member States).[57] The reviewed evidence, nevertheless, gives tenuous support for harmonising the presumption of innocence standards on the premise that it would enable the operation of mutual recognition. On the contrary, it was accepted in the ULB Study report that there is little evidence that Member States' courts relied on a failure to observe fundamental rights on the presumption of innocence in order to refuse or delay recognition.[58]

This finding accords with evidence from stakeholders that suggests there are few cases that show mistrust across borders on the ground of failure to protect the right to the presumption of innocence of suspects or the accused.[59] Surveys of

[53] SWD (2013) 478 (n 46) 4–5, 18–20, 30; Presumption of Innocence Directive (n 10) recitals 2–5.

[54] The Commission referred to evidence by Lord Justice Thomas to the UK Parliament's Scott Baker inquiry, 'A Review of the United Kingdom's Extradition Arrangements', presented to the Home Secretary on 30 September 2012, to support the presence of judicial unease about divergent standards.

[55] SWD (2013) 478 (n 46) 12–19 and annex IV.

[56] See above section II for this point.

[57] JUSTICE, 'European Arrest Warrants – ensuring an effective defence' (2012).

[58] G Vernimmen-Van Tiggelen and L Surano, 'Analysis of the Future of Mutual Recognition in Criminal Matters in the European Union', Call for tenders JLS/D3/2007/03, European Commission – 20 November 2008, 10–11, 22–23.

[59] This observation is supported by evidence given by JUSTICE to an online survey conducted by the Centre for Strategy and Evaluation Services (CSES) in connection to its report, 'Study of financial and other impacts for an Impact Assessment of a Measure Covering the Right to be Presumed Innocent for Suspected or Accused Persons in Criminal Proceedings', referred to in the impact assessment, SWD (2013) 478 (n 46) 33–34.

judges and prosecutors in the JUSTICE report suggest that there is a high level of mutual trust between the judicial authorities of the Member States.[60] This analysis finds support in the UK House of Lords subsidiarity opinion to the directive, which underlined that the evidence invoked by the Commission failed to demonstrate how the Member States' uneven application of the standards in the ECHR caused obstacles to the functioning of mutual recognition.[61] The case law referred to in the impact assessment is also insufficient to substantiate concerns relating to the operation of mutual recognition arising from divergent standards on the presumption of innocence. The high-profile EAW case law from national courts relates to examples where refusal of execution was considered on account of the application of existing human rights standards in the issuing state rather than the absence of formal standards.[62] The other judgments from the Court of Justice concern the construction of the mandatory and optional grounds of refusal which are provided for in the EAW Framework Decision[63] as well as the double criminality requirement.[64]

It is opportune here to illustrate an instance where harmonisation of procedural rights may satisfy the mutual recognition criterion in Article 82(2) TFEU. This concerns the effects of decisions rendered in the absence of the person concerned at the trial (*in absentia*). It is apparent from the negotiations of the Presumption of Innocence Directive and the judgment in *Melloni*[65] that there were mutual recognition concerns arising from divergent procedural standards in trials *in absentia*. The point of disagreement among the Member States and the Commission particularly concerned the scope of protection for a right to be heard in *in absentia* trials.[66]

Melloni is an enlightening example.[67] In this case, the Spanish national court in charge of executing the arrest warrant considered refusing to surrender a person, on the ground that there was a different constitutional standard of protection in

[60] On account of factors such as the capacity of the justice systems, the right to a fair trial, the level of independence of the judiciary: P Albers and others, 'Final Report – Towards a common evaluation framework to assess mutual trust in the field of EU judicial cooperation in criminal matters', March 2011, 330.

[61] House of Commons, 'Reasoned Opinion of the House of Commons concerning a Draft Directive on the Strengthening of Certain Aspects of the Presumption of Innocence and the Right to be Present at Trial in Criminal Proceedings, 3–4.

[62] 19 January 2010, *R (Gary Mann) v City of Westminster Magistrates' Court & Another* [2010] EWHC 48 (Admin); ECtHR 1 February 2011, No 360/10, *Garry Norman MANN v Portugal and the United Kingdom*; 9 September 2011, *Sofia City Court v Dimintrinka Atanasova-Kalaidzheiva* [2011] EWHC 2335 (Admin); 16 May 2011, Oberlandsgericht München, *Klaas Carel Faber*; 30 May 2012, Supreme Court of the United Kingdom, *Assange (Appellant) v The Swedish Prosecution Authority (Respondent)* [2011] UKSC 22 on appeal from [2012] EWHC 2849 (Admin).

[63] Case C-192/12 *Melvin West* EU:C:2012:404; Case C-168/13 PPU *Jeremy F* EU:C: 2013:358.

[64] *Advocaten Voor de Wereld* (n 4).

[65] *Melloni* (n 4).

[66] See Council docs 12955/14; 13304/14; 13538/14; 15837/14; 11112/15; 13471/15 for examples of such contestation.

[67] LFM Besselink 'The Parameters of Constitutional Conflict after *Melloni*' (2014) 39 *European Law Review* 531 for comprehensive criticism of the Court's stance on the protection of fundamental rights.

the issuing Member State's legislation, compared to the executing state.[68] The important facts here are that the conditions for accepting arrest warrants for convictions delivered *in absentia* had been harmonised by the EAW Framework Decision[69] and that the proceedings in the Italian courts were in conformity with the conditions for delivering *in absentia* judgments in that decision. The Court of Justice rejected conferring powers on the executing judicial authority to place further limits on the principle of mutual recognition pursuant to the Spanish constitutional provision when the EU legislator had already exhaustively harmonised the rules on the protection of the fundamental right at issue as this would encroach upon the primacy and effectiveness of EU law.[70]

The key point from the *Melloni* judgment is that divergent standards of protection with reference to judgments delivered *in absentia* may frustrate the operation of mutual recognition. In this area, Member States disagree markedly about what is required for the presumption of innocence principle to be respected.[71] The debate pertaining to trials *in absentia* is even more underscored in the *Melloni* judgment, where the Spanish constitutional court had concerns about surrendering the suspect even where there were harmonised EU rules on the conditions for accepting judgments *in absentia*.[72]

On the basis of the examples of EU legislation (the Presumption of Innocence Directive and the Victims' Rights Directive) considered in this section, there are some general points to be made. The examination of these examples evinces the failure of the EU legislator to engage in a compelling analysis of the nexus between harmonisation, the creation of mutual trust and the operation of mutual recognition. The analysis also throws into sharp relief the apparent dissonance between the broad claims made by the Commission and the evidence and reasons advanced to substantiate those claims. Overall, this suggests that the EU legislator needs to dig deeper to demonstrate the benefits of a harmonisation measure for the operation of a specific mutual recognition instrument.

D. Challenging the Mutual Recognition Justification for Exercising EU Competence in Domestic Criminal Procedure

The previous subsection suggested that it is very difficult for the EU legislator to prove that EU legislation conforms to the mutual recognition criterion. Based on

[68] In the particular case, the Spanish Constitution as interpreted by the Spanish Constitutional Court provided for an unconditional opportunity for a convicted party to challenge a decision of surrender followed by a conviction *in absentia* to safeguard his rights of defence.

[69] See EAW Framework Decision (n 3) Art 4 (1)(a).

[70] *Melloni* (n 4) paras 55–63.

[71] As one example, it seems that certain Member States (when the directive was prepared) allowed accused persons to waive their right to be present at their trial, whilst in other states the presence of the defendant appears to be mandatory in practice for more serious offences: *see* SWD (2013) 478 (n 46) 25–27, 69–70, annex V.

[72] The German Report in 'Criminal procedural laws across the European Union' (n 47) 58–59 points out some of those divergences with reference to presumption of innocence.

these findings, it is appropriate to consider the normative justification for having EU competence in the area of criminal procedure. The debate reverts to examine the EU legislator's central claim for action in this area which is that harmonisation *per se* creates: (1) mutual trust; and therefore (2) a smoother operation of mutual recognition. This assertion is rejected on the basis of a simple contention which is that harmonisation does not contribute significantly to the 'facilitation' of mutual recognition.

Turning first to the relationship between mutual trust and harmonisation, it appears that 'trust-building' in the EU area of judicial cooperation[73] is an intricate exercise requiring the presence of several social and normative conditions. Sociological research suggests that trust-building may be viewed as a learning experience whereby judges – after several personal meetings – can obtain the requisite knowledge to decide whether they wish to trust other Member State officials when executing MR instruments.[74] The 'progressive development of a European judicial culture' includes initiatives such as training seminars for judges from various EU Member States and the building of judicial networks,[75] which are pertinent examples of such trust-building measures. These initiatives intend to build trust by addressing the ignorance of potential 'trustors' – judges, prosecutors of the Member States – about the 'trustees', ie the courts issuing the MR request.

Reverting to the relationship between harmonisation of procedural standards and the building of mutual trust, there are currently no empirical studies substantiating the nature of the relationship. Given this, it is appropriate to build the discussion on the general insights from the social sciences. These findings suggest that the role of law in affecting human behaviour is ambiguous.[76] In line with this, it is surmised that the 'journey to the unknown' for the court executing an MR instrument is not primarily related to a lack of knowledge of the legal system of the country of origin.[77] The journey is 'perilous' because the 'executing' court does not have full information about what exactly has happened before the court first seized of the matter, and how that court applied the law. By applying mutual recognition,

[73] Interestingly, it seems that the Court of Justice's development of 'autonomous concepts' has helped to engender more trust among Member States: see V Mitsilegas, 'Autonomous Concepts, Diversity Management and Mutual Trust in Europe's Area of Criminal Justice' (2020) 57 *Common Market Law Review* 45.

[74] T Wischmeyer, 'Generating trust through law? Judicial cooperation in the European Union and the "principle of mutual trust"' (2016) 17 *German Law Journal* 339, 353, 356.

[75] European Network of Councils for the Judiciary, 'Mutual Confidence 2009–2010 – Report and Recommendations' (2010): www.encj.eu/images/stories/pdf/mutualconfidence/mc2009-2010en.pdf; Commission, 'Building Trust in EU-Wide Justice: A New Dimension to European Judicial Training', COM (2011) 551 final.

[76] See eg JT Scholz and N Pinney, 'Duty, Fear, and Tax Compliance: The Heuristic Basis of Citizenship Behavior' (1995) 39 *American Journal of Political Science* 490; R Paternoster, 'How Much Do We Really Know about Criminal Deterrence?' (2010) 100 *Journal of Criminal Law and Criminology* 765, 818–23.

[77] J Dugard and C Van den Wyngaert, 'Reconciling Extradition with Human Rights' (1998) 92 *American Journal of International Law* 187; Mitsilegas (n 33) 1281–82.

another Member State, however, recognises the judicial act in its interpretation and application of all relevant provisions in a given case.[78] The key issue from a 'mutual trust' perspective thus appears to be the subjective attitude of judges, including their sensitivities to other states' fundamental rights records.

This argument finds support in the EU legislator's official portrayal of the 'trust' problem. A review of the preparatory documents to recently adopted EU legislation suggests that the real 'trust' problem relates to divergent applications of existing fundamental rights standards rather than the absence of formal standards.[79] It is claimed that Member States do not perceive that they can trust the adequacy of other Member States' criminal justice systems for the purposes of mutual recognition. This perception is reinforced by the fact that Member States diverge in the way they comply with the procedural safeguards of the ECHR and by the fact that the European Court of Human Rights has found a significant number of violations against Member States.[80]

However, it should be recognised that harmonisation may – under certain conditions – be beneficial in building trust. It can positively influence systemic trust by safeguarding normative expectations in legal systems as well as reinforcing shared values.[81] Furthermore, the more knowledge judges in a Member State can obtain about other legal systems, the more likely it is that trust will be acquired to enable the enforcement of MR instruments.[82] This argument coheres with an informed understanding of 'rational' mutual 'trust'[83] as an 'impersonal abstract system'[84] devised to cope with a lack of full information on the criminal law rules in other Member States. Rational trust is nonetheless subject to the Member State's commitment to meet our expectations, which in this context rests on the entity's testimonial reputation, output regularities and performance evaluations.[85] 'Executing' judges' subjective perceptions of other states' ability to adhere to central fundamental rights precepts, and their belief that the individuals they

[78] S Lavenex, 'Mutual recognition and the monopoly of force: limits of the single market analogy' (2007) 14 *Journal of European Public Policy* 762, 764–72, for this observation.

[79] SWD (2013) 478 (n 46) 10–11, 13–29; Commission, 'Commission Staff Working Document – Proposal for a Council Framework Decision on the right to interpretation and translation in criminal proceedings, Accompanying the Proposal for a Framework Decision on the right to interpretation and to translation in criminal proceedings, Impact Assessment, SEC (2009) 915, 9–16; SEC (2011) 580 (n 32) 6–20.

[80] ibid.

[81] E Xanthoupolou, 'Mutual Trust and Rights in the Criminal and Asylum Law: Three Phases of Evolution and the Uncharted Territory Beyond Blind Trust' (2018) 55 *Common Market Law Review* 489, 497–98, 505–7; N. Luhmann, *Law as A Social System* (Oxford: Oxford University Press, 2004) 180–99.

[82] See Case C-578/16 PPU *CK and Others v Republika Slovenija* EU:C:2017:127, paras 80–89 for an example of the Court of Justice underlining 'knowledge' as central for the building of 'mutual trust' within the scope of EU asylum law.

[83] See A Giddens, *The Consequences of Modernity* (Polity Press, 1990); N Luhmann, 'Familiarity, Confidence, Trust: Problems and Alternatives' in D Gambetta (ed), *Trust: Making and Breaking Cooperative Relations* (University of Oxford, 2000, electronic edn) ch 6 for a discussion of 'rational' trust.

[84] Giddens (n 83) 26–27, 34–35.

[85] ibid.

are to surrender will be subject to a proper procedure which respects those basic precepts, are central for the operation of mutual recognition.[86] Harmonisation of procedural standards can never *in itself* eradicate judges' basic instinct to be suspicious when executing MR requests based on criminal proceedings which in a particular case do not hold up to central fundamental rights standards.[87]

The second contention is that mutual recognition is likely to work effectively even in the absence of harmonisation. To explain this point, it is useful to consider the distinctive role of law within the EU system of judicial cooperation on the basis of the 'compliance' literature.[88] It is argued here that national courts, which are responsible for executing MR instruments, have 'internalised' an obligation to loyally conform to EU rules. It appears rational to assume that judges' primary motivations for complying with EU law and executing MR instruments without objections are functional, and legalistic. In this regard, it is envisaged that national judges are sensitive to the signals that the Court of Justice sends about the proper application of EU law.[89] The Court's case law on mutual recognition is instructive in this respect, stating clearly that the mutual recognition principle must be applied effectively and unequivocally as a logical consequence deriving from mutual trust.[90] Since Member States are required to trust each other's rules and that they are correctly applied, they consequently need to recognise each other's decisions.[91] The Court of Justice reinforced this line of case law in *Melloni*, holding that Article 53 of the Charter of Fundamental Rights cannot be employed by Member States to impose further limits on the operation of the principle of mutual recognition not envisaged by the relevant MR instrument as this would undermine the principle of primacy by allowing a Member State to disapply rules which are fully in line with EU law.[92] The clear pronouncement of primacy by the Court in *Melloni* provides further ammunition to national courts to loyally enforce the mutual recognition principle as envisaged by the various MR instruments.

The core argument is further supported by a review of a selective sample of national case law on the EAW from national courts in Sweden, Ireland and

[86] R Hardin, *Trust and Trustworthiness* (Russell Sage Foundation, 2002) ch 1: TR Tyler, 'Public Trust and Confidence in Legal Authorities: What Do Majority and Minority Group Members Want from the Law and Legal Institutions?' (2001) 19 *Behavioural Science and Law* 215.

[87] Xanthoupolou (n 81) 490–92, 499–505.

[88] See for a selection of relevant contributions: A Nollkaemper, 'The Role of National Courts in Inducing Compliance with International and European Law – A Comparison' in M Cremona (ed), *Compliance and Enforcement of EU Law* (Oxford: Oxford University Press, 2012); L Conant, 'Compliance and What EU Member States Make of It' in M Cremona (ed), *Compliance and Enforcement of EU Law* (Oxford: Oxford University Press, 2012).

[89] R Romeu, 'Law and Politics in the Application of EC Law: Spanish Courts and the ECJ 1986–2000' (2006) 43 *Common Market Law Review* 395; Conant (n 88) 10–11.

[90] Case C-396/11 *Radu* EU:C:2013:39, paras 33–35 *Melloni* (n 4) paras 36–38.

[91] Joined Cases C-187/01 and C-385/01 *Gözütok and Brügge* EU:C:2002:516, Opinion of Advocate General Ruiz-Jarabo Colomer, para 124.

[92] *Melloni* (n 4) paras 58–65.

Germany.[93] The reviewed case law suggests that divergent standards in criminal procedure have a negligible relevance for the operation of the principle of mutual recognition. National courts do not lightly abandon the principle of mutual recognition and have been keen to uphold EU law on the basis of mutual trust.[94] Whilst the national courts at issue recognise that an EAW may be suspended on account of the national authorities' application of common rights standards, this appears to provide a very high threshold for judicial intervention;[95] ie real and substantive defects in the system of justice, where fundamental rights were likely to be placed at risk, or actually denied.[96] This approach mirrors the Court of Justice's rulings in *Aranyosi and Căldăraru* and *LM*, where a refusal to surrender suspects was considered because of serious fundamental rights breaches (the prohibition against torture and persecution or a risk of a flagrant denial of justice pertaining to the independence of a Member State's judiciary)[97] in the issuing Member State. Mutual trust *in abstracto* thus seems to be sufficient for Member States' judges when contemplating the execution of MR instruments.

This analysis is coherent with Janssen's finding that national judicial authorities perform their controlling activities in a spirit of cooperation in line with the provisions of the relevant MR instruments.[98] National judges arguably see it as their duty to apply those instruments faithfully and not second-guess the assessments of the Member States issuing the MR requests. The fact that the principle of mutual recognition may be sidelined in more exceptional situations of 'egregious'

[93] The sample included a review of approximately 30 judgments from Irish, German and Swedish appeal and supreme courts on the EAW. The German sample has been extracted from the general report *Criminal Procedural Law across the European Union* (n 45).

[94] The judgments, NJA 2009 s 350; NJA 2005 s 897; NJA 2007 s 168; RÅ 2010 ref 45; HFD 2013 ref 42; NJA 2017 s 300; NJA 2010, N 36; NJA 2011, N 34; NJA 2007, N 15, from the Swedish Supreme Court and Supreme Administrative Court offer support for this proposition. See also *Minister for Justice and Equality v O'Connor* [2018] IESC 47; *Minister for Justice v Brennan* [2007] 3 IR 732; *Balmer v Minister for Justice and Equality* [2016] IESC 25; *Minister for Justice and Equality v Buckley* [2015] IESC 87; *Minister for Justice and Equality v Shannon* [2012] IEHC 91; *Minister for Justice v McArdle* [2015] IESC 56; *Minister for Justice Equality & Law Reform v Stapleton* [2007] IESC 30 for judgments of Irish courts in support of the statement.

[95] Whilst German courts stand out as being more prone to refuse to execute an EAW, on the basis of the German Federal Constitutional Court's strong decision of 15 December 2015, order no 2735/14, it still seems that the leading principle in the case law is mutual trust: see eg BVerfG, Beschluss vom 06 September 2016 – 2 BvR 890/16 LG; LG Hamburg, Beschluss vom 21 November 2012, BGH 1 StR 310/12, HRRS 2013, Nr 314; OLG Köln, Beschluss vom 21 May 2012, 2 SsRs 2/12= NZV 2012, 45; OLG Karlsruhe, Beschluss vom 31 January 2017 -1 Ws 235/16.

[96] See *Minister for Justice v Brennan* (n 94); *Balmer v Minister for Justice and Equality* (n 94) para 44, and Swedish judgments: NJA 2007 s 168 and NJA 2017 s 975 (Swedish Supreme Court) for support for this approach. A judgment by the German Federal Constitutional Court, BvR 890/16 (n 95), suggests that the core content of the principle of human dignity must be infringed before an EAW's execution will be suspended.

[97] This test is most likely drawn from the ECtHR's case law: see ECtHR 7 July 1989, No 14038/88, *Soering v United Kingdom*, paras 89–91; ECtHR 21 January 2011, No 30696/09, *MSS v Belgium and Greece*.

[98] See C Janssens, *The Principle of Mutual Recognition in EU Law* (Oxford: Oxford University Press, 2013) 141–44, 190–91, 212; Van Tiggelen and Surano (n 58) 9.

fundamental rights violations does not change the key proposition, which is that national judges tend to execute MR instruments pursuant to the requests of the issuing state. Given all this, there appears to be a marginal role for harmonisation to play in enabling the application of this principle.

III. The Cross-Border Justification in Domestic Criminal Procedure – Article 82(2) TFEU

Having examined mutual recognition as a constraint to EU action under Article 82(2) TFEU, the following section analyses to what extent the cross-border justification can be used to harmonise domestic criminal procedure. Article 82(2) TFEU states that that the EU is competent in this field 'to the extent necessary to facilitate mutual recognition of judgments … and police and judicial cooperation in criminal matters having a *cross-border dimension*'.

Peers has argued that this competence cannot be confined to matters which have a specific relationship with cross-border proceedings, as with the EU's civil law powers. The Treaty drafters intentionally chose a broader wording for the criminal law power ('cross-border dimension') in Article 82(2) TFEU than the wording of the civil law power in Article 81(1) TFEU ('cross-border implications'), which in practice signifies that there have to be two states involved in respect of the latter power. Furthermore, the EU's specific competence in Article 82(2) TFEU would be rendered meaningless if it could only be used in cross-border proceedings as Article 82(1) TFEU already sets out a power to regulate proceedings of a purely cross-border nature. Peers has added another pragmatic argument to defend why EU harmonisation cannot be limited to cross-border criminal proceedings. Taking the example of rules on individual rights, it will be hard *in practice* to limit their impact to cross-border cases. The suspects might all be in the country when the investigation commences, but then they might have moved at some stage in the proceedings of the investigation, at which point there is a cross-border element.[99]

Peers' argument is supported by EU legislative practice. The Presumption of Innocence Proposal is a case at point. In this proposal, the Commission has sustained that Article 82(2) TFEU provides the legal basis for legislation applicable not only to cross-border criminal proceedings but also to domestic cases. It argues that a precise prior categorisation of criminal proceedings as cross-border is impossible in relation to the majority of cases and that all previous proposals on procedural rights of defendants followed this logic as they provided for certain rights to be applicable in all criminal proceedings.[100] The pragmatic argument

[99] See S Peers, *EU Justice and Home Affairs Law* (Oxford: Oxford University Press, 2016) 136–37.
[100] See SWD (2013) 478 final (n 46) 29.

was also endorsed in the discussions before the House of Lords' European Union Committee. It was argued that it would be impractical to limit minimum standards for criminal procedure to cross-border cases as cases may start this way, end up being domestic only, or the converse, by which time the application of EU minimum standards will be too late.[101]

The argument for a broader understanding of the cross-border dimension criterion is compelling from a systematic and practical perspective. It is surely correct that the wording of Article 82(2) TFEU is wider than the one for the civil law power in Article 81 TFEU, corresponding to the wording of Article 83(1) TFEU.[102] It is nonetheless maintained that Article 82(2) TFEU requires the EU legislator to show that the proposed legislative act is directly concerned with a cross-border situation or harmonises national procedural rules that have clear implications for cross-border judicial cooperation. Whilst it is difficult to define cross-border cases, there are two alternative ways of doing this. The first is to have a wide definition including as a cross-border case any case which has a transnational element involving not only proceedings with an offender or perpetrator from another Member State, but also crimes involving a victim or offender from a third country and complex crimes where the evidence is in another country than the one where the suspect and accused are citizens.[103] The second one, which is argued for here, is to have a narrower definition and only apply EU minimum procedural rights for defendants and victims in 'pure' cross-border scenarios, where either a victim or a suspect is involved in a trial in another State than the state in which they are citizens and situations where evidence must be mutually recognised for a trial in another Member State than where it is collected.

It is apposite here to offer some examples to illustrate the argument. If the envisaged measure regulates issues that have a markedly local dimension, the measure is not in line with Article 82(2) TFEU. The proposed definition would mean that migrant EU workers who are victims or offenders in another Member State than their home Member State would be entitled to protection from the EU regime. This covers typical free movement cases which, for example, might involve a lorry driver who is arrested in another Member State as a result of a traffic accident[104] or *Cowan* situations[105] where a person becomes a victim in another Member State than their own. It is also clear that all discussions on mutual recognition of evidence and mutual recognition instruments such as arrest warrants and prohibition orders[106] fall under the heading of clear cross-border cases.[107]

[101] See *The European Union's Policy on Criminal Procedure* (n 36) 81; House of Lords' European Union Committee, *The European Union's Policy on Criminal Procedure*, 30th Report of Session 2010–12 (London: Stationery Office, 2012), HL Paper 288, Bar Council of England and Wales – Written Evidence, 6–7, for similar recognition of this practice.

[102] See below ch 4 for a comprehensive discussion of this provision.

[103] See Commission, 'Study on Cross Border Legal Aid Project', JLS/2008/E4/009, Final Report, 8.

[104] See Commission's legal aid study (n 103) 8 for these examples.

[105] Case C-186/87 *Cowan v Trésor public* EU:C:1989:47; Case C-164/07 *Wood* EU:C:2008:321.

[106] The MR instruments falls, with the exception of evidence, under the scope of Art 82(1) TFEU.

[107] See *The European Union's Policy on Criminal Procedure* (n 36), Viviane Reding – Oral Evidence, Q 55, 122; Commission's legal aid study (n 103) 8.

What is then the rationale behind this stringent reading? First, it appears clear that the intention of the Treaty drafters was that cooperation should be restricted to 'pure' cross-border cases. Working Group X, which was responsible for drafting the provisions in Title V, suggested that Article 82 TFEU should only permit the adoption of common rules on *specific* elements of criminal procedure to the extent that such rules relate to *procedures with transnational implications* and are needed to ensure the full application of mutual recognition regimes.[108] It appeared that many Convention members had insisted that the exercise of EU competence should only be allowed in matters where this was justified by a cross-border dimension, which entailed that Article 82(2) TFEU was specifically revised to add the wording 'cross-border dimension'.[109]

The democratic underpinnings for the transnational interests theory discussed in Chapter 2 also favour this interpretation. If one considers in which situations it is important to have special protection for victims and offenders, those situations are limited to scenarios where the victim and the offender are involved in a trial in another Member State than their own. Suspects and victims in a trial involving cross-border elements have much less capacity or possibilities, because of cultural and language barriers, to defend themselves or in the case of victims obtain recognition, protection and support. Nor are Member States likely to give special protection to cross-border victims or defendants.[110] It is precisely the cross-border elements of domestic criminal procedure, ie transnational victimhood or rights for cross-border offenders, which makes the EU a more legitimate body than Member States to act on a matter.[111]

It is also argued that free movement concerns fall within the category of legitimate justifications for EU action under Article 82(2) TFEU. In addition to the transnational nature of the issue to be regulated, the most common way of defending why EU action rather than Member State action on a matter is warranted is on the basis that it facilitates free movement.[112] It has been suggested that harmonisation of national criminal procedure is needed to ensure the exercise of the free movement of persons within the EU. Differences in national procedural rules reduce access to justice, affect legal certainty and thus constitute obstacles to the fundamental freedoms.[113]

[108] See European Convention, CONV 426/02, 'Final report of Working Group X "Freedom, Security and Justice"', Brussels, 2 December 2002, 11. Emphasis added to underline that the idea was to limit cooperation to 'cross-border' cases.

[109] See European Convention, CONV 727/03, 'Draft sections of Part Three with comments', Brussels, 27 May 2003, 32.

[110] See above ch 2, section III; J Öberg, 'Subsidiarity and EU Procedural Criminal Law' (2015) 5 *European Criminal Law Review*.

[111] See Bar Council of England and Wales (n 101) 13; R Lang, 'The EU's New Victims' Rights Directive: Can Minimum Harmonization Work for a Concept Like Vulnerability'? (2013) 22 *Nottingham Law Journal* 90, 94.

[112] See M Poiares Maduro, 'Reforming the Market or the State? Article 30 and the European Constitution: Economic Freedom and Political Rights' (1997) 3 *European Law Journal* 55, 76–77.

[113] See Commission, 'Proposal for a Directive of the European Parliament and of the Council establishing minimum standards on the rights, support and protection of victims of crime', Brussels, 18.5.2011, COM(2011) 275 final 2–3; SWD (2013) 478 (n 46) 8–9, 17–19; A Weyembergh, 'The

The Court's case law on the scope of the fundamental freedoms supports a broad interpretation of EU competence to harmonise domestic criminal procedures. The *Cowan* judgment is the leading ruling. This case was concerned with a British citizen, Cowan, who had, after being injured in an assault suffered during a brief stay in Paris, applied for compensation from the French Trésor Public for this injury. Cowan was, however, denied compensation because he did not satisfy the conditions for obtaining the compensation as he was neither resident in France nor a national of a country which had entered into a reciprocal arrangement with France. Cowan argued that the French rules on obtaining compensation prevented tourists from going freely to another Member State to receive services there, thus infringing Article 18 TFEU.[114]

The Court held that the principle of equality precludes a Member State from making the award of a right to a person in a situation governed by Union law subject to the condition that they hold a residence permit or be a national of a country which has entered into a reciprocal agreement with that Member State. The Court also found that the prohibition of discrimination was applicable since Cowan's situation was governed by the rules on the freedom to provide services, which includes the freedom for the recipients of services such as tourists to go to another Member State in order to receive a service there. The French Government, however, submitted that the right to obtain compensation, because it was a manifestation of the principle of national solidarity, could be restricted to persons who are either nationals of that State or foreign nationals resident on the territory of that State. The Court disagreed and held that the free movement to receive services includes a right to be protected from harm in the Member State in question on the same basis as that of nationals and persons residing there. The French Government also argued that the contested rules falling within the law of criminal procedure were outside the scope of the Treaty. The Court nevertheless held that although the rules of criminal procedure in principle are matters for which the Member States are responsible, such rules may neither discriminate against persons who exercise their free movement nor restrict the fundamental freedoms guaranteed by EU law. The Court concluded that the French rules were contrary to the prohibition of discrimination laid down in the Treaties.[115] On the basis of this ruling, and if we assume that there is congruence between the scope of the fundamental freedoms and the scope of the EU's harmonisation competence, it seems that the EU legislator can also justify EU harmonisation of domestic criminal procedures with reference to free movement concerns.

The free movement rationale is also premised on the idea of transnational interests discussed in Chapter 2, which suggests that EU action on this field can correct the dysfunctional workings of national political processes by giving 'virtual'

Functions of Approximation of Penal Legislation within the European Union' (2005) 12 *Maastricht Journal of European and Comparative Law* 149, 166–67.

[114] See Case C-186/87 *Cowan v Trésor public* (n 105) paras 2–6, 8.

[115] ibid, paras 10–20.

political rights to foreigners where they have a legitimate concern (eg where the interests of 'free' movers crossing the borders are not sufficiently considered).[116] As noted previously, the employment of the free movement justification must nonetheless be circumscribed. The most important limit is to ask for evidence for substantiating the rationale for EU action and that such action is more effective than Member State action following a subsidiarity-inspired reading of the cross-border criterion.[117] Firstly, a mere finding of disparities between national rules and an abstract risk of distortions of competition are not, according to the Court of Justice as stated in the *Tobacco Advertising* judgment, sufficient reasons to justify the choice of acting at EU level.[118] The transnational interests argument suggests that EU harmonisation can only take place if the Union legislator shows that there are national divergences which give rise to externalities or transnational 'market failures'[119] or a concrete risk of failure in the form of distortions to competition or obstacles to the fundamental freedoms.[120] Potential obstacles do not justify Union action, unless it is shown that it is 'likely' that divergent criminal procedural criminal laws cause obstacles to free movement of persons.[121] Overall, the argument here suggests that the exercise of EU competence under Article 82(2) TFEU is limited to regulation of cross-border proceedings involving in particular situations of obstacles to the fundamental freedoms.

The final part of this section analyses in depth a piece of legislation, the Victims' Rights Directive, to illustrate the application of the cross-border criterion in Article 82(2) TFEU. The purpose of this Directive is to develop mutual trust between criminal justice authorities, by ensuring that the rights of victims are fully respected and protected throughout the EU and that victims have effective access to justice and restoration.[122] It sets forth several rights for victims and their family members encompassing a right to information, support,[123] procedural rights

[116] See above ch 2, section III.

[117] See Art 5(3) TEU; European Council, 'Conclusions adopted at Edinburgh European Council, Annex 1 to Part A: Overall Approach to the Application by the Council of the Subsidiarity Principle and Article 3b of the Treaty on European Union', Bulletin of the European Communities 12-1992, 11–12 December 1992, 20.

[118] See Case C-376/98 *Germany v Parliament and Council (Tobacco Advertising)* [2000] ECR I-08419, paras 83–84, 106–7.

[119] 'Market failure' can generally be defined as 'deviations from perfect markets due to some element of the functioning of the market structure'; see World Trade Organization (WTO) Secretariat, 'World Trade Report 2004 – Exploring the linkage between the domestic policy environment and international trade', ch 3, 150–51: www.wto.org/english/res_e/booksp_e/anrep_e/wtr04_2c_e.pdf. It includes for example protectionist trade barriers, distortions to competition, regulatory costs and inefficiencies arising from multiple regimes and the externalities arising from negative effects occurring in one state as a result of an activity that is regulated or not regulated in another Member State.

[120] See J Öberg, 'Subsidiarity as a Limit to the Exercise of EU Competences' (2017) 36 *Yearbook of European Law* 391 developing the argument on transnational market failures in detail.

[121] See Case C-376/98 *Tobacco Advertising* (n 118) paras 84–85, 106–7.

[122] See Victims' Rights Directive (n 10) Art 1(1); SEC (2011) 580 final (n 32) 21; European Council, 'The Stockholm Programme: An Open and Secure Europe Serving and Protecting Citizens' (2010) OJ C 115/1, 2.3.4, 3.1.1, 3.4.1.

[123] See Victims' Right Directive (n 10) ch 2, Arts 3–9.

when participating in criminal proceedings[124] and right to protection.[125] The rights set out in the Directive apply in cross-border as well as domestic cases.[126] The following examines to what extent the EU Commission correctly exercised its competence in conformity with the cross-border criterion when it adopted the Victims' Rights Directive.

The Commission has proposed two separate justifications for why the Victims' Rights Directive conforms to the cross-border criterion. First, there is according to the Commission significant 'transnational aspects' of victimisation which 'cannot be dealt with satisfactorily by action by Member States'. There is a large number of EU citizens who live, work and travel around the EU and fall victim to crime whilst abroad. Around 11.3 million EU citizens live in a foreign EU State, and a large majority of EU citizens who travel abroad on holidays chose another EU country. Assuming they suffer crime at the same rate as nationals, this means that around 1.7 million citizens (15% of the total) living abroad fall victim to crime every year.[127]

The cross-border argument is in principle a compelling justification. It is well recognised that cross-border victims have specific needs[128] that do not necessarily coincide with those of national victims.[129] Because of these particularities, it is clear why the Union has a special interest in protecting cross-border victims. Secondly, the Commission sustains that free movement concerns can justify harmonisation of victim rights. Victims may not be subject to the same rights in their country of residence compared to their home country, or in a country where they temporarily travel or visit, which risks impeding the free movement of persons and services as recognised by the case law of the Court of Justice.[130] Furthermore, the Commission argues that action at EU level would produce clear benefits by enabling economies of scale to be achieved in relation to the development of training programmes, development and dissemination of information programmes. Action at EU level would also produce 'clear benefits' in terms of effectiveness of the action since new EU legislation will have greater enforcement mechanisms to ensure that legislation is in fact implemented and enable the deficits of previous legislation to be rectified.[131]

[124] ibid, ch 3, Arts 10–17.

[125] ibid, ch 4, Arts 18–24.

[126] ibid, Art 1(1).

[127] See SEC (2011) 580 (n 32) 18.

[128] Such as a need for translation and interpretation (Victims' Rights Directive (n 10) Arts 5(2) and 7) as well as specific protection and legal support to bring proceedings and participating without physically being present at the trial; see Victims' Rights Directive, Arts 3(g) and 17.

[129] See I Wieczorek, 'A Needed Balance Between Security, Liberty and Justice. Positive Signals Arrive From the Field of Victims' Rights' (2012) 2 *European Criminal Law Review* 141, 143, 147.

[130] See SEC (2011) 580 (n 32) 18. In addition to having a right to non-discriminatory treatment as regards the possibilities of obtaining state compensation (Case C-186/87 *Cowan v Trésor public* (n 105) paras 10–19) victims or close relatives of deceased EU citizens are also entitled to equal treatment as regards victims' compensation schemes for crimes committed outside the territory of the host state (Case C-164/07 *Wood* (n 105) paras 11–16).

[131] See SEC (2011) 580 (n 33) 20.

At face value it appears that the justifications in the Victims' Rights Proposal are legitimate to defend the need for EU action on victims' rights. There are at least two rationales: the free movement aspect and the transnational nature of victimisation which offers adequate justifications for EU action. Nevertheless, if we examine the legislative background documents in more detail, it becomes clear that the reasons stated for action do not justify the scope of the proposed action. In particular, it is not explained why the EU on the basis of the stated reasons should have a general right to regulate purely internal situations, ie situations where the victim is victimised in their own Member State and where the judicial proceedings take place in that Member State.[132] The Commission's proposal exceeds the cross-border criterion by regulating rights of all victims, regardless of whether they are victimised abroad and whether the proceedings are conducted abroad.[133]

The essence of my criticism goes to the rationales for EU action: the free movement argument which is based on the alleged cross-border aspects of victimisation. However, in cases where victimisation has no cross-border implications, the logic for harmonisation of local victims' rights on the basis of free movement concerns fails.[134] Local victims' rights are simply not needed for the functioning of the fundamental freedoms. Even if there were a link between the regulation of victims' rights in domestic proceedings and the functioning of the internal market, the Commission has failed to account for such a link.[135] Given this failure and the fact that it seems almost impossible to envisage any scenario where local victims' rights would have any impact on the fundamental freedoms, it appears that the reasoning fails to adhere to the required 'adequacy' standard and thus the cross-border criterion in Article 82(2) TFEU.

IV. Conclusions

The first part of this chapter considered mutual recognition as justification for EU action in the field of criminal procedure. It argued that mutual recognition is not only a principle promoting integration in the field of criminal justice but also a substantive limit to the scope of EU legislative activity in this area. A narrow reading was suggested of Article 82(2) TFEU requiring the EU legislator to make it 'likely' that a specific EU harmonisation measure makes a positive contribution to the operation of mutual recognition. The subsequent part of the chapter challenged, from a

[132] See P Asp and others, 'A Manifesto on European Criminal Policy' (2013) 11 *Zeitschrift für Internationale Strafrechtsdogmatik* 430 444; P Rock, *Constructing victims' rights; the Home Office, New Labour, and victims* (Oxford: Oxford University Press, 2004) 513–14.

[133] That the Victims' Rights Directive (n 10) applies to all victims is clear from Arts 1 and 2.

[134] See European Union's Policy on Criminal Procedure (n 36), S Peers, Oral Evidence, Q 16, 140.

[135] See House of Lords' European Union Committee, *The European Union's Policy on Criminal Procedure*, EU Sub-Committee E (Justice and Institutions), EU Criminal Procedure Policy, Valsamis Mitsilegas – Supplementary Written Evidence, 30th Report of Session 2010–12, 111–12, 114.

principled perspective, the 'instrumental' justification for exercising EU competence to enable mutual recognition. On the basis of sociological and legal research on 'trust-building' and an analysis of the EU legislator's account of the 'trust' problem, it was argued that there is a very narrow role for harmonisation in creating mutual trust. Furthermore, general compliance research, and national case law on the EAW, propose that national judges in principle seem to have 'internalised' an obligation to loyally enforce the MR instruments in a spirit of confidence.[136]

The second section examined the cross-border justification in Article 82(2) TFEU. It was argued that the EU's competence for regulation of national procedural rules should be limited to 'clear' cross-border cases – ie where the defendant or the victim's suspect is not a citizen of the Member State in which they are tried; in cases where the crime is committed abroad; in cases where evidence must be mutually recognised for a trial in another Member State than where it is collected. The EU only has a legitimate interest in regulating the situations in cross-border cases. It was suggested that the EU legislator should demonstrate that there is a problem of insufficient protection of defence and victims' rights having a cross-border dimension which gives rise to obstacles or potential obstacles to the fundamental freedoms. The EU legislator would also have to show that the envisaged EU action, given the scope or scale of the action, gives or is likely to give benefit in addressing the problem compared to Member State action.[137] On the basis of this conceptualisation of the cross-border criterion, a general criticism was put forward against discretely selected EU proposals in the field of defence rights and victims' rights that cover both domestic and cross-border proceedings. A particular case study of the Victims' Right Directive was conducted. It was suggested that the Victims' Rights Proposal failed to offer compelling reasoning to substantiate how and why harmonisation of victims' rights would facilitate the fundamental freedoms.[138]

This brings us to the ramification of the argument, which puts into the limelight the legitimate rationales for EU legislation in this area. A limited reading of EU competence under Article 82(2) TFEU suggests a 'careful' approach to EU intervention in the field of criminal procedure. The post-Lisbon proliferation of legislative activity to strengthen procedural rights of individuals marks a distinctive shift from a state-centred focus on mutual recognition to harmonisation and a system that puts fundamental rights at the forefront.[139] The argument here is, however, critical to several of these instances of EU legislation (such as the Victims' Rights Directive and the Directive on the Presumption of Innocence) which provide self-standing human rights standards with a feeble link between the rights proposed and their necessity for the operation of mutual

[136] See above section II.
[137] See above section III (A).
[138] See above section III.
[139] See V Mitsilegas, 'The Symbiotic Relationship between Mutual Trust and Fundamental Rights in Europe's Area of Criminal Justice' (2015) 6 *New Journal of European Criminal Law* 457, 475–77.

recognition and the fundamental freedoms. The EU legislator should look for evidence and data on contestation on the scope of fundamental rights protection and the scope of criminal definitions among the Member States' leading national courts to not execute MR instruments.[140] Such a policy will also look for evidence of problems and issues pertaining to the absence of sufficient protection for cross-border defendants and victims in criminal proceedings. Those instances are informative in showing where the EU legislator might intervene to provide added value in enhancing the legitimacy of national criminal procedural law.[141]

The example of harmonisation of procedural standards in this chapter also illustrates the general argument. In cross-border situations, there is a clear interest for the EU to intervene to protect the legitimate interests of individual defendants (who exercised their right to free movement) who otherwise would not have a voice in the national democratic procedure. However, in purely national situations which do not have any cross-border dimension, it is more ambiguous whether the EU per se is better placed to strike the balance between the necessities of law enforcement and defence rights.[142] There are many different opinions on what is just, on what is advisable, and on what is suitable, and Member States disagree considerably on what is a fair level of procedural minimum rights for defendants and victims and do so for valid cultural and moral reasons. A Member State can for example argue that divergence in procedural protection for offenders should lead to a strengthening of those rights by filling in those gaps in States with no or weak protection. Some Member States may on the other hand perceive that strengthening offenders' rights will impair the effectiveness of the criminal justice system and reduce the chances of clearing up crimes. Whilst formal justice[143] is often invoked as a justification for common standards,[144] it is difficult to defend harmonisation with reference to substantive justice arguments within the EU context given the absence of a common conception of what this might entail.[145] The cross-border criterion precludes the EU legislator from substituting the fairness and justice of policy choices made

[140] Not only data on time delays and implementation deficits; see Commission, 'Report from the Commission to the European Parliament and the Council On the implementation since 2007 of the Council Framework Decision of 13 June 2002 on the European arrest warrant and the surrender procedures between Member States', COM (2011) 175 final.

[141] See above section II (B) for a discussion of judicial review of legislation adopted under Art 82(2) TFEU.

[142] See Kumm (n 31) 519–20.

[143] J Rawls, *A Theory of Justice* (Cambridge: Belknap Press of Harvard University Press, revised edn 1999) 50–51, 208–9 suggests that formal justice entails that similar cases are treated similarly and that distinctions between persons must be justified by reference to the relevant legal rules and principles.

[144] A Weyembergh, 'Approximation of criminal laws, the Constitutional Treaty and the Hague Programme' (2005) 42 *Common Market Law Review* 1567, 1581.

[145] See J Vogel 'Why is the harmonisation of penal law necessary? A comment' in A Klip and H van der Wilt (eds), *Harmonisation and Harmonising Measures in Criminal Law* (Amsterdam: Royal Netherlands Academy of Science, 2002) 60–61.

by Member States, and justice cannot thus in itself justify EU harmonisation of national procedural criminal standards. This approach accepts reverse discrimination, meaning that unless there is a cross-border situation, victims or suspects would have to accept the rules to which they are nationals and may be differently treated depending on whether they are involved in a transnational context.[146] But this is, and has always been, the central way of delimiting EU competences in regulating the affairs of the Member States.

[146] See Art 82(2) TFEU.

4

Justification for EU Action in Substantive Criminal Law

I. Introduction

How powers are divided between the Member States and the Union in the politically sensitive field of criminal law is a pivotal question of federalism.[1] For a long time it was also apparent that concerns for state integrity and political sensitivity made criminal law a matter beyond the sphere of EU integration.[2] Whilst the European Union by means of successive Treaty revisions in Maastricht, Nice and Amsterdam had evolved significantly and assumed powers over several new policy areas, no explicit power to harmonise in criminal law had been conferred on the Union before the Lisbon Treaty. The Maastricht Treaty had constructed a general EU judicial cooperation mechanism to address the collective action problem of serious transnational organised crime by means of the third pillar.[3] Instead of harmonising domestic criminal law, the Member States prioritised at the 1999 Tampere European Council the introduction of the principle of mutual recognition as the main driver for EU criminal policy.[4]

The absence of a clear Community competence to harmonise domestic criminal law did not, however, settle the matter. The Commission assumed its role as a 'supranational entrepreneur'[5] and argued for a Community criminal law competence on the basis that it was needed for the effective enforcement of EU policies.[6] The Council and the Member States disagreed, arguing that the absence of an express

[1] R Barkow, 'Federalism and Criminal Law: What the Feds Can Learn from the States' (2011) 109 *Michigan Law Review* 519.

[2] See Michael Dougan, 'From the Velvet Glove to the Iron Fist: Criminal Sanctions for the Enforcement of Union Law' in Marise Cremona (ed), *Compliance and the Enforcement of EU Law* (Oxford: Oxford University Press, 2012) 74–78, 91–92; S Lavenex and W Wallace, 'Justice and Home Affairs – Towards a European Public Order' in H Wallace and others (eds), *Policy-Making in the European Union* (Oxford: Oxford University Press, 2005).

[3] Commission, White Paper to the European Council, *Completing the Internal Market* (Milan, 28–29 June 1985), COM (85) 310 final, paras 11, 29, 53–56.

[4] Council, 'Presidency Conclusions, Tampere European Council, 15-16 October 1999', point 33.

[5] C Kaunert, '"Without the Power of Purse or Sword": The European Arrest Warrant and the Role of the Commission' (2007) 29 *Journal of European Integration* 387.

[6] See Case C-176/03 *Commission v Council* EU:C:2005:542, paras 19–21; Case C-440/05 *Commission Communities v Council* EU:C:2007:625, paras 24–25, 28–39.

conferral of competence in the Treaties in conjunction with concerns for sovereignty militated against recognising such a competence in the first pillar.[7] The Court of Justice was called on to determine the issue. The Court accepted the Commission's argument and recognised, in two prominent judgments, *Environmental Crimes*[8] and *Ship-Source Pollution*,[9] that the Community had a competence to impose criminal sanctions if this was essential for the effective enforcement of EU environmental policy. The debate on the existence of a first pillar competence was ultimately brought to an end by the Lisbon Treaty, which explicitly conferred a competence on the EU to impose criminal sanctions to enforce substantive Union policies.[10]

The Lisbon Treaty's new competence in Article 83 TFEU to harmonise domestic substantive criminal law in relation to offences and sanctions has formalised the general national division between 'core' and 'regulatory criminal law'. Article 83(1) TFEU first deals first with the former category of offences, whilst Article 83(2) TFEU addresses the post-*Environmental Crimes* EU competence in criminal law which is 'essential' to effectively enforce existing EU policies.[11] The author has previously extensively analysed the EU's regulatory criminal law competence in Article 83(2) TFEU,[12] and the key focus in this chapter will therefore be on examining the scope and justifications for exercising the power in Article 83(1) TFEU.

Article 83(1) lists 10 offences[13] for which the EU has a right to establish minimum rules concerning the definition of criminal offences and sanctions. These offences are considered to be of a 'particularly serious nature', and the provision assumes that these offences deserve criminalisation because of the general harm and damage incurred by such offences without any need to establish that harm. The rationale for employing Article 83 TFEU is of central relevance as it is one of the more contested provisions of the Lisbon Treaty. The German Federal Constitutional Court has prominently in its *Lisbon Judgment*, due to the sensitive nature of criminal law for state sovereignty, expressed its reservations in relation to an excessive use of the Union's new criminal law powers.[14] On the basis of the reinforced Treaty mandate, we have also witnessed, post-Lisbon, notable legislative activity in this area, entailing the adoption of no less than eight directives

[7] See Case C-176/03 *Commission v Council* (n 6) paras 26–27.

[8] See Case C-176/03 *Commission v Council* (n 6) paras 47–48. The criminal law competence was conferred on the basis of Art 175 of the Consolidated Version of the Treaty Establishing the European Community [2002] OJ C 325/33 ('EC', 'EC Treaty').

[9] See Case C-440/05 *Commission v Council* (n 6) paras 66–69. The Court inferred the competence on the basis of Art 80(2) EC.

[10] See Art 83(2) TFEU.

[11] See P Asp, *The Substantive Criminal Law Competence of the EU – Towards an Area of Freedom, Security & Justice – Part 1* (Stockholm: Jure, 2013) 19–20.

[12] J Öberg, *Limits to EU Powers: A Case Study of EU Regulatory Criminal Law* (Oxford: Hart Publishing, 2017).

[13] 'Terrorism, trafficking in human beings and sexual exploitation of women and children, illicit drug trafficking, illicit arms trafficking, money laundering, corruption, counterfeiting of means of payment, computer crime and organised crime.'

[14] See Judgment of German Federal Constitutional Court of 30 June 2009, *Lisbon Judgment*, Case 2 BvE 2/08, 5/08, 2 BvR 1010/08, 1022/08, 1259/08, 182/09 (2009), para 226.

on criminalisation in a number of different areas.[15] Whilst Article 83 TFEU has settled the controversy of the existence of EU competence to harmonise criminal law, it is still debatable how this competence should be exercised.

This chapter thus proceeds to analyse the justifications for EU legislative activity in substantive criminal law on the basis of Article 83(1) TFEU. First, it analyses harm-based theoretical accounts as justifications for harmonisation of EU substantive criminal law, examining as case studies the recent proposals for criminalisation of gender-based violence, the EU proposal on criminalisation of hate speech and hate crime (II). Subsequently, it considers in depth the transnational criterion, supranational public goods and market failures as rationales for harmonisation of substantive criminal law. On the basis of the examples of gender-based violence, hate speech and the EU proposal criminalising violation of EU restrictive measures, it argues that EU action can only be directed to problems where criminal law protects supranational public goods or addresses market failures. The chapter finally addresses dysfunctional judicial cooperation and discusses and criticises mutual recognition as a justification for harmonisation of substantive criminal law under Article 83 TFEU.

II. The EU's Substantive Criminal Law Competence in Article 83(1) – Principle of Harm

A. Particularly Serious Crimes

When examining the EU's core criminal law competence in Article 83(1) TFEU, it is appropriate to commence with the wording of the provision. Pursuant to this provision:

> The European Parliament and the Council may, by means of directives … establish minimum rules concerning the definition of criminal offences and sanctions in the areas of

[15] Directive 2014/57/EU of the European Parliament and of the Council of 16 April 2014 on criminal sanctions for market abuse [2014] OJ L 173/79; Directive (EU) 2017/541 of the European Parliament and of the Council of 15 March 2017 on combating terrorism and replacing Council Framework Decision 2002/475/JHA and amending Council Decision 2005/671/JHA [2017] OJ L 88/6; Directive 2013/40/EU of the European Parliament and of the Council of 12 August 2013 on attacks against information systems and replacing Council Framework Decision 2005/222/JHA [2013] OJ L 218/8; Directive 2011/92/EU of the European Parliament and of the Council of 13 December 2011 on combating the sexual abuse and sexual exploitation of children and child pornography, and replacing Council Framework Decision 2004/68/JHA [2011] OJ L 335/1; Directive (EU) 2019/713 of the European Parliament and of the Council of 17 April 2019 on combating fraud and counterfeiting of non-cash means of payment and replacing Council Framework Decision 2001/413/JHA [2019] OJ L 123/18; Directive 2014/62/EU of the European Parliament and of the Council of 15 May 2014 on the protection of the euro and other currencies against counterfeiting by criminal law and replacing Council Framework Decision 2000/383/JHA [2014] OJ L 151/1; Directive (EU) 2018/1673 of the European Parliament and of the Council of 23 October 2018 on combating money laundering by criminal law [2018] OJ L 284/22; Directive (EU) 2017/1371 of the European Parliament and of the Council of 5 July 2017 on the fight against fraud to the Union's financial interests by means of criminal law [2017] OJ L 198/29.

> *particularly serious crime* with a *cross-border dimension* resulting from *the nature or impact of such offences* or from a *special need* to combat them on a common basis.
>
> These areas of crime are the following: *terrorism, trafficking in human beings and sexual exploitation of women and children, illicit drug trafficking, illicit arms trafficking, money laundering, corruption, counterfeiting of means of payment, computer crime and organised crime.*
>
> On the basis of developments in crime, the Council may adopt a [unanimous] decision identifying other areas of crime that *meet the criteria specified in this paragraph*.'

This provision strongly enshrines two of the key normative justifications for EU criminal law discussed in this book: the 'cross-border' criterion and the 'harm-based' principle. These criteria ((i) 'particularly serious crime' that has a (ii) 'cross-border dimension') are cumulative and both need to be satisfied for all new offences that are added to the list.[16]

Procedurally, the provision also imposes a two-step procedure for adopting EU legislation. The first step is that the Council unanimously adopts, after obtaining the consent of the European Parliament (EP), a decision identifying a certain offence (eg hate speech) as another area of crime that meets the criteria set out in Article 83(1) TFEU '[o]n the basis of developments in crime'. Such a decision will extend the list of areas of crime to include this offence as an EU crime This will therefore provide a legal basis enabling the EP and the Council to adopt a directive on criminalisation for this selected offence in line with the ordinary legislative procedure.[17]

As mentioned above in Chapter 2, there is a constitutional endorsement of the harm principle in the Treaties as Article 83(1) TFEU offers the EU powers to criminalise in the areas of '*particularly serious crime*'.[18] The harm principle is also more generally endorsed as a guiding principle by the EU institutions in respect of the EU's substantive criminal law competence with an emphasis on an evidence-based reading of the principle. The Council has stated in its 2009 'Conclusions on model provisions' that the 'criminal provisions should focus on conduct causing actual harm or seriously threatening the rights or essential interest which is the object of protection; that is, avoiding criminalisation of a conduct at an unwarrantably early stage'.[19] The Commission's Communication from 2011 stressed that criminalisation should proceed based on clear factual evidence about the serious nature or

[16] Asp, *Substantive Criminal Law Competence of the EU* (n 11) 18–20.

[17] Art 83(1) TFEU; S Peers, 'EU foreign policy sanctions: extending and using EU criminal law powers to enforce them', 2 December 2022, EU Law Analysis: http://eulawanalysis.blogspot.com/2022/12/eu-foreign-policy-sanctions-extending.html.

[18] eg 'terrorism, trafficking in human beings and sexual exploitation of women and children, illicit drug trafficking, illicit arms trafficking, money laundering, corruption, counterfeiting of means of payment, and organised crime'.

[19] Council, 'Council Conclusions on model provisions, guiding the Council's criminal law deliberations' (2979th Justice and Home Affairs Council meeting, Brussels, 30 November 2009) 3.

grave effects of the crime in question.[20] The EP, on the other hand, argued that the necessity of new substantive criminal law provisions must be demonstrated by the factual evidence, making it clear that criminalisation should focus on the conduct that causes 'significant pecuniary or non-pecuniary damage' to society or individuals.[21]

In terms of the enumeration of so-called eurocrimes, Article 83(1) TFEU offers evidence of the harm principle as the leading consideration as the list thus reflects an 'EU-wide consensus about the harmfulness of the crimes' registered therein as similar conduct has already been recognised as deserving of criminalisation in the predominant majority of the EU Member States.[22] The harm evidently transpires through the listed 'EU crimes', namely, terrorism, trafficking in human beings and sexual exploitation of women and children, illicit drug trafficking, illicit arms trafficking, money laundering, corruption, counterfeiting of means of payment, computer crime and organised crime.[23] As regards some of the offence types on the list, the generic requirement of 'particularly serious' will almost automatically be satisfied. For example, trafficking in human beings and terrorism in standard cases are offences that almost always or at least in standard cases must be considered to be particularly serious. In relation to other offence types on the list, however, the requirements are not necessarily fulfilled. Computer crimes do not have to be particularly serious (eg small-scale file sharing or minor data trespassing). Asp has, however, argued that it is not sufficient that the crimes are on the list but that they also need to conform to the generic requirements (particularly serious offence with a cross-border dimension) relying on the fact that those conditions are placed in subsection 1 of Article 83(1) TFEU.[24]

Whilst Asp employs a well-executed textual reading of Article 83(1) TFEU, there are additional considerations that need to be taken into account. First, it is very difficult to appreciate why the Member States would have bothered to set out this list of offences if the intention was not that these offences were considered by those states to satisfy the general requirements. An alternative reading is that the list indicates offences that are considered to be 'particularly serious' and of a 'cross-border dimension' without this having to be proven when a legislative initiative concerns one of those offences. This is a supported by a historically sensitive construction of the Treaties. Working Group X, responsible for drafting

[20] 'Communication from the Commission to the European Parliament, the Council, the European Economic and Social Committee and the Committee of the Regions – Towards an EU Criminal Policy: Ensuring the effective implementation of EU policies through criminal law', COM (2011) 573 final, 3, 7–10.

[21] European Parliament, 'Resolution of 22 May 2012 on an EU approach to criminal law' P7_TA(2012)0208, 2; N Peršak, 'Principles of EU criminalisation and their varied normative strength: Harm and effectiveness' (2021) 27 *European Law Journal* 463, 469.

[22] Peršak (n 21) 475–76; V Mitsilegas, *EU Criminal Law After Lisbon: Rights, Trust and the Transformation of Justice in Europe* (Oxford: Hart Publishing, 2016) 58–62.

[23] Peršak (n 21) 468–69.

[24] Asp (n 11) 83–85.

the Constitutional Treaty, contended that the centre of attention of the Union's competence in criminal law should be serious crime of a transnational dimension or implications and the need to prosecute certain types of crime at Union level.[25] In terms of those kinds of offences, the Group believed that a certain degree of harmonisation was necessary as they could not be addressed effectively by the Member States acting alone.[26] The Working Group pointed to the Treaty of Amsterdam for more concrete examples of such serious transnational offences where the Union had an explicit power to adopt measures 'relating to … criminal acts and to penalties in the fields of organised crime, terrorism and illicit drug trafficking'.[27] The Treaty, however, also implicitly suggested a power for harmonisation in the areas of trafficking in persons and offences against children, illicit drug and arms trafficking, corruption and fraud.[28] The Tampere European Council mentioned specifically harmonisation in the areas of 'financial crime (money laundering, corruption, Euro counterfeiting), drugs trafficking, trafficking in human beings, particularly exploitation of women, sexual exploitation of children, high tech crime and environmental crime'.[29] This suggests that there has been some support from the original contention among the Member States that there exists a list of crimes that is intrinsically of a particularly serious nature and of a cross-border dimension.

Notwithstanding these considerations, the following strives to exhaustively analyse some discrete examples of EU criminal law legislation on the assumption also that new criminalisation proposals in the areas of crime listed in Article 83(1) need to satisfy the criterion of 'particularly serious crime' and the 'cross-border' criterion. Recent legislative practice (which has in some detail discussed the proposals on the basis of these criteria) gives support for this approach in the analysis. The addition of new crimes in Article 83(1) TFEU compared to the crimes mentioned in the Amsterdam Treaty also gives some support for the reading that new criminalisation in these areas needs to be scrutinised on the basis of these 'generic' criteria ('particularly serious crime' of a 'cross-border dimension').[30] Furthermore, a more conventional reading of the subsidiarity principle in Article 5(3) TEU also suggests that the offences proposed under Article 83(1) TFEU in already enumerated crime areas need to be in line with the cross-border dimension.[31]

[25] CONV 69/02, 'Justice and Home Affairs – Progress report and general problems', Brussels, 31 May 2002.

[26] CONV 426/02, 'Final report of Working Group X "Freedom, Security and Justice"', Brussels, 2 December 2002, 9–10; CONV 727/03, 'Draft sections of Part Three with comments', Brussels, 27 May 2003.

[27] Art 31(e) of the pre-Lisbon version of the Treaty on European Union [2002] OJ C 325/5.

[28] Art 29 of the pre-Lisbon version of the Treaty of European Union.

[29] European Council, Tampere European Council, 15 and 16 October 1999, Presidency Conclusions. Many of these offences are now in the list in Art 83(1) TFEU.

[30] Asp (n 11), 83-85.

[31] See J Öberg, 'Subsidiarity as a Limit to the Exercise of EU Competences' (2017) 36 *Yearbook of European Law* 391.

B. Gender-Based Violence and Violence against Women

In the following subsections, some more recent straightforward examples of how the harm principle can be applied within the EU context will be analysed, looking first at the EU proposal on gender-based violence and violence against women. In May 2021, the European Parliament (EP) drafted a report suggesting that gender-based violence should be added to the list of new crimes under Article 83(1) TFEU.[32] As gender-based violence is not enumerated in the eurocrimes list, the provision requires that the Council would have to adopt a unanimous decision identifying gender-based violence as an area of crime that meets this criterion after having obtained the consent of the EP.[33]

Since it nonetheless was impossible to obtain unanimity in the Council, the proposal by the EP to add gender-based violence has not been taken further. The Commission instead tweaked the legal basis and submitted a new proposal, claiming that criminalisation in combating violence against women and domestic violence could be encompassed within the list of eurocrimes in Article 83(1) TFEU under the areas of 'sexual exploitation' and 'computer crimes'.[34] The proposal is currently under negotiations with the EP and the Council, but at the time of writing the approach of the Commission and the EP is that the directive at least should criminalise the following offences: rape,[35] female genital mutilation, non-consensual sharing of intimate or manipulated material, cyber stalking, cyber harassment and cyber incitement to violence and hatred.[36]

In respect of the assessment of the principle of harm and the criterion of 'particularly serious crime' the following can be stated. It seems apparent that violence against women and gender-based violence in general imposes very serious harm to individuals and society in the sense discussed above.[37] The EP Draft Report and the Commission Proposal in 2022 substantiated a wide range of adverse psychological, economic and social impacts that gender-based violence has on victims, including stress, anxiety, panic attacks, low self-esteem, post-traumatic stress disorder, higher rates of depression, alcohol and drug abuse.[38] Physical or sexual

[32] European Parliament, 'Draft Report with recommendations to the Commission on identifying gender-based violence as a new area of crime listed in Article 83(1) TFEU', (2021/2035(INL)), 30.4.2021.

[33] Art 83(1) TFEU, para 2.

[34] Commission, 'Proposal for a Directive of the European Parliament and of the Council on combating violence against women and domestic violence', COM(2022) 105 final, 8–9.

[35] The Council's General Approach does not include the rape offence, see Council Doc 9305/23 of 17 May 2023.

[36] COM(2022) 105 final (n 34) arts 5–10, 35–36; European Parliament, Draft European Parliament Legislative Resolution on the proposal for a directive of the European Parliament and of the Council on combating violence against women and domestic violence (COM(2022)0105 – C9-0058/2022 – 2022/0066(COD)).

[37] See above ch 2.

[38] See EP Draft Report (n 32); COM(2022) 105 final (n 34); see also J Öberg, 'Gender-based violence as a crime under Article 83(1) TFEU'; Public Exchange of View of the European

violence against women and domestic violence are pervasive throughout the EU and are estimated to affect one in three women in the EU. In an EU-wide survey, 33% of women indicated having experienced physical and/or sexual violence, 22% intimate partner violence, 18% stalking and 55% sexual harassment, since the age of 15 years.[39]

Violence against women and domestic violence cause substantial pain and suffering to the victims and result in large costs to the economy and society as a whole. The European Institute for Gender Equality (EIGE) carried out a recent study in 2021 on the costs of gender-based violence. The study considered three main sources of costs: direct cost of services (use of services provided to mitigate the harm caused by violence including the use of health services to treat the physical and mental harms; the criminal justice system, specialist services such as protection and support services); lost economic output (victim's decreased ability to look for a job or productivity on the job and the time taken off work to handle the consequences of the crime); and physical and emotional impacts measured as a reduction in the quality of life. On this basis, the 2021 EIGE study estimated that total yearly costs of gender-based violence against women in the EU-27 stands at €290 billion (extrapolating the costs computed by the UK Home Office) and almost €152 billion for domestic violence. These costs consist in large part of physical, psychological and emotional impacts (55.57%), criminal justice system (20.43%) and lost economic output (13.93%). These costs do not include the societal costs of gender-based cyber violence, which have been estimated at €49–€89 billion.[40]

Whilst it is difficult to estimate with certainty the costs of gender-based violence, it appears uncontroversial to claim that gender-based violence is a serious crime satisfying the harm principle. It is not only a private wrong to individuals causing physical and emotional harm, but also an undermining of women generally as autonomous individuals, thus deserving of a larger censure from the community.[41]

Parliament LIBE and FEMM committees on a 'Proposal for a Council decision to add gender-based violence in the areas of crime listed in Article 83 TFEU': www.europarl.europa.eu/committees/sv/exchange-of-views-on-adding-gender-based/product-details/20210527EOT05581.

[39] European Union Agency for Fundamental Rights, 'Violence against women: an EU-wide survey. Main results report', 2014, Strasbourg, 3.3.2014: https://fra.europa.eu/en/publication/2014/violence-against-women-eu-wide-survey-main-results-report#; COM(2022) 105 final (n 34).

[40] EP Draft Report (n 32) 3–5; European Parliamentary Research Service, W van Ballegooij and J Moxom, 'Cost of Non-Europe Report – Equality and the Fight against Racism and Xenophobia', Brussels, European Parliament, 2018: www.europarl.europa.eu/RegData/etudes/STUD/2018/615660/EPRS_STU(2018)615660_EN.pdf; European Parliamentary Research Service, N Lomba, C Navarra, M Fernandes, 'Combating Gender-based Violence: Cyber Violence: European added value assessment', Brussels: European Parliament, March 2021: www.europarl.europa.eu/RegData/etudes/STUD/2021/662621/EPRS_STU(2021)662621_EN.pdf; European Parliamentary Research Service, N Lomba, C Navarra, M García Muñoz and M Fernandes, 'Gender-based violence as a new area of crime listed in Article 83(1) TFEU, European added value assessment', Brussels: European Union, 14 June 2021: www.europarl.europa.eu/thinktank/en/document/EPRS_STU(2021)662640.

[41] Along the lines advanced by Anthony Duff in his public goods theory as discussed above in ch 2, section I.

It thus appears clear that gender-based violence satisfies the criterion of being a 'particularly serious crime' as required by Article 83(1) TFEU.

C. Hate-Based Speech and Hate Crime

Another relevant case study for the application of the harm principle is the Commission's recent communication on criminalising hate-based speech and hate crime. This initiative is the end-product of the EU's long-term efforts to fight racism – as recently illustrated by President von der Leyen's recent State of the Union speech.[42] The combating of racism and xenophobia is included in the tasks of the Union,[43] and Article 67 TFEU envisages that this objective could be achieved 'if necessary' 'through the approximation of criminal laws'. The Commission's initiative on hate-based speech and hate crime has obtained broad support from the Council,[44] but the Commission has yet to submit a concrete proposal to extend the list of eurocrimes to this area of crime.

In terms of the assessment of the harm principle and the criterion of 'particularly serious crime', the Commission has claimed in its communication that all manifestations of hate speech are incompatible with the values of respect for human dignity, freedom, democracy, equality, rule of law and respect for human rights upon which the EU is founded.[45] Hate speech affects not only the individual victims but is claimed to undermine the very foundations of our society, weakening mutual understanding and respect for diversity on which democratic societies are built.[46] Hate speech and hate crime have serious and often long-lasting consequences on victims' physical and mental health and well-being; they are targeted because of their immutable characteristics or because of one that is at the core of their identity. Crimes triggered by hatred send messages of devaluation and rejection of whole groups and communities.[47] Acts of hate speech and hate crime are thus not only a private wrong but a public wrong[48] perceived by the whole community and society.[49]

[42] Commission, 'Communication from the Commission to the European Parliament and the Council – A more inclusive and protective Europe: extending the list of EU crimes to hate speech and hate crime', COM(2021) 777 final; U von der Leyen, 'State of the Union 2020, Letter of Intent', Brussels, 16 September 2020: https://state-of-the-union.ec.europa.eu/state-union-2020_en.

[43] Art 67(3) TFEU.

[44] Press Release, 'Justice and Home Affairs Council, 3-4 March 2022': www.consilium.europa.eu/en/meetings/jha/2022/03/03-04/.

[45] Arts 2 and 6 TEU and Charter of Fundamental Rights of the European Union [2010] OJ C 83/389.

[46] COM (2021) 777 final (n 42) 3.

[47] COM (2021) 777 final (n 42) 6–12.

[48] SS Marshall and RR Duff, 'Criminalization and sharing wrongs' (1998) 11 *Canadian Journal of Law and Jurisprudence* 7, 7–9; S Coutts, 'Supranational public wrongs: The limitations and possibilities of European criminal law and a European community' (2017) 54 *Common Market Law Review* 771, 787–89.

[49] The particular gravity of such conduct has been consistently acknowledged by the European Court of Human Rights; European Court of Human Rights judgment of 14.1 2020, *Beizaras and Levickas*

Hate speech has a chilling effect on freedom of expression and impacts adversely on the readiness of citizens to engage in politics and to exercise official functions with public visibility, such as members of parliament, mayors and politicians, as evidenced by various reports. While hate speech and threats are directed against all journalists,[50] statistics demonstrate that female journalists and politicians are subject to more threats than their male counterparts.[51] Evidence points to a 'pyramid of hate' or a 'ladder of harm',[52] starting from acts of bias and discrimination, moving up towards bias-motivated violence, such as murder, rape, assault, terrorism, violent extremism. There is overwhelming evidence suggesting that various groups are particularly targeted by hate speech and hate crime including people of Asian origin,[53] Roma origin,[54] sub-Saharan or north African backgrounds, Jews,[55] people with disabilities[56] and older people,[57] who experience higher rates of discrimination, harassment and violence motivated by hatred.[58]

v Lithuania, para 111; European Court of Human Rights judgment of 10.7.2008, *Soulas and Others v France*, para 47; European Court of Human Rights judgment of 9.2.2012, *Vejdeland and Others v Sweden*, para 59.

[50] Eurobarometer 452 showed that three quarters of journalists have experienced hate speech on social media and that half of them hesitates to engage in the public debate due to this: European Commission, 'Media pluralism and democracy – Special Eurobarometer 452', Last update 9 March 2021: https://wayback.archive-it.org/12090/20210728081045/https:/digital-strategy.ec.europa.eu/en/library/media-pluralism-and-democracy-special-eurobarometer-452.

[51] J Bayer J and P Bard, 'Hate speech and hate crime in the EU and the evaluation of online content regulation approaches', Study commissioned by the European Parliament's Policy Department for Citizens' Rights and Constitutional Affairs, July 2020: www.europarl.europa.eu/RegData/etudes/STUD/2020/655135/IPOL_STU(2020)655135_EN.pdf; Inter-Parliamentary Union (IPU) and Parliamentary Assembly of the Council of Europe (PACE), 'Sexism, harassment and violence against women in parliaments in Europe', Issues Brief October 2018: www.ipu.org/resources/publications/issue-briefs/2018-10/sexism-harassment-and-violence-against-women-in-parliaments-in-europe.

[52] SELMA Hacking Hate, 'Hacking Online Hate: Building an Evidence Base for Educators', 2019: https://hackinghate.eu/assets/documents/hacking-online-hate-research-report-1.pdf; Council of Europe, European Commission Against Racism and Intolerance, 'Hate speech and violence': www.coe.int/en/web/european-commission-against-racism-and-intolerance/hate-speech-and-violence.

[53] European Union Agency for Fundamental Rights, 'EU-MIDIS II: Second European Union Minorities and Discrimination Survey', 2017: https://fra.europa.eu/sites/default/files/fra_uploads/fra-2017-eu-midis-ii-main-results_en.pdf.

[54] European Union Agency for Fundamental Rights, Survey, 'Roma and Travellers in Six Countries', 2020: https://fra.europa.eu/sites/default/files/fra_uploads/fra-2020-roma-travellers-six-countries_en.pdf.

[55] European Union Agency for Fundamental Rights, Survey 'Experiences and perceptions of antisemitism – Second survey on discrimination and hate crime against Jews in the EU', 10 December 2018: https://fra.europa.eu/en/publication/2018/experiences-and-perceptions-antisemitism-second-survey-discrimination-and-hate.

[56] European Union Agency for Fundamental Rights, 'Equal protection for all victims of hate crime. The case of people with disabilities', 30 March 2015: https://fra.europa.eu/en/publication/2015/equal-protection-all-victims-hate-crime-case-people-disabilities.

[57] World Health Organization, 'Elder Abuse', 2021: www.who.int/news-room/fact-sheets/detail/abuse-of-older-people.

[58] COM (2021) 777 final (n 42) 8–11.

D. Overall Assessment of the Harm Criterion

It seems that both the proposals on violence against women and hate-based speech are 'adequately reasoned' and contain 'relevant evidence' supporting the propositions on the damage caused by these offences.[59] It is contended that at least in serious cases these offences satisfy the criterion of being 'particularly serious crimes'. This is apparent in respect of violence against women but also in the graver forms of hate-based speech inciting violence and serious threats to bodily harm.[60] It is difficult to impose a higher standard of legality for satisfying the harm criterion in Article 83(1) TFEU.

Contrasting the assessment of the proposal on violence against women and the proposal on hate-based speech and hate crime with another adjacent piece of EU legislation, it is less clear that the Commission proposal for criminalisation of violation of Union restrictive measures satisfies the harm criterion.[61] The Commission (and the Council) claim this to be a 'particularly serious crime' since it can perpetuate threats to international peace and security, undermine the support for democracy and human rights resulting in significant economic, societal and environmental damage. They also argue that because of such violations, individuals and entities whose assets are frozen continue to be able to access their assets or continue to access state funds that were misappropriated and use them to purchase arms with which they commit their crimes.[62]

The reasoning on the damages of those offences is on the whole scant, reaching only the minimum threshold of Article 296 TFEU.[63] Furthermore, the Commission has invoked very little evidence (which probably exists) to substantiate its propositions on the damage of violations of EU restrictive measures. It is thus highly questionable that this proposal at this stage – on the basis of the advanced reasoning and evidence – will satisfy the threshold of constituting a 'particularly serious crime'.

III. The Cross-Border Criterion as a Justification of EU Substantive Criminal Law

The following section of the chapter addresses the second justification set out by Article 83(1) TFEU for the EU to exercise its criminal law competence: ie the

[59] See ch 3, section II (B) for this process-based test review of EU legislation.

[60] See *Beizaras and Levickas v Lithuania* (n 49) para 111.

[61] Commission, 'Proposal for a Directive of the European Parliament and of the Council on the definition of criminal offences and penalties for the violation of Union restrictive measures', COM(2022) 684 final.

[62] Council Decision (EU) 2022/2332 of 28 November 2022 on identifying the violation of Union restrictive measures as an area of crime that meets the criteria specified in Article 83(1) of the Treaty on the Functioning of the European Union [2022] OJ L 308/18, recitals 10–16; COM (2022) 684 final (n 61) 3–8.

[63] M Shapiro, 'The Giving Reasons Requirement', *University of Chicago Legal Forum* (1992) 179.

cross-border criterion. This criterion suggests that the offence in question may have a cross-border dimension resulting either from the nature of such offences, the impact of such offences or a special need to combat them on a common basis.[64] This criterion is in the paradigmatic example satisfied when the offence as such involves the crossing of borders, eg smuggling of goods and the smuggling of human beings. The cross-border dimension may also result from the impact of the offence in question where the offence typically affects more than one state, including serious environmental offences and forgeries of the euro (neither of those offences stop at the borders). In addition, the cross-border dimension can, according to the Treaty, result from 'a special need to combat the offences on a common basis' which cannot be detached from the nature or impact of the offences. Such a special need does not already exist where the institutions have formed a corresponding political will.[65]

The cross-border justification is a key argument in debates on comparative federalism on when and to what extent the central legislator rather than the state legislator should intervene through criminal law. The general argument from the US federalism discourse is that the more integrated national economies and market, the more crimes crossing borders, the more increasing effects of states' enforcement efforts on other states causing spillover benefits in other states and intensified pressures of the race to the bottom, the stronger the case for centralised legislation.[66]

Sevenster has offered a compelling argument for how the cross-border dimension of criminal activity may support harmonisation within the EU context. She argues in favour of harmonisation of criminal laws on the basis of 'Delaware effects'[67] which could occur if economic norms were equal, but the penal legislation in Member States showed great divergence. Feeble criminal enforcement or loopholes in states' criminal enforcement systems would thus create 'safe havens' because potential perpetrators are provided with an incentive to exploit those jurisdictions.[68] Sevenster has suggested that Member States, in the absence of harmonisation, could enter into a suboptimal 'deregulatory race'[69] to attract business to their own jurisdiction. Divergences in criminal laws may create such races if the Member State with the most lenient penal system attracts most production.

[64] See Art 83(1) TFEU, para 1.

[65] *Lisbon Judgment* (n 14) para 359; Asp (n 11) 86.

[66] T Stacy and K Dayton, 'The Underfederalization of Crime' (1997) 6 *Cornell Journal of Law & Public Policy* 247, 276.

[67] Denominated after the competitively more flexible legislation for companies in the state of Delaware: see WL Cary, 'Federalism and Corporate Law: Reflections upon Delaware' (1974) 83 *Yale Law Journal* 663, 668, 701–5; L Arye Bebchuk, 'Federalism and the Corporation: The Desirable Limits on State Competition in Corporate Law' (1992) 105 *Harvard Law Review* 1435, 1443–44.

[68] See HG Sevenster, 'Criminal Law and EC Law' (1992) 29 *Common Market Law Review* 29.

[69] All the jurisdictional competition literature is originally based on the seminal article by C Tiebout, 'A Pure Theory of Local Expenditures' (1956) 64 *Journal of Political Economy* 416. Tiebout argues that under a stylised set of assumptions, competition among local governments might lead to efficient levels of taxation and of supply of public goods.

It is envisaged that Member States will not, because of perverse incentives such as a fear of placing one's own companies at a disadvantage, strictly enforce violations of common EU rules.[70]

The transnational argument has been used regularly by the EU legislator to substantiate harmonisation of national criminal laws.[71] It can be illustrated by examining the Commission's proposals to harmonise criminal laws in relation to EU regulatory schemes. In these proposals, the Commission has assumed that differences in Member States' sanctioning regimes may create a regulatory 'race to the bottom' in order to attract investment and firms. This argument envisages that firms, in the absence of harmonisation, will be subject to different costs for compliance because of divergent regulatory standards, putting firms in a jurisdiction with stringent regimes under a competitive disadvantage.[72] Firms under a criminalisation regime may for example incur additional costs – eg costs for adopting internal compliance mechanisms and costs for advisers to ensure compliance with the relevant rules – that would not be incurred by firms in a state with a lenient enforcement regime.[73]

The Commission's harmonisation argument envisages a rational actor model whereby offenders calculate their own interests and try to minimise the risk of sanctions. Assuming a context of inter-jurisdictional competition and transnational profit-driven crimes, Teichman has elaborated on this argument and suggested that firms and individuals are likely to rationally locate illegal activities to jurisdictions with feeble enforcement regimes. If one jurisdiction raises the price of committing a crime within it, either by increasing the sanction or the probability of detection, then neighbouring states become more attractive crime targets which will cause those states to adjust their sanctions and probabilities of

[70] See Sevenster (n 68) 53–55, 59–60. See also J Vogel, 'Why is the harmonisation of penal law necessary? A comment' in A Klip and H van der Wilt (eds), *Harmonisation and Harmonising Measures in Criminal Law* (Amsterdam: Royal Netherlands Academy of Science, 2002) 60–61 for a similar argument. R Van den Bergh, 'The subsidiarity principle in European Community law: some insights from law and economics' (1994) 1 *Maastricht Journal of European and Comparative Law* 337, 337–50 explains superbly the general economic rationale of the argument.

[71] Directive 2008/99/EC of the European Parliament and of the Council of 19 November 2008 on the protection of the environment through criminal law [2008] OJ L 328/28, recital 2, Directive 2009/123/EC of the European Parliament and of the Council of 21 October 2009 amending Directive 2005/35/EC on ship-source pollution and on the introduction of penalties for infringements [2009] OJ L 280/52, recital 14; Commission, 'Proposal for a Directive of the European Parliament and of the Council on criminal sanctions for insider dealing and market manipulation', Brussels, 20.10.2011, COM (2011) 654 final, 3, 5, recital 7; COM (2011) 573 final (n 20) 5.

[72] See Commission, 'Commission Staff Working Document, Accompanying Document to the Proposal for a Directive of the European Parliament and of the Council on the protection of the environment through criminal law, Impact Assessment', SEC (2007) 160, 24; Commission, 'Communication from the Commission to the European Parliament, the Council, the European Economic and Social Committee and the Committee of the Regions: Reinforcing sanctioning regimes in the financial services sector', COM(2010) 716 final, 10.

[73] See Case C-376/98 *Germany v European Parliament and Council (Tobacco Advertising)* EU:C:2000:544, para 109; Case C-300/89 *Commission v Council (Titanium Dioxide)* EU:C:1991:244, paras 12, 23.

detection to prevent criminal activity from moving to their state.[74] Furthermore, whilst a state's regulatory efforts may produce positive externalities in other states, the regulating state will only be able to partly capture those benefits, leading that state to underregulate and incline towards a suboptimal level of law enforcement.[75]

The case for federal legislation on gun control and criminalisation has been defended on a similar basis, suggesting that when one state decides to regulate such purchases, a divergent decision by nearby states has the external effect of substantially undermining the regulation. Instead of complying with one state's regulatory requirements, sellers and or purchasers can circumvent gun control laws by travelling to other states that do not have such requirements, thus undermining the preferences of the regulating states. In the case of child support, the problem of externalities justifies a role for a federal legislator when the child and the noncustodial parent who owes support are located in different states since that parent's state will incur much of the cost of enforcement while the benefits will accrue in another state. The theory of federalism predicts that the efforts of the noncustodial parent's state to collect from the parent will be suboptimal.[76]

The general proposition here, however, rejects that harmonisation of national criminal laws can readily be justified with reference to jurisdictional competition considerations. This argument finds support in the literature accounted for in the previous chapter on regulatory scholarship and competitive federalism.[77] This literature suggests that EU harmonisation, to be justified, first needs to establish the presence of a collective action problem or transnational market failure deserving regulation at centralised level.[78] Furthermore, central EU legislative action must be more effective than Member State action, which is typically the case for policies involving significant economies of scale and externalities across countries and where Member States do not have the required capacity or expertise

[74] D Teichman, 'The Market for Criminal Justice: Federalism, Crime Control, and Jurisdictional Competition' (2005) 103 *Michigan Law Review* 1831, 1831–35.

[75] DL Shapiro, *Federalism: A dialogue* (Evanston: Northwestern University Press, 1995) 42, 44; Stacy and Dayton (n 66) 289–91; J Le Boeuf, 'The Economics of Federalism and the Proper Scope of the Federal Commerce Power' (1994) 31 *San Diego Law Review* 555, 567; C Sunstein, *The Partial Constitution* (Cambridge: Harvard University Press, 1993) 151.

[76] Stacy and Dayton (n 66) 285, 304, 306–7. Similar considerations – and arguments on equality and underenforcement – apply according to Stacy and Dayton to the Violence Against Women Act of 1994 and gun and gun control violence, Stacy and Dayton, 296, 299, 303; AC Dailey, 'Federalism and Families' (1995) 143 *University of Pennsylvania Law Review* 1787, 1882–83.

[77] See above ch 2, section III (B).

[78] See eg R Revesz, 'Rehabilitating Interstate Competition: Rethinking the "Race to the Bottom" Rationale for Federal Environmental Regulation' (1992) 67 *New York University Law Review* 1210; WE Oates, 'An Essay on Fiscal Federalism' (1999) 37 *Journal of Economic Literature* 1120, 1134–37; CM Radaelli, 'The Puzzle of Regulatory Competition' (2004) 24 *Journal of Public Policy* 1; D Vogel, 'Trading up and governing across: transnational governance and environmental protection' (1997) 4 *Journal of European Public Policy* 556; L Enriques and M Gatti, 'The Uneasy Case for Top-Down Corporate Law Harmonization in the European Union' (2006) 27 *University of Pennsylvania Journal of International Economic Law* 939.

to address a certain policy area (eg serious transnational crime).[79] This body of literature also claims that the stylised assumptions of the jurisdiction competition literature (such as 'suboptimal', 'regulatory races') are rarely satisfied in empirical reality.[80] Evidence from regulatory scholarship indicates that race to the bottom models have overestimated the role played by regulatory standards in market behaviour, suggesting that other non-regulatory variables play a more significant role in deciding location for companies.[81]

All this suggests that claims of the existence of distortions of competition require empirical support to justify harmonisation in the field of criminal law. Taking the example used by Sevenster,[82] of 'Delaware effects' arising from feeble enforcement regimes in certain states, such potential distortions cannot per se be employed to support EU intervention. There must thus be concrete evidence as to the existence of transnational externalities, such as safe havens, or clear indications that states compete with each other by lenient sanctioning systems to substantiate the case for EU harmonisation.[83]

Criminal law scholars have also challenged the 'safe havens' argument on the basis of limited evidence that sanctioning regimes play a role for potential perpetrators when choosing jurisdiction to commit criminal offences. It has been proposed that the severity of sanctions and definition of offences are negligible competitive parameters compared with other key factors such as wage costs, infrastructure, tax and duty rules, proximity to primary producer.[84] Melander has convincingly challenged the key premise of Teichman's jurisdictional competition argument[85] which is that offenders possess extensive knowledge on the criminal justice systems of the Member States. Furthermore, if offenders had such information, the Member States with the mildest criminal justice systems should be the primary haven for criminal organisations. The criminal justice systems in the Nordic countries have in comparison to the rest of European been marked by more lenient sanctions and should consequently be a paradise for criminals.[86] However, there is limited evidence that organised crime has been a serious concern for the Nordic countries

[79] See in particular B Coeuré and J Pisani-Ferry, 'The Governance of the European Union's International Economic Relations: How Many Voices?' in A Sapir (ed), *Fragmented Power: Europe and the Global Economy* (Brussels: Bruegel, 2007) 36–42.

[80] See Enriques and Gatti (n 78) 953, 969, 978, 998.

[81] See Radaelli (n 78) 2–3, 5–6, 8; Vogel, 'Trading up and governing across' (n 78) 557–59, 561.

[82] See Sevenster (n 68), outlining the theoretical argument for EU criminal law harmonisation and the Commission's argument with respect to criminalisation in the field of environment and market abuse; SEC (2007) 160 (n 72) 24; COM(2010) 716 final (n 72) 10.

[83] Öberg, 'Subsidiarity as a limit' (n 31).

[84] See T Elholm, 'Does EU Criminal Cooperation Necessarily Mean Increased Repression?' (2009) 17 *European Journal of Crime, Criminal Law and Criminal Justice* 191; PH Robinson and JM Darley, 'Does Criminal Law Deter? A Behavioural Science Investigation' (2004) 24 *Oxford Journal of Legal Studies* 173, 205–6.

[85] Teichman, 'The Market for Criminal Justice' (n 74).

[86] S Melander, 'Ultima Ratio in European Criminal Law' (2013) 3 *European Criminal Law Review* 45, 56–57.

in the past.[87] Although Melander's argument is compelling, it cannot be excluded that political economy theories at least to some extent can explain the location of cross-border organised crime.[88]

To substantiate the more general critique towards the overly flexible use of the cross-border justification, the following will analyse the three recent proposals in EU substantive criminal law that were discussed in the previous section: the proposal on violence against women, the proposal to criminalise hate crime and hate-based speech and the proposal to criminalise violations of EU restrictive measures.

A. Violence against Women

The proposal on violence against women criminalises certain forms of violence that disproportionately affect women and strengthens victims' rights, employing the existing legal bases in Articles 82(2) and 83(1) TFEU. Whilst the proposal also covers victims' rights, the discussion here will focus on the criminalisation of gender-based violence as the 2012 Victims' Rights Directive[89] is subject to comprehensive scrutiny in the previous chapter.

The Commission's case for EU legislation on violence against women – in addition to existing comprehensive Member State national legislation in this field – is that divergences remain in respect of cyber violence, sexual violence and non-consensual dissemination of private images. For example, it appears that the use of force or threats as an essential element of rape is required in 16 Member States instead of focusing on lack of consent. Furthermore, female genital mutilation is not a specific criminal offence in nine Member States, forced marriages are not explicitly criminalised in seven Member States, whilst forced sterilisation has been introduced as a specific criminal offence in only four Member States.[90]

As mentioned above, this Commission proposal is a revised version of the European Parliament's previous proposal to add gender-based violence as a specific crime under Article 83(1) TFEU (which has been dropped due to the unanimity

[87] L Korsell and P Larsson, 'Crime and Justice in Scandinavia' (2011) 40 *Crime and Justice* 519. There is nonetheless tentative evidence that this trend is changing and that organised crime, at least politically, is becoming a concern in some Nordic countries: see Government of Sweden: 'Regeringens första 100 dagar: Kriminalitet', published 26 January 2023: www.regeringen.se/artiklar/2023/01/regeringens-forsta-100-dagar-kriminalitet/.

[88] See D Teichman and T Broude, 'Outsourcing and insourcing crime: The political economy of globalized criminal activity' (2009) 62 *Vanderbilt Law Review* 795, 807–10.

[89] Directive 2012/29/EU of the European Parliament and of the Council of 25 October 2012 establishing minimum standards on the rights, support and protection of victims of crime, and replacing Council Framework Decision 2001/220/JHA [2012] OJ L 315/57.

[90] Commission, 'Commission Staff Working Document: Impact Assessment Report, Accompanying the Document Proposal for a Directive of the European Parliament and of the Council on combating violence against women and domestic violence', SWD(2022) 62 final, 20–22.

requirement for adding new crimes to the list of eurocrimes).[91] The legal framing of the Commission's rebooted proposal is also new as the current proposal suggests that violence against women should be contained within the scope of the term 'sexual exploitation of women and children and computer crime'.[92] The Commission claims that the term 'sexual exploitation' in Article 83(1) TFEU can be 'understood as any actual or attempted abuse of a position of vulnerability including profiting monetarily, socially or politically from a sexual act with another person'. The criminal offences of rape and female genital mutilation presuppose these elements as these are exploitative practices performed for the purpose of asserting male domination over women and their sexuality. The term 'computer crime' in Article 83(1) TFEU is claimed to cover offences intrinsically linked to the use of information and communication technologies which can amplify the severity of the offence in terms of quantity, intensity, target selection and duration.[93]

Assessing the conformity of the proposal with the cross-border criterion is, however, a complex exercise. Whilst the proposal for violence against women at first sight seems to be more generally about 'violence against women' and 'domestic violence',[94] it appears from a close reading of the proposal that it only seeks to criminalise three types of offences: (i) rape,[95] (ii) female genital mutilation,[96] (iii) non-consensual sharing of intimate or manipulated material[97] and (iv) cyber harassment, cyber stalking and cyber incitement to violence.[98] The assessment is made even more confusing because the Commission's general argument on subsidiarity and the need for EU action centres generally on violence against women. The Commission argues that violence against women is widespread in the EU having an impact on millions of people in the EU, leading to violations of fundamental rights and causing considerable costs. In addition, cyber violence against women has emerged as a new form of violence spreading and amplifying beyond individual Member States. The internet is claimed to be an inherently cross-border environment, where content hosted in one Member State can be accessed from another Member State and where action by Member States acting individually will be insufficient to solve this problem. Furthermore, even if Member States have addressed violence against women in legislation, these EU legislative measures can increase the effectiveness of national legislation by enabling EU-level enforcement and monitoring. The initiative would also oblige the six Member States who have not ratified the Istanbul Convention to undertake measures that are sufficient to tackle this kind of violence.[99]

[91] EP Draft Report (n 32).
[92] See Art 83(1) TFEU, 1st sentence.
[93] COM (2022) 105 final (n 34) 8; SWD(2022) 62 final (n 90) 1–3.
[94] COM (2022) 105 final (n 34) arts 4a and 4b, 34.
[95] ibid, Art 5.
[96] ibid, Art 6.
[97] ibid, Art 7.
[98] ibid, Arts 8–10.
[99] SWD(2022) 62 final (n 90) 31–34, 51–52; COM (2022) 105 final (n 34), 8–9.

Whilst the argument that cyber violence has an inherent cross-border dimension is compelling, it is difficult to envisage how other types of violence against women (including rape, female genital mutilation and non-consensual sharing of intimate material) can have such a dimension. As recognised by the Commission, only 3% of women victims of all physical violence reported the violence to have taken place abroad, so this problem concerns approximately 100,000 women in Europe annually. Cross-border violence against women is thus of a comparatively insignificant phenomenon compared to conventional violence against women.[100]

Overall, there is limited reasoning or evidence in the Commission's preparatory documents to the effect that rape, female genital mutilation and non-consensual sharing of intimate material would be cross-border offences by nature. As mentioned above, a crime can be considered to have a cross-border dimension by nature when the offence as such, due to the offence description, involves the crossing of borders. Whilst such a cross-border element could be substantiated with regard to the cyber offences and non-consensual sharing of intimate material in certain cases, it is typically not existent in terms of rape and female genital mutilation.[101] Those offences do not involve the crossing of borders in the typical case. Those offences do not either have – in standard cases – impacts or implications which transcend borders like, for example, (serious) environmental offences and forgeries of the euro.[102] In terms of image-based sexual abuse committed through information and communication technologies, its borderless nature suggests that national responses cannot adequately respond to it, thus satisfying the cross-border criterion. In the case of image-based sexual abuse and the technologies involved, It seems that the non-consensual creating, taking and/or sharing of a sexual image occurs within national borders whilst in certain cases its harms may spread beyond them.[103]

Thus, on the basis of the test of 'adequate reasoning and relevant evidence',[104] it does not appear that the proposal on violence against women in its entirety satisfies the 'cross-border' criterion in Article 83(1) TFEU. This does not exclude the legality of the proposal as the forms of violence against women listed in the directive as criminal offences could be contained within the terms of 'sexual exploitation' and 'computer crime' which are part of the list in Article 83(1) TFEU.

[100] European Union Agency for Fundamental Rights, 'Crime, Safety and Victims' Rights', 19 February 2021: https://fra.europa.eu/en/publication/2021/fundamental-rights-survey-crime. This survey collected data from 35,000 people and focuses on respondents' experiences as victims of selected types of crime, including violence and harassment.

[101] Öberg, 'Gender-based violence as a crime under Article 83(1) TFEU' (n 38).

[102] Asp, *Substantive Criminal Law Competence of the EU* (n 11) 86–90.

[103] L Arroyo Zapatero and M Munoz De Morales Romero, 'Droit penal européen et Traité de Lisbonne: le cas de l'harmonisation autonome (article 83.1 TFEU)' in G Giudicielli-Delage and C Lazerges (eds), *Le Droit Penal de l'Union Europeenne au Lendemain du Traité de Lisbonne* (Paris: Societé de Legislation Compareé, 2012) 113; C Rigotti and C McGlynn, 'Towards an EU criminal law on violence against women: The ambitions and limitations of the Commission's proposal to criminalise image-based sexual abuse' (2022) 13 *New Journal of European Criminal Law* 452, 470.

[104] See above ch 3, section II (B) for an account of this test.

Rape and female genital mutilation could reasonably be contained within the concept of sexual exploitation,[105] whilst the cyber offences in the proposal could be contained within the broad term of computer crime.[106] Nonetheless, the argument on the cross-border criterion still holds force as the proposed EU act on violence against women (if the cross-border criterion cannot be applied directly in respect of crimes in the list such as 'computer crime' and 'sexual exploitation') would still – as regards the offences of rape, female genital mutilation and standard cases of non-consensual sharing of intimate images – be contrary to the subsidiarity principle.[107]

B. Hate Speech and Hate Crime

The next section examines the cross-border justification in respect of the Commission's 2021 Communication on hate-based speech and hate crime.[108] In its Communication, the Commission has claimed that the cross-border dimension of hate speech and hate crime is evidenced by the nature and impact of these phenomena as well as by the existence of a special need to combat them on a common basis. The Commission's argument on the cross-border nature of hate speech online is compelling as the nature of the internet entails that such hate speech is accessible to everybody anywhere.[109] However, the Commission has also argued that hate messages expressed offline (eg in written press) have a cross-border dimension on the basis of their impact as they are easily reproduced and disseminated across borders.[110] It also points to the fact that the hateful messages

[105] Arts 5 and 6, see COM(2022) 105 final (n 34) 35–36.

[106] ibid, Arts 7–10.

[107] which requires the case for EU action to be justified on the basis of the (cross-border) 'scope and nature of the action': see Art 5(3) TEU; Öberg, 'Subsidiarity as a limit' (n 31).

[108] COM (2021) 777 final (n 42).

[109] European Commission, Directorate-General for Justice and Consumers, P Ypma, C Drevon, C Fulcher and others, 'Study to support the preparation of the European Commission's initiative to extend the list of EU crimes in Article 83 of the Treaty on the Functioning of the EU to hate speech and hate crime: final report' (Luxembourg: Publications Office of the European Union, 2021): https://op.europa.eu/en/publication-detail/-/publication/f866de4e-57de-11ec-91ac-01aa75ed71a1/language-en, s 4.2.4; C Arroyo López and R Moreno López, 'Hate Speech in the Online Setting' in S Assimakopoulos, FH Baider and S Millar (eds), *Online Hate Speech in the European Union: A Discourse-Analytic Perspective* (Cham: Springer Nature, 2017): https://link.springer.com/content/pdf/10.1007%2F978-3-319-72604-5.pdf, 11; PRISM, 'Hate Crime and Hate Speech in Europe: Comprehensive Analysis of International Law Principles, EU-wide Study and National Assessments': https://sosracismo.eu/wp-content/uploads/2016/07/Hate-Crime-and-Hate-Speech-in-Europe.-Comprehensive-Analysis-of-International-Law-Principles-EU-wide-Study-and-National-Assessments.pdf, 17.

[110] European Commission, Directorate-General for Justice and Consumers, P Ypma, C Drevon, C Fulcher and others, 'European Commission, Study to support the preparation of the European Commission's initiative to extend the list of EU crimes in Article 83 of the Treaty on the Functioning of the EU to hate speech and hate crime, Annex VI – Synopsis Report of the consultation activities': https://op.europa.eu/en/publication-detail/-/publication/1473b895-57e8-11ec-91ac-01aa75ed71a1/language-en, 10–11.

are developed and propagated by networks with members from several countries and can also lead to radicalisation and the creation of violent extremist groups, which cross borders and are unified in their ideology.[111] The psychological impact on individuals and society can go beyond borders by provoking an environment of fear and affect not only individuals but wider communities in different countries.[112]

In respect of the Commission's 2021 Communication, it requires some more nuanced analysis to substantiate that the tackling of hate speech and hate crime is in line with the cross-border criterion. Hate-based speech may certainly take place online, cross virtual borders and in certain cases have a cross-border impact.[113] The preparatory documents and the Commission's supporting study pointed to quite compelling evidence that online hate speech by nature and also offline hate speech may have a transnational dimension.[114] This is a different conclusion to an earlier assessment by Turner[115] of the proposals for an EU Framework Decision,[116] which according to her suggested that the Commission's justification for this proposal went far beyond the notion of addressing merely transnational crimes. She observed that the problem of hate crime was already being addressed under the auspices of a Protocol to the Council of Europe Cyber-Crime Convention[117] and that the proposal swept broadly, covering conduct both online and off. She also suggested that the argument on the need to harmonise to enhance judicial cooperation and avoid criminals escaping to safe havens was not backed up by any evidence.[118]

It seems that the Commission's 2021 Communication on hate speech and hate crime – contrary to the 2008 proposal – is more compelling in establishing

[111] SELMA Hacking Hate (n 52); 'Commission Supporting study: final report' (n 109) ss 4.2.4 and 4.3.4.

[112] COM (2021) 777 final (n 42),14–15, 20–21.

[113] Commission Supporting study: final report' (n 109) 79–80, 87; European Commission, Directorate-General for Justice and Consumers, P Ypma, C Drevon, C Fulcher and others, 'European Commission, Study to support the preparation of the European Commission's initiative to extend the list of EU crimes in Article 83 of the Treaty on the Functioning of the EU to hate speech and hate crime, Annex VII – Analysis and synthesis of all the information and quantitative and qualitative data collected': https://op.europa.eu/en/publication-detail/-/publication/8ef232d3-57e4-11ec-91ac-01aa75ed71a1/language-en, 43–51.

[114] Analysis and synthesis (n 109) 79–80, 87; Annex VII – Analysis and synthesis (n 113) 43–51; European Commission, Directorate-General for Justice and Consumers, P Ypma, C Drevon, C Fulcher and others, 'European Commission, Study to support the preparation of the European Commission's initiative to extend the list of EU crimes in Article 83 of the Treaty on the Functioning of the EU to hate speech and hate crime, Annex 1 – Literature List: https://op.europa.eu/en/publication-detail/-/publication/4a18bedb-57dc-11ec-91ac-01aa75ed71a1/language-en.

[115] JI Turner, 'The Expressive Dimension of EU Criminal Law' (2012) 60 *American Journal of Comparative Law* 555.

[116] Commission, Proposal for a Council Framework Decision on Combating Racism and Xenophobia, COM (2001) 664 final, 5.

[117] ibid 6.

[118] Council Framework Decision 2008/913/JHA of 28 November 2008 on combating certain forms and expressions of racism and xenophobia by means of criminal law [2008] OJ L 328/55, recitals 3–4. European Parliament, 'Report on the Proposal for a Council Framework Decision on Combating Certain Forms and Expressions of Racism and Xenophobia by Means of Criminal Law',15, A6-0444/2007, 14 November 2005 (Minority opinion pursuant to Rule 48(3) of the Rules of Procedure by Koenraad Dillen); Turner (n 115) 568–69, 572.

a cross-border dimension of hate crime.[119] The remaining quibble with the Communication is that hate-based speech and hate crimes in standard cases just occur in a clear national context with national victims and national offenders.[120] In respect of the contention that offline hate speech and hate crime have a clear cross-border dimension, we are still referring to impacts and effects which are 'indirect' and where it is difficult to establish a causal relationship between the crime and the claimed cross-border implications. The Supporting Study referred to four examples of these effects:

(1) Hateful messages in public can be reproduced and become easily available throughout the EU.
(2) The ideologies behind hate speech messages are developed internationally and are cross-border phenomena because they can be rapidly shared through social media.
(3) Hate crime offences may be developed by networks with members from several countries (within the EU) that inspire, organise, or plan physical attacks against specific groups.
(4) The spillover effect of hate crimes on society may provoke follow-up hate crimes in other Member States.[121]

None of these examples, however, substantiate concrete implications or effects of hate speech or hate crime. We are rather looking at cross-border effects which may emerge or are 'likely to emerge' in the future, to use the terminology of the European Court of Justice.[122] Whilst there is a more compelling argument that these effects are likely to occur in respect of offline hate speech, there is not sufficiently compelling evidence which can substantiate that those effects would occur in respect of hate crime. Hate crime must be conceived as an offence which in the typical case does not carry cross-border effects or implications.[123] Furthermore, the Communication did not sufficiently clearly establish that national authorities were unwilling or unable to address racist crimes and that the EU would perform better in combating these offences. Finally, the argument on a special need to combat hate crime on a common basis offers very limited additional support for the cross-border nature of this offence. The supporting study suggests that the impact and seriousness of the offence are so severe, and the consequences so grave, that common action at the EU level is required to prevent these consequences and protect the wider EU society. However, this element overlaps with 'cross-border impact' as both of these concepts refer to the way an offence affects the wider EU society,[124] and it is highly unclear how the claimed seriousness of the offence and

[119] 'Commission Supporting study: final report' (n 109) 113–17.
[120] ibid 116–19.
[121] Annex VI – Synopsis Report of the consultation activities (n 110) 11–12.
[122] Case C-376/98 *Germany v European Parliament and Council (Tobacco Advertising)* EU:C:2000:544, para 86.
[123] Turner (n 115) 568–69.
[124] 'Commission Supporting study: final report' (n 109) 118–20.

the political ambition to combat hate crime could make this offence into a cross-border offence.[125]

In sum, it seems that the EU Commission's Communication on hate speech and hate crime is not fully in line with the cross-border criterion. Whilst it could be substantiated that there was 'adequate reasoning' and 'relevant evidence' to support that online and offline hate speech is at least 'likely' to have cross-border implications, it was not clearly demonstrated that hate crime[126] is an offence of a cross-border nature or an offence carrying clearly substantiated cross-border effects.

C. Violations of EU Sanctions

The final example examining the cross-border justification concerns the EU Council's recent decision to extend criminal law competence to cover EU foreign policy sanctions[127] and the Commission's subsequent proposal to harmonise the criminal law of Member States on this issue.[128] The rationale behind the Commission's criminalisation proposal is that restrictive measures are inconsistently enforced, undermining the EU's ability to speak with one voice which is particularly urgent within the context of Russia's military aggression against Ukraine. The EU has put in place a series of restrictive measures against Russian and Belarusian individuals and entities, some dating back to 2014.[129] However, the new Council Regulation on restrictive measures in respect of the Ukraine war[130] only obliges Member States to adopt effective, proportionate and dissuasive penalties but does not provide for any criminal law response in respect of violation of restrictive measures.[131] The effective enforcement of restrictive measures, including through criminal law measures aimed at addressing the violation of restrictive measures, is envisaged to support this policy.[132] Peers has sensibly argued that the criminal law proposal on Union restrictive measures is not an unwarranted extension of competence but should be understood as part of the EU's response to the Russian invasion of Ukraine. Whilst those measures will not end the invasion, they could make some contribution to the effective implementation of those sanctions

[125] Asp (n 11) 89–90 for this reading of the cross-border requirement.

[126] See 'Commission Supporting study: final report' (n 109) 116–20 for the reasoning in this regard.

[127] Council Decision (EU) 2022/2332 (n 62); Council, 'General Approach: Proposal for a Directive of the European Parliament and of the Council on the definition of criminal offences and penalties for the violation of Union restrictive measures', Council Doc 9312/23, 17 May 2023.

[128] COM (2022) 684 final (n 61).

[129] Council Decision (EU) 2022/2332 (n 62) recitals 10–16.

[130] Council Regulation (EU) 2022/1273 of 21 July 2022 amending Regulation (EU) No 269/2014 concerning restrictive measures in respect of actions undermining or threatening the territorial integrity, sovereignty and independence of Ukraine [2022] OJ L 194/1.

[131] COM (2022) 684 final (n 61) 2–7.

[132] Art 2 TEU.

which have been established to oppose the invasion and send a political message that the EU is stepping up its enforcement.[133]

The objective of the proposal is to ensure common definitions of offences related to the violation of Union restrictive measures and the availability of criminal penalties for those offences. In respect of the cross-border criterion, the Commission claims that violations of EU restrictive measures have an inherently cross-border dimension, suggesting that the objectives of the proposal can be better achieved at EU level than Member State level, by reason of the scale and effects of the conduct at stake.[134] Not only are they usually committed by natural persons and legal entities operating on a global scale, but, in some cases, Union restrictive measures (eg restrictions on banking services) even forbid cross-border operations.[135] Hence, by definition, their violation is conduct with a cross-border dimension requiring a common EU response. It is also argued that the different definitions of and penalties for the violation of Union restrictive measures under Member States' national laws hinder the consistent and effective application of Union policies on restrictive measures[136] and can lead to forum shopping by offenders because they could choose to conduct their activities in those Member States that provide for less severe penalties for the violation of EU restrictive measures.[137]

In terms of the assessment of the cross-border criterion, there is a case for considering the enforcement of violations of sanctions of restrictive measures as a European public good. First, it is difficult to deny that a violation of a restrictive measure is an attack against clear common EU policies. Furthermore, these are typically situations where the underlying restrictive measure itself is of a cross-border character.[138] The underlying measure can consist of travel bans, financial sanctions, asset freezing, restrictions on admission, restrictions on offering financial services, prohibitions on arms exports, prohibitions on bank transfers.[139] Also, whereas many Member States have legislation in place to enforce violations of this legislation, it appears that the EU is better placed to enforce this legislation. As the underlying restrictive measures relate to EU sanctions towards individuals and companies, it seems that Member States do not have the same incentives to protect

[133] Peers, 'EU foreign policy sanctions' (n 17).
[134] Art 5(3) TEU.
[135] Commission, 'Communication from the Commission to the European Parliament and the Council – Towards a Directive on criminal penalties for the violation of Union restrictive measures', COM(2022) 249 final, 3–4.
[136] Provided for by Art 83(1) TFEU.
[137] COM(2022) 684 final (n 61) 7–8; COM(2022) 249 final (n 135) 1–2.
[138] See European Commission, Sanctions Map, last updated 15 September 2023: https://sanctionsmap.eu/#/main.
[139] European Commission, 'Overview of sanctions and related resources', last updated 7 September 2023: https://finance.ec.europa.eu/eu-and-world/sanctions-restrictive-measures/overview-sanctions-and-related-tools_en#what-are-sanctions-restrictives-measures.

those interests as the Union.[140] This is substantiated by the fact that only half of the Member States had made violations of EU restrictive measures explicitly a criminal offence.[141] Overall, there is consequently 'adequate reasoning' and 'relevant evidence' which can substantiate that the Commission's proposal on criminalising violations of EU restrictive measures is in line with the cross-border criterion in Article 83(1) TFEU.

IV. Mutual Recognition as a Justification for Harmonisation of Substantive Criminal Law

Turning from the cross-border rationale for EU action, this section discusses mutual recognition as a justification for EU action in substantive criminal law. The wording of Article 82(1) TFEU – 'Judicial cooperation in criminal matters in the Union shall be based on the principle of mutual recognition' – suggests that a key objective of harmonisation of substantive criminal law under Article 83 TFEU is to facilitate the operation of mutual recognition.[142] This wording gives constitutional support for claiming that the EU's competence to legislate on criminal law is 'conditional' on the need to demonstrate that legislation facilitates the proper operation of mutual recognition (and other forms of judicial cooperation).[143] Whilst mutual recognition has been the motor of European integration in criminal matters since Tampere, its potential as a justification for EU action under Article 83 TFEU is underexplored.[144]

The justification for substantive criminal law harmonisation on this premise is that the effective operation of mutual recognition is based on mutual trust and that such a state of trust is premised on a certain degree of similarity as regards substantive rules on criminal behaviours.[145] Harmonisation of substantive criminal law could be employed to address problems caused by the double criminality requirement or other types of obstacles applicable in relation to different MR instruments. It has even been contended that mutual recognition requires some degree of harmonisation for Member States' judges to be prepared to recognise the decisions of other Member States' authorities given that divergences in substantive criminal law are closely connected to moral and ethical standards.[146]

[140] Eurojust, Genocide Network, 'Prosecution of sanctions (restrictive measures) violations in national jurisdictions: a comparative analysis', The Hague, December 2021, Annex: www.eurojust.europa.eu/sites/default/files/assets/genocide_network_report_on_prosecution_of_s anctions_restrictive_measures_violations_23_11_2021.pdf.

[141] ibid 22–24.

[142] Arts 67(3), 67(4) TFEU provide support for the centrality of mutual recognition in the system of judicial cooperation post-Lisbon.

[143] See CONV 426/02 (n 26) 10–12.

[144] See V Mitsilegas, 'The Constitutional Implications of Mutual Recognition in Criminal Matters in the EU' (2006) 43 *Common Market Law Review* 1277, 1307–9.

[145] See Art 83 TFEU.

[146] See P Asp, *The Procedural Criminal Law Cooperation of the EU – Towards an area of freedom, security & justice – Part 2* (Stockholm: Jure, 2016) 20–23, 53–54; Commission, 'Communication from the

A selective review of EU measures adopted post-Lisbon suggests that the need for enhancing mutual recognition or judicial cooperation is regularly employed as a justification for harmonisation. The conventional harmonisation argument is that divergences in definitions and with respect to the level of sanctions impede international judicial cooperation and create risks of forum-shopping. It is particularly claimed that minimum sanctions over a certain period (eg 12 months)[147] makes it possible to ensure that sentenced perpetrators can be surrendered with the help of MR instruments such as the EAW.[148] Moreover, it is argued that common definitions of criminal offences would facilitate common benchmarks for cross-border information exchange and thus enhance judicial cooperation within the EU.[149]

The most advanced 'judicial cooperation' argument can be extracted from the preparatory documents to the Directive on Attacks against Information Systems.[150] The Commission argued here that harmonisation of the definitions of criminal offences involving attacks against information systems would enable cooperation between judicial authorities of the Member States.[151] Given the potential of tools such as botnets to spread large-scale attacks by infecting thousands of computers a day, it was argued to be imperative that swift cooperation among the Member States in respect of sharing information was established to ensure that they can take effective measures towards such attacks. The claim for harmonisation was also based on the need to avoid a situation of 'forum-shopping', where countries without adequate criminal penalties would become the weakest link and targets for large-scale attacks. When the negotiations of the Directive on Attacks against Information Systems took place in 2009 and 2010, there were a number of Member States which did not have in place comprehensive criminal law legislation and penalties addressing botnets (and similar tools) used to conduct attacks against information systems. Furthermore, only qualification as a serious offence

Commission to the Council and the European Parliament, Mutual Recognition of Final Decisions in Criminal Matters' COM (2000) 495 final, 2–4.

[147] See Council, 'Council Framework Decision 2002/584/JHA of 13 June 2002 on the European arrest warrant and the surrender procedures between Member States – Statements made by certain Member States on the adoption of the Framework Decision' [2002] OJ L 190/1, Art 2(1).

[148] Commission, 'Proposal for a Directive of the European Parliament and of the Council on preventing and combating trafficking in human beings, and protecting victims, repealing Framework Decision 2002/629/JHA', COM (2010)95 final, 8; Commission, 'Proposal for a Directive of the European Parliament and of the Council on the fight against fraud to the Union's financial interests by means of criminal law', COM (2012) 363 final, 10, 14; COM (2011) 654 final (n 71) 3, 7; Commission, 'Proposal for a Directive of the European Parliament and of the Council on the protection of the euro and other currencies against counterfeiting by criminal law, and replacing Council Framework Decision 2000/383/JHA', COM(2013) 42 final, 3 and 12; Commission, 'Proposal for a Directive of the European Parliament and of the Council on attacks against information systems and repealing Council Framework Decision 2005/222/JHA', COM(2010) 517 final, 10–11.

[149] Commission, 'Proposal for a Directive of the European Parliament and of the Council on combating terrorism and replacing Council Framework Decision 2002/475/JHA on combating terrorism', COM(2015) 625 final, 4, 10, 12.

[150] Directive on Attacks against Information Systems (n 15).

[151] COM(2010) 517 final (n 148) 10–11; Directive on Attacks against Information Systems (n 15), recitals 27–28.

would allow for judicial cooperation and provision of adequate resources by law enforcement agencies involving the tracking of computer data by specialised officers, the application of specific high-tech tools and the use of special investigative techniques.[152]

Nonetheless, there is a compelling critique[153] towards employing mutual recognition as a justification advanced for harmonisation of substantive criminal law.[154] If we consider the discussed example of the Directive on Attack against Information Systems, there is very scarce empirical evidence that differing definitions of criminal offences in relation to information attacks have ever been a problem in respect of judicial cooperation measures. Whilst higher criminal penalties potentially may prevent forum-shopping, there is no evidence in the preparatory documents to the Directive suggesting that the functioning of mutual recognition would be impeded by the absence of common criminal law definitions in respect of cybercrimes. The Commission has not even contended that divergent definitions would constitute a concrete obstacle to the operation of mutual recognition.[155]

The argument here suggests that is implausible that divergent definitions of criminal offences ever could constitute an obstacle to the operation of mutual recognition. It is posited that national judges will enforce MR instruments, regardless of whether they trust the law in the Member States issuing the relevant instrument. The far-reaching compliance by national courts to the principle of mutual recognition[156] suggests that mutual trust is secondary to the national courts' loyalty toward the application of the principle of mutual recognition in EU law.[157]

If we adopt a broader perspective on harmonisation and consider positive benefits for judicial cooperation, there might be a stronger argument for EU action. There is some force in the claim that higher penalties may enhance swifter judicial cooperation as this would entail that measures such as the EAW and other MR instruments would require automatic acceptance of requests for judicial cooperation. It is, nevertheless, significant to underline, when analysing the Commission's argument for harmonisation, that criminalisation in itself is not

[152] Commission, 'Commission Staff Working Document, Accompanying document to the Proposal for a Directive of the European Parliament and of the Council on attacks against information systems, and repealing Council Framework Decision 2005/222/JHA Impact Assessment', SEC(2010) 1122 final, 15–18, 42, 46; the call for harmonisation has received general political legitimacy by the Council of Europe's Global Project on Cybercrime; see more recently: Council of Europe, Project Cybercrime @ Octopus, 22 April 2019: https://rm.coe.int/summary-of-the-cybercrime-octopus/1680968ab0.

[153] The previous chapter developed this critique in detail.

[154] J Ouwerkerk, 'The Potential of Mutual Recognition as Limit to the Exercise of EU Criminalisation Powers' (2017) 7 *European Criminal Law Review* 5, 7.

[155] SEC(2010) 1122 final (n 152).

[156] J Öberg, 'Trust in the Law? Mutual Recognition as a Justification to Domestic Criminal Procedure' (2020) 16 *European Constitutional Law Review* 33, 57–58.

[157] R Colson, 'Domesticating the European Arrest Warrant: European Criminal Law between Fragmentation and Acculturation' in R Colson and S Field (eds), *EU Criminal Justice and the Challenges of Legal Diversity. Towards A Socio-Legal Approach to EU Criminal Policy* (Cambridge: Cambridge University Press, 2016) 213–18.

sufficient to facilitate judicial cooperation. What seems to be required in the area of attacks against information systems is markedly higher penalisation to trigger effective judicial cooperation.[158]

However, also in this instance where higher common penalties may trigger more expedient cooperation, it is questionable whether the mutual recognition argument for harmonisation of substantive criminal law is sufficiently convincing. A general critique towards this line of thinking is that the recognition of key MR instruments does not require the verification of double criminality for a list of 32 offences enumerated in the EAW[159] and the EEW[160] framework decisions. Since the 'list' covers, in principle, all offences mentioned in Article 83 TFEU, it is not compelling to argue that harmonisation with respect to these offences is required to facilitate judicial cooperation. It is for example undisputable that 'computer-related' crimes – which the Directive on Attacks against Information Systems is concerned with – are encompassed within this list.[161] This suggests that Member States for those enumerated offences are obliged to comply with MR requests irrespective of whether the underlying offences constitute a crime in the domestic legal order.[162] On this basis, it is difficult to appreciate how harmonisation of the offence definitions would be required to enable the operation of mutual recognition. The only exceptional instance would be where a certain offence in the executing state would have such a low penalty scale that it would not reach the threshold of a maximum period of at least three years required by the EEW and the EAW framework decisions.[163] Whilst this problem might theoretically occur, there is limited evidence substantiating that this problem is of such a magnitude that it would compel a substantive harmonisation effort by the EU legislator. It appears rather that the key issue, when it comes to the execution of judicial cooperation instruments, is concerned with an absence of procedural standards or illegitimate application of such standards.[164]

V. Conclusions

This chapter examined the normative justifications for harmonisation of EU substantive criminal law. The chapter first considered the harm criterion as enshrined in Article 83(1) TFEU and the notion of 'particularly serious crime'. Whilst the harm criterion is a conventional justification for criminalisation in

[158] COM(2010) 517 final (n 148) 7–8, 10–11.
[159] EAW Framework Decision (n 147) Art 2(2).
[160] Council Framework Decision 2008/978/JHA of 18 December 2008 on the European evidence warrant for the purpose of obtaining objects, documents and data for use in proceedings in criminal matters [2008] OJ L 350/72, Art 14(2).
[161] EEW Framework Decision (n 160) Art 14(2); EAW Framework Decision (n 147) Art 2(2).
[162] EAW Framework Decision (n 147) Art 2(4).
[163] EEW Framework Decision (n 160) Art 14(2); EAW Framework Decision (n 147) Art 2(2).
[164] See Öberg, 'Trust in the Law' (n 156).

criminal law theory, it does not offer very much guidance in establishing why the EU rather than the Member States should regulate a certain issue. It is difficult to ascertain whether a certain offence is of merely a serious nature or particularly serious nature and what level of empirical evidence is needed to substantiate that criminalisation of a certain offence is in line with the harm principle. It was nonetheless contended that the proposal on violence against women and the proposal on hate crime and hate-based speech satisfied the criterion of constituting 'particularly serious offences' on the basis of the quantity and quality of evidence substantiating the damage of these offences to the individual and society.[165]

The second section – building on the European public goods and transnational interests framework in Chapter 2 – considered in detail the cross-border justification for harmonisation of substantive criminal law as enshrined in Article 83(1) TFEU. It first analysed the Treaty provision and argued that this condition needs to be applied stringently both for adding new offences to the list in Article 83 and for criminalisation in the areas of enumerated eurocrimes. It proceeded to examine the general case for harmonising criminal law with reference to cross-border assumptions. It was argued that the EU legislator's general assumption that divergences between Member States' enforcement and sanctioning regimes leads to distortions in the form of safe havens and a race to the bottom is often misplaced. There is a strong body of literature instead suggesting that differences in sanctioning regimes or differences in criminalisation have limited impact on the choice of location for firms or criminals or on the tendency of Member States to engage in regulatory races.[166]

The final part of this section examined the cross-border justification with respect to three distinctive proposals: the Commission's proposal on hate crime and hate speech, the Commission's proposal on violence against women and the criminalisation of violation of EU restrictive measures. Overall, the Commission's argument on the cross-border nature of cyber violence and online (and offline) hate speech was compelling and substantiated with sufficient empirical studies and evidence. It was nonetheless not demonstrated clearly how domestic sexual violence such as rape or conventional hate crimes were offences of a cross-border nature or offences carrying cross-border implications as required by Article 83(1) TFEU.[167] In respect of the proposal to criminalise violations of EU restrictive measures, it was substantiated clearly how these offences – given the typically underlying cross-border nature of the restrictive measure – were of a more intrinsic cross-border nature satisfying the conditions of legality in the aforementioned legal basis.

The final part of the chapter considered mutual recognition as a justification for harmonisation of substantive criminal law. Admittedly, the overarching Treaty objective of harmonisation of substantive criminal law in Article 82(1) assumes

[165] See above section II.
[166] See above section III (A).
[167] See above section III (A)–(C).

that such harmonisation will enhance 'judicial cooperation' (and mutual recognition). There is, however, limited empirical evidence supporting the need for such EU harmonisation for enabling the realisation of those objectives. In particular, it was observed that the execution of key MR instruments such as the EEW and EAW does not require verification of double criminality for a list of 32 offences covered by those framework decisions. Examining in detail the proposal for harmonisation in the area of attacks against information systems, it was found that there is no compelling reasoning or evidence to support that criminalisation has any noticeable impact on the recognition of MR instruments or judicial cooperation.[168]

Without giving a judgement here[169] on whether this is a justified approach, it appears that the EU is conducting recently a more markedly 'expressive' and value-based approach to criminalisation, taking a stand against certain conduct even if it has no significant cross-border dimension. The EU's action in such cases is explained by a need to reaffirm the Union's core values expressing commitment to human rights and equal treatment. EU legislators chose the criminal label to send a message – that the entire community believes racist conduct and violence against women is reprehensible and that the Union cares for the well-being of groups who are likely to be victims of such crimes, thus strengthening the Union's political identity and thus claiming deeper bonds of allegiance over time.[170]

[168] See above section IV.

[169] The expressive use of EU criminal law is discussed in a more detailed way below in the concluding ch 7.

[170] Turner (n 115) 572–73.

5

The Normative Justifications for a European Public Prosecutor

I. Introduction

The European Public Prosecutor's Office (EPPO), which recently has commenced its operation, appears to be an emblem for the transformation of EU criminal law from an intergovernmental paradigm to a strong supranational polity. The fashioning of such a body in this sensitive policy field has, however, been a contested process.[1] The seeds for the EPPO were prefigured in the mid-1990s in the work of Corpus Juris. This project had suggested a scheme of measures to counter the non-enforcement of offences against the EU's budget, including suggestions of a single set of offences applicable throughout the Union, a common set of procedural rules for the prosecution of such offences and the establishment of a European public prosecutor.[2] The rationale for creating such a body emerged from legitimate concerns over extensive mismanagement and misappropriation of EU funds.[3] This, in conjunction with the strategic importance of protecting the EU budget, made a compelling case for establishing a centralised European prosecution authority.[4]

It is, however, well known that the vision of the EPPO as an integrated prosecution agency must be singled out as a very sensitive issue in political terms.[5] Member States have voiced strong opposition towards the establishment of such an office, viewing the EPPO as a further encroachment on national sovereignty, and expressed concerns over the far-reaching implications of such an office on

[1] Described as a 'rocky' road' in V Mitsilegas, *EU Criminal Law After Lisbon: Rights, Trust and the Transformation of Justice in Europe* (Oxford: Hart Publishing, 2016) ch 4.

[2] M Delmas Marty and JAE Vervaele, *The Implementation of the Corpus Juris in the Member States – Penal Provisions for the Protection of European Finances* (Antwerp/Oxford/Groningen: Intersentia, 2001).

[3] M Wade, *EuroNEEDs – Evaluating the need for and the needs of a European Criminal Justice System – Preliminary Report* (Freiburg: Max Planck Institute for Foreign and International Criminal Law, 2011) for an extensive report analysing the need for a European Public Prosecutor.

[4] See Commission, 'Commission Staff Working Document, Impact Assessment, Accompanying the Proposal for a Council Regulation on the establishment of the European Public Prosecutor's Office' SWD (2013) 274, 7–8.

[5] A Weyembergh and C Briere, 'Towards a European Public Prosecutor', Policy paper for the European Parliament, LIBE Committee, November 2016, 9.

the functioning of national criminal justice systems.[6] More importantly, prior to Lisbon there was no Treaty mandate to create such an office,[7] meaning that it was impossible to constitutionally defend the establishment of such a supranational prosecutor.

Nevertheless, the prospect of creating a European Public Prosecutor derived real impetus from the successful negotiation of the new Article 86 TFEU, which was enshrined in the Lisbon Treaty. This provision provides the Council with a competence to 'establish a European Public Prosecutor's Office … in order to combat crimes affecting the financial interests of the Union' by a unanimous decision. The EPPO shall 'be responsible for investigating, prosecuting, and bringing to judgment … the perpetrators of, and accomplices in, offences against the Union's financial interests' and 'exercise the functions of prosecutor in the competent courts of the Member States in relation to such offences'.[8] Whilst Article 86 TFEU does not in itself establish the EPPO, it provides the legal basis for the Council Regulation which then created it.[9]

The EPPO represents a highly symbolic achievement in terms of its potential for a fundamental system change for the EU's area of criminal justice. It departs markedly from the conventional Member State-centric view that intergovernmental cooperation should remain a dominating principle of governance in the AFSJ.[10] By establishing the EPPO, a supranational body has effectively assumed such competences (for example powers to independently prosecute offences in domestic courts) that traditionally belong to the central government of a federal state.[11]

This chapter critically examines the justification for having a centralised European Public Prosecutor. The first part of chapter offers a comprehensive conventional legal analysis of the scope of the EPPO's powers in light of the argument on European public goods advanced in Chapter 2. The analysis particularly centres on the question of exclusivity, pre-emption and the type of enforcement powers enjoyed by the EPPO. The second part of the chapter discusses in detail

[6] The yellow card issued by national parliaments against the EPPO Proposal is compelling evidence for this proposition: Commission, 'Communication from the Commission to the European Parliament, the Council and the National Parliaments on the review of the proposal for a Council Regulation on the establishment of the European Public Prosecutor's Office with regard to the principle of subsidiarity, in accordance with Protocol No 2' COM (2013) 851 final.

[7] Although such an office was suggested by the failed European Convention Draft Treaty Establishing a Constitution for Europe [2004] OJ C 310/121, Arts 3–274.

[8] See Art 86(1)–(2) TFEU; CONV 426/02, 'Final report of Working Group X "Freedom, Security and Justice"', 19–20 for the thinking behind the provision.

[9] Council Regulation (EU) 2017/1939 of 12 October 2017 implementing enhanced cooperation on the establishment of the European Public Prosecutor's Office [2017] OJ L 283/1.

[10] For a small selection of recent literature: P Asp (ed), *The European Public Prosecutor's Office – Legal and Criminal Policy Perspectives* (Stockholm: Jure, 2015); K Ligeti, *Toward a Prosecutor for the European Union: Volume 1* (Oxford: Hart Publishing, 2012); W Geelhoed, LH Erkelens, AWH Mei (eds), *Shifting Perspectives on the European Public Prosecutor's Office* (The Hague: TMC Asser Press, 2018).

[11] JA Vervaele, 'The European Public Prosecutor's Office (EPPO): Introductory Remarks' in W Geelhoed, L Erkelens and AWH Meij (eds), *Shifting Perspectives on the European Public Prosecutor's Office* (The Hague: TMC Asser Press, 2018) 11–12.

the way in which the EPPO's powers and the exercise of these may constitute a threat to state sovereignty from a legitimacy perspective. The chapter particularly examines to what extent the EPPO constitutes a desirable example of a 'federal' European criminal law. The final section of the chapter considers critically as an alternative to a centralised prosecutor a model of judicial cooperation based on the structure of Eurojust under Article 85 TFEU and the recent Eurojust Regulation. Within this enquiry, it also examines whether the powers of Eurojust should be expanded and be made binding in order for the agency to effectively satisfy its working tasks. The conclusions summarise the key insights of the chapter and offers some reflections on those findings.

II. The European Public Prosecutor's Competencies under Article 86 TFEU and the EPPO Regulation

A. Substantive Scope of Competence

Article 86(1) TFEU currently limits the powers of the EPPO to prosecute crimes 'against the Union's financial interests'. It is clear that the substantive jurisdiction of the EPPO, as derived from the EU Directive on the fight against fraud to the Union's financial interests by means of criminal law ('PIF Directive') and the 'inextricably linked offences', is potentially very broad.[12] The PIF offences cover a broad range of illegal behaviours, encompassing passive and active corruption, fraud, embezzlement, subsidy abuse and money laundering[13] as well as 'offences regarding participation in a criminal organisation' if the focus of such an organisation is to commit any of the PIF offences.[14]

A more significant question is to what extent there is a compelling justification for the EPPO to prosecute not only offences against the financial interests of the Union but also to have a competence to prosecute 'ancillary' offences.[15] The relevant provision in the EPPO Regulation prescribes that the 'EPPO shall also be competent for any other criminal offence that is *inextricably linked* to' one of the PIF offences.[16] It is apparent that Article 86 TFEU does not explicitly confer powers on the EPPO to prosecute ancillary offences. The question is thus whether such competences can, by implication, be inferred on the basis of the doctrine of

[12] EPPO Regulation (n 9) Art 22.

[13] Directive (EU) 2017/1371 of the European Parliament and of the Council of 5 July 2017 on the fight against fraud to the Union's financial interests by means of criminal law [2017] OJ L 198/29, Arts 3 and 4.

[14] EPPO Regulation (n 9) Arts 22(2) and 22(3).

[15] See A Nieto Martín and M Muñoz de Morales Romero, 'The Office of the European Public Prosecutor and Related Offences: Deconstructing the Problem' in P Asp (ed), *The European Public Prosecutor's Office – Legal and Criminal Policy Perspectives* (Stockholm: Jure, 2015).

[16] Regulation (EU) 2017/1939 (n 9) Art 22(3).

'implied powers'[17] as being inherent in the original power in Article 86 TFEU and necessary to achieve the objective of effectively fighting crimes against the EU's financial interests.[18]

The Commission defended the scope of the Regulation on this basis, arguing that the principle of *ne bis in idem* requires an extension of competence beyond the PIF offences to prosecute inextricably linked offences. Parallel prosecution of PIF offences and inextricably linked offences based on identical facts by both the EPPO and the national prosecution service would defeat the purpose of the EPPO Regulation. In the case of such prosecutions, the *ne bis in idem* principle[19] would oblige the EPPO or the national prosecution service to close the proceedings once a final criminal conviction, prosecutorial case disposal or a final acquittal had been delivered based on the same facts.[20] The Commission's original proposal survived the negotiations, and the current provision entails that the EPPO is competent for 'ancillary' offences where offences are inextricably linked and the PIF offence is preponderant in terms of the seriousness of the offence concerned and where the inextricably linked offence is deemed to be instrumental in the commission of one of the PIF offences.[21]

The wide notion of 'ancillary' competence endorsed by the EPPO Regulation is, however, difficult to align with a principled reading of Article 86 TFEU based on the idea of 'transnational interests'.[22] The baseline premise for the idea of transnational interests is, as mentioned above, that EU action would correct the dysfunctional workings of national political processes by giving 'virtual' political rights to foreigners where they have a legitimate concern.[23] However, the theory of transnational interests may also – as in the case of the EPPO's competence – refer to core EU interests, such as the protection of the EU budget. The financial interest of the EU is a genuine supranational interest, as the budget is central for the existence of the Union. The EPPO is, for this purpose, entrusted with the objective of protecting the common interests of the EU budget, which go beyond the territories of individual Member States.[24] The need to confer the EPPO with these competencies arises from the nature of the crimes in question, which by affecting the Union's

[17] Case C-176/03 *Commission v Council* EU:C:2005:542, paras 48–51; Case 22/70 *Commission v Council (ERTA)* EU:C:1971:32, paras 16–22, 28–32.

[18] Art 325 TFEU.

[19] Charter of Fundamental Rights, Art 50 and Convention Implementing the Schengen Agreement of 14 June 1985 between the Governments of the States of the Benelux Economic Union, the Federal Republic of Germany and the French Republic on the gradual abolition of checks at their common borders, 22.9.2000 [2000] OJ L 239/19, Art 54.

[20] COM(2013)851 final (n 6) paras 2.6, 4–12; Case C-467/04 *Gasparini* EU:C:2006:610; European Court of Human Rights, judgment of 10.2.2009 (No 14939/03) *Sergey Zolotukhin v Russia* (Grand Chamber), para 82.

[21] Regulation (EU) 2017/1939 (n 9) recitals 54–56, Arts 22(3) and 25(3).

[22] See above ch 2, section III.

[23] C Joerges and J Neyer 'From intergovernmental bargaining to deliberative processes: The constitutionalisation of comitology' (1997) 3 *European Law Journal* 273, 293, 295.

[24] See Nieto Martín and Morales Romero (n 15) 132–33; Wade (n 3).

own financial interests inevitably have a Union dimension. Furthermore, and as conceded by the opinions of national parliaments,[25] the criminal justice authorities of Member States are systematically predisposed – because of loyalties to the state's criminal enforcement interests – to deprioritise the protection of the EU's financial interests.[26]

Thus, there is a compelling justification for the EPPO to have competencies to prosecute the PIF offences. The degree of legitimacy for EU intervention in terms of inextricably linked offences is, however, substantially reduced. Unlike the situations where there are offences against the EU's financial interests, Member States have no competing interests in relation to ancillary offences. In fact, Member States may be well placed to enforce such 'national' offences given their understanding of the local situation.[27] Furthermore, there is a legitimate national economic interest in prosecuting the inextricably linked offences such as VAT or national subsidy abuse cases.[28]

The *ne bis in idem* argument must, however, be taken seriously. By not conferring powers on the EPPO to prosecute ancillary offences, it is apparent that there may be instances where the EPPO would have to drop its pursuit of a specific investigation on the basis that a national prosecutor had already prosecuted those inextricably linked offences and those had ended in a final discharge or acquittal. However, it is argued that the EPPO would nonetheless be able to function effectively with the powers it has been conferred with to prosecute the PIF offences. The offences in the PIF Directive, which constitute the basis for the EPPO's powers

[25] Seimas of the Republic of Lithuania, Committee on European Affairs, 'Opinion on the European Commission Proposal for a Council Regulation on the Establishment of the European Public Prosecutor's Office', 16 July 2014, No V-2014-4174L; Joint Committee on Justice, Defence and Equality (Ireland), 'Reasoned Opinion of Joint Committee on Justice, Defence and Equality, COM(2013)534 Proposal for a Council Regulation on the establishment of the European Public Prosecutor's Office', October 2013; Chamber of Deputies (Romania), 'Reasoned opinion finding the lack of conformity of the Proposal for a Council Regulation on the establishment of the European Public Prosecutor's Office with the principle of subsidiarity' COM(2013)534 (courtesy translation); Dutch Senate of the States General, 'Reasoned opinion (breach of subsidiarity) on the proposal for a Council regulation on the establishment of the European Public Prosecutor's Office (DOC(2013)534)', 17 October 2013, 153768.01.

[26] See J Öberg, 'National Parliaments and Political Control of EU Competences – A Sufficient Safeguard of Federalism?' (2018) 24 *European Public Law* 695 for discussion. There is also empirical evidence that national investigators and prosecutors may not always have the ability to appreciate the full extent of a case. This might mean that cases which are truly 'European' will not be handed over to the EPPO, with the consequence that they are not sufficiently investigated: Wade (n 3) 14–30, 144–50.

[27] National parliaments made this point clearly in their reasoned opinions; see Chamber of Deputies (Romania), 'Reasoned opinion' (n 25); Dutch Senate of the States General, 'Reasoned opinion' (n 25); Seimas of the Republic of Lithuania, Committee on European Affairs, 'Opinion' (n 25); Senate of the Republic of Poland, 'Opinion of the European Union Affairs Committee of the Senate of the Republic of Poland on the proposal for a Council regulation on the establishment of the European Public Prosecutor's Office', COM (2013)534, adopted at the meeting of 9 October 2013 (courtesy translation); Statement by the Committee on Justice, 'Reasoned Opinion of Swedish Parliament – Subsidiarity check on the proposal on the establishment of the European Public Prosecutor's Office', 2013/14: JuU13.

[28] Nieto Martín and Morales Romero (n 15) 135–36 outlines these legitimate interests when discussing ancillary competence.

pursuant to the Regulation, are broadly defined, covering – to some extent – ancillary offences. The definition encompasses all actions (such as the use or presentation of false and incorrect statements or documents) which are intended to make an unlawful gain by causing a loss to the EU's financial interest, and covers procurement-related and non-procurement related expenditure,[29] including corruption offences committed by national officials that are likely to damage the Union's financial interest as well as offences by national officials who are entrusted with the management of funds and who misappropriate them and damage the Union's financial interest.[30]

Given the wide design of the EPPO's powers, there is no convincing rationale for conferring an additional competence on the EPPO to prosecute 'inextricably linked offences'. The *ne bis in idem* concerns cannot change this observation. The *ne bis in idem* principle in EU law retains as a relevant criterion the identification of the material facts (the existence of a set of concrete circumstances) which are inextricably linked together in time and space.[31] It is very difficult to envisage situations where the EPPO would be impeded – because of a previous proceeding for a similar national offence – in prosecuting a PIF offence.[32] In most instances where a national offence involved facts that would coincide with a PIF offence, the national prosecutors would be required to give priority to the exercise of the EPPO's powers by ceding to the EPPO the decision whether to bring proceedings in respect of that criminal conduct.[33] In this respect, national authorities must refrain from taking any decision that may have the effect of precluding the EPPO from exercising its right of evocation. Where the EPPO exercises this right, national authorities shall refrain from carrying out further acts of investigation in respect of the same offence.[34]

For all these reasons, there is no compelling normative justification for the EPPO to be conferred with a competence to prosecute 'inextricably linked offences'.

B. Nature of the EPPO's Powers

The nature of the EPPO's powers is another contentious question. Article 86 TFEU does not explicitly address this issue. It only states that the EPPO shall 'be responsible for investigating, prosecuting and bringing to judgment … the perpetrators of … offences against the Union's financial interests' and 'exercise the functions

[29] See PIF Directive (n 13) Art 3(2).

[30] See PIF Directive (n 13) Arts 4(2) and 4(3); and EPP Regulation (n 9) Art 22(1).

[31] Case C-436/04 *Van Esbroeck* EU:C:2006:165 para 36.

[32] This is notwithstanding the broad reading of the *ne bis in idem* principle in the CISA convention advanced by the Court of Justice: Case C-467/04 *Gasparini and Others* (n 20) paras 23–33; Case C-436/04 *Van Esbroeck* (n 31) paras 30–40.

[33] EPPO Regulation (n 9) Arts 24 and 25(1) for the national authorities' obligations in this regard.

[34] ibid Art 27.

of prosecutor in the competent courts of the Member States in relation to such offences'.

The Commission's original proposal of exclusive competence was the product of an innovative vision of a 'federal' prosecution authority at EU level.[35] By granting the EPPO exclusive competence, the Commission sent a strong signal to Member States that only the EPPO would be competent to investigate and prosecute the 'European' offences associated with fraud against the EU budget.[36] The issue of 'exclusivity' was widely contested when the EPPO Proposal was subsequently brought to the Member States.[37] Exclusive competence implies that the EPPO would have held a monopoly on investigating and prosecuting those offences that fall within its substantive scope of competence, that is the PIF offences.[38] If enacted, this would have meant that national authorities would have to surrender their competence in relation to such offences. This approach proved too sensitive in terms of national sovereignty, and subsequent negotiations in the Council shifted to a more 'cooperative' design of concurrent competence for the EPPO on the basis of the Greek presidency's proposal. This model provides that both the EPPO and national prosecution authorities are competent to enforce crimes against the EU budget, without an explicit priority for the EPPO.[39] As thing stand, the current EPPO Regulation has opted for this model of concurrent competence, with a right of evocation for the EPPO.

Irrespective of the current design of the EPPO Regulation, it is opportune to discuss the extent to which there exists a compelling normative justification for 'implied' exclusive competence. The argument for 'implied' exclusive competence is that 'exclusivity' would be indispensable for the EPPO effectively to fight crimes against the EU's financial interests.[40] Implied exclusivity is a well-known concept in the field of EU external relations law.[41] In a line of case law that commenced with the seminal *ERTA* judgment, the Court of Justice has endorsed a broad test for finding EU exclusive competence to negotiate and conclude international agreements. The Court has held that exclusive competence is based on the 'purpose of preserving the effectiveness of Community law and the proper functioning of the

[35] Commission, 'Proposal for a Council Regulation on the establishment of the European Public Prosecutor's Office', COM (2013) 534 final, Art 14.

[36] Art 4(2) TFEU. See the discussion in V Mitsilegas, 'EU Criminal Law after Lisbon' (n 1) 104–5, 109, 122–23.

[37] See discussion in J Öberg, *Limits to EU Powers: A Case Study of EU Regulatory Criminal Law* (Oxford: Hart Publishing, 2017) 167–82.

[38] See EPPO Regulation (n 9) Art 22 for an outline of the EPPO's substantive competence.

[39] Council, 'From Presidency to the Council, Proposal for a Regulation on the establishment of the European Public Prosecutor's Office' (Draft Regulation, 5766/17, 31 January 2017), Arts 17 and 20. See V Mitsilegas, 'EU Criminal Law After Lisbon' (n 1) 103–13 for a discussion of the recent Council proposals.

[40] Which is the key objective of Art 86 TFEU.

[41] See Opinion 1/76 *Draft Agreement establishing a European laying-up fund for inland waterway vessels*, EU:C:1977:63; Opinion 1/03 *Competence of the Community to conclude the new Lugano Convention*, EU:C:2006:81, for examples of 'implied' exclusive competence.

systems established by its rules'.[42] The test for implied exclusivity is a wide one, encompassing a potential risk that the objectives of common EU rules would be frustrated. Given the requirement to consider the future state of EU law,[43] it seems inevitable that this test – generally – will entail a finding of exclusive competence.[44]

Because of the special nature of EU external relations law (where the need for uniformity is imperative at all stages of the negotiation of international agreements),[45] it is questionable whether this broad reading of implied exclusive competence could be transposed to the field of EU criminal law. In this area, particularly given the fact that it is an area where national sovereignty is affected in a very significant manner by EU actions,[46] a more cautious approach to exclusivity is warranted.

On the basis of the argument on European public goods advanced above, there is a tentative case for exclusivity. It is evident that the effective pursuit of the tasks of the EPPO – ie the effective protection of the EU's financial interests[47] – under Article 86 TFEU might be jeopardised unless the EPPO is conferred with exclusive competence.[48] Exclusivity would be based on the observation that Member States' concurrent exercise of competence could endanger the operation of the EPPO and thereby defeat the purpose of providing for an efficient and coherent prosecution of the PIF offences.[49] Member States' judicial authorities do not have the expertise, capacity or incentives to provide sufficient protection for the Union's financial interests. With exclusive competence, the EPPO would be able to more effectively direct investigations, by having an overview of all the available information, and would thus be able to determine where the investigation could most successfully be pursued.[50]

C. Exercise of Competence – If not Exclusivity, Pre-Emption?

Whilst there may be a normative justification for exclusivity, the current Regulation, however, proceeds, as mentioned, from a model of concurrent

[42] Opinion 1/03 *Lugano Convention* (n 41) paras 126, 128, 131. See also Opinion 3/15 *Marrakesh Treaty*, EU:C:2017:114, para 124.

[43] Opinion 1/03 *Lugano Convention* (n 41) paras 126, 128, 131.

[44] M Chamon, 'Implied exclusive powers in the ECJ's post-Lisbon jurisprudence: the continued development of the ERTA doctrine' (2018) 55 *Common Market Law Review* 1109, 1125, 1135–38, 1141.

[45] See B Van Vooren and R Wessel, *EU External Relations Law: Text, Cases and Materials* (Cambridge: Cambridge University Press, 2014) chs 4 and 6.

[46] Judgment of Federal Constitutional Court of 30 June 2009, *Lisbon Judgment*, Case 2 BvE 2/08, 5/08, 2 BvR 1010/08, 1022/08, 1259/08, 182/09 (2009), paras 352–56.

[47] Art 325 TFEU.

[48] This is one of the key justifications for recognising an implied legislative power; Joined Cases 281, 283–285, 287/85 *Germany and Others v Commission* EU:C:1987:351, para 28.

[49] Coherent and effective application of EU law is the central argument for conferring exclusive competence on the EU: Opinion 1/03 *Lugano Convention* (n 41) paras 122, 126, 128; Opinion 1/76, *Draft Agreement* (n 41) paras 3–7; Case 22/70 *ERTA* (n 17) paras 16–31.

[50] COM (2013) 534 final (n 35) 2–3; SWD (2013) 274 (n 4) 6–9, 25–27.

competences between the EPPO and national prosecution authorities.[51] The EPPO does, however, have 'priority' in prosecuting the PIF offences where it decides to exercise competence and also a 'right of evocation' for investigations started by national prosecution authorities. The key provision in the EPPO Regulation states that the 'EPPO shall exercise its competence either by initiating an investigation … or by deciding to use its right of evocation …'. If the EPPO decides to exercise its competence, the 'national authorities shall not exercise their own competence in respect of the same criminal conduct'.[52] The EPPO shall take its decision on whether to exercise its right of evocation no later than five days after receiving information from national authorities of an offence falling within the EPPO's jurisdiction. During this period, 'the national authorities shall refrain from taking any decision … that may have the effect of precluding the EPPO from exercising its right of evocation'.[53]

The rules on exercising competence in the EPPO Regulation are based on the idea that the Member States have a 'dormant' competence to prosecute PIF offences 'to the extent' that the EPPO has decided not to exercise its competencies. The rules in the Regulation also mean that powers to prosecute offences falling outside the PIF Directive and the EPPO's remit under the Regulation (VAT fraud under €10m,[54] minor PIF offences or inextricably linked offences where those offences have a stronger link to national law[55]) remain within the power of national prosecutors. The rules on exercising competence in the EPPO Regulation will, however, ultimately give priority to the EU level. Thus, if the EPPO exercises competence or employs its right of evocation, the case will be handled by the EPPO. This means that the EPPO's competence in practice might *become* exclusive in case of a conflict with national authorities.[56] This is, however, defensible in light of the principle of sincere cooperation, which states that the Member States shall take any appropriate measures to ensure fulfilment of the obligations resulting from the acts of the Union.[57] For this purpose, those authorities must refrain from any measure which could jeopardise the attainment of the EPPO's objectives, which are to effectively prosecute offences against the EU's financial interests.[58]

It is argued that the EPPO Regulation strikes the correct balance on the basis of the normative argument on transnational interests. It confers the EPPO with a right of evocation and priority in terms of more serious PIF offences that have a strong Union dimension and defers to national prosecutors the prosecution of

[51] Concurrent competence was subject to controversy in the early negotiations of the EPPO Regulation. See Council doc 9834/1/14, 3–4, 23–25 and Council docs 15862/1/14; 6318/1/15; 16993/14; 7070/15; 7876/15; 7876/15.

[52] EPPO Regulation (n 9) Art 25(1).

[53] EPPO Regulation (n 9) Art 27.

[54] See EPPO Regulation (n 9) Art 22(1).

[55] See in particular the complex rules in EPPO Regulation (n 9) Arts 25(2) and 25(3).

[56] EPPO Regulation (n 9) Art 25(1); Art 2(2) TFEU.

[57] Art 4(3) TEU.

[58] EPPO Regulation (n 9) Arts 25(1), 27 and 28.

offences that have a markedly 'local' dimension.[59] This suggests that the core remit for the EPPO and its right of evocation concerns prosecution of the 'real' PIF offences[60] where, because of the implications of those offences for the EU budget, there is a strong Union interest to prosecute these offences.[61] The rules on exercise of competences thus strive to ensure that the EPPO performs its main task of protecting the interests of the EU budget, whilst also respecting the powers of national authorities in this sensitive area where they enjoy stronger legitimacy to prosecute the offences at issue.

D. The Type of Powers Conferred Upon the EPPO

It is apparent that the EPPO stands out among other EU agencies in having been conferred with very significant powers. The Treaties suggests that the EPPO is intended to have competences equivalent to those of a national prosecutor without any need to act through a national authority. In that respect the EPPO shall have binding powers to undertake investigations,[62] and carry out acts of prosecution (ie dismiss cases, allocate cases, reallocate cases and reopen investigations) for offences that fall within the EPPO's jurisdiction.[63] The decision whether to indict the accused person should – in principle – be made by the competent Permanent Chamber on the basis of a draft decision by the European Delegated Prosecutor (EDP) to ensure a coherent prosecution policy.[64] The EDP shall subsequently have powers to bring a case to judgment, in particular the power to present trial pleas, participate in taking evidence and exercise all available remedies in national law.[65] The EPPO would be in charge of the whole process from the initial criminal investigation to the formal prosecution, and be vested with all corollary powers such as giving instructions to national police forces in the course of the investigations. For this purpose, the EPPO will be empowered to employ coercive measures such as searching premises, private homes, and personal property, and requiring the production of documents, freezing instrumentalities or proceeds of crime, and will have powers to request the arrest or pre-trial detention of suspects.[66] However, the EPPO should rely on national law enforcement authorities for the execution of coercive measures,[67] who will carry out such acts pursuant to the instructions of the EPPO.[68]

[59] Reflecting the negotiations of the Council, see Council doc ST 18120/13, 4–5.

[60] EPPO Regulation (n 9) Arts 22(1) and 25(2).

[61] EPPO Regulation (n 9) Arts 22(3), 25(2) and 25(3).

[62] EPPO Regulation (n 9) Art 26.

[63] Art 86(2) TFEU. In principle all of these powers lie with the Permanent Chambers: EPPO Regulation (n 9) Arts 10(3) and 10(4).

[64] EPPO Regulation (n 9) recital 78, Arts 35 and 36.

[65] EPPO Regulation (n 9) Art 13(1).

[66] EPPO Regulation (n 9) Arts 30(1) and 33(1).

[67] EPPO Regulation (n 9) recital 69.

[68] EPPO Regulation (n 9) recital 87.

The argument on transnational interests and European public goods offers a solid justification for the EPPO being conferred with those powers. It is evident that the effective protection of the EU's financial interests[69] under Article 86 TFEU requires that the EPPO is provided with real and binding powers. Unless the EPPO is conferred those competencies, the whole purpose of having a European prosecutor which provides for an efficient and coherent prosecution of the PIF offences would be defeated.[70] With comprehensive and binding enforcement powers, the EPPO is able to effectively direct prosecutions and investigations of the 'European' PIF offences. The establishment of the EPPO suggests a significant transformation of the 'enforcement' paradigm according to which EU law relies on Member States for enforcement. Within the EPPO's jurisdiction, its operations will remove borders between national criminal justice systems creating an integrated single area of criminal prosecution.[71]

III. Normative Justifications for Intrusions by the EPPO into State Sovereignty

The fact that the prosecutors in EPPO will exercise independent executive powers in the territory of the Member State gives us reason to analyse the relationship between the EPPO, state sovereignty and criminal law.

The key problem with national sovereignty is closely related to the historical relationship of the Member States and the EU within European integration and the states' disinclination to delegate criminal law powers to the EU.[72] As the Treaty stipulates, the EU should pay due respect to the Member States' legal and constitutional traditions,[73] particularly given the fact that the nation state is regarded as the most legitimate entity for adopting legislation on criminal law. Germany's Federal Constitutional Court has stated that nothing more strongly embodies the exercise of sovereign authority than the right to define and enforce the rules of criminal law, since a criminal justice system embodies a legal community which expresses a code of conduct that is anchored in its moral values.[74]

[69] Art 325 TFEU.

[70] Coherent and effective application of EU law is also the central argument for conferring exclusive competence on the EU: Opinion 1/03 *Lugano Convention* (n 41) paras 122, 126, 128; Case 22/70 *ERTA* (n 17) paras 16–31.

[71] J Monar, 'Eurojust and the European Public Prosecutor Perspective: From Cooperation to Integration in EU Criminal Justice?' (2013) 14 *Perspectives on European Politics and Society* 339, 352.

[72] HG Sevenster, 'Criminal Law and EC Law' (1992) 29 *Common Market Law Review* 29; M Dougan, 'From the Velvet Glove to the Iron Fist: Criminal Sanctions for the Enforcement of Union Law' in Marise Cremona (ed), *Compliance and the Enforcement of EU Law* (Oxford: Oxford University Press, 2012); C Fijnaut, 'Police Co-operation and the Area of Freedom, Security and Justice' in N Walker (ed), *Europe's Area of Freedom, Security, and Justice* (Oxford: Oxford University Press, 2004).

[73] Arts 67, 82(2), 82(3) and 83(3) TFEU.

[74] Lisbon Judgment of the German Constitutional Court (n 46) paras 252–53, 355–56.

A reasonable analysis of the relationship between national sovereignty and EU criminal law also necessarily involves a discussion of the meaning of sovereignty. According to the classic concept of sovereignty, which was introduced by Jean Bodin toward the end of the 16th century, the state has the ultimate claim to authority which cannot be divided.[75] Subsequent discussions of sovereignty have departed from that narrow definition. As Lenaerts has maintained, there is simply 'no nucleus of sovereignty that the member states can invoke against the [Union]'.[76] By definition, the Member States have surrendered part of their sovereign powers in selected areas as confirmed by the principle of conferral.[77] The principles of primacy and direct effect – which have been established by Court of Justice case law – clearly reinforce that national sovereignty within the EU is not absolute as per Bodin's definition.[78]

Furthermore, the traditional concept of sovereignty does not acknowledge the independent roles of EU agencies and institutions through which Member States – in addition to national agencies and institutions – exercise their sovereignty.[79] Furthermore, key EU legal acts such as regulations and directives that are adopted by qualified majority in the Council are binding for Member States, even if they vote against them.[80] Even though Member States formally have the right to leave the Union,[81] this carries a very high political cost and is more of a divorce than an exercise of legal sovereignty[82] – as illustrated by the United Kingdom's painstaking Brexit procedure. All this seems to suggest that sovereignty as an argument for limiting EU competence can only be applied in areas with minor or no cross-border elements.

It is within this context that it should be analysed how the creation of the EPPO and its operations can involve a threat to national sovereignty. The establishment of the EPPO entails primarily that EU citizens will be deprived of making political decisions via their national parliaments in areas of criminal law in matters that involve severe restraints on the exercise of their individual rights. As noted above, the EDPs will be competent to exercise enforcement powers such as filing charges against suspects and deciding on coercive measures, with similar powers as national prosecutors under domestic law.[83]

Nonetheless, it is posited that these constraints of sovereignty are warranted in the case of the EPPO. It is legitimate to argue – on the basis of the argument on

[75] JH Franklin, *Bodin on sovereignty* (Cambridge: Cambridge University Press, 2012).

[76] K Lenaerts, 'Constitutionalism and the Many Faces of Federalism' (1990) 38 *American Journal of Comparative Law* 205.

[77] Art 5(2) TFEU.

[78] Case 6/62 *Van Gend en Loos* EU:C:1963:1; Case 6/64 *Costa v Enel* EU:C:1964:66.

[79] Statens Offentliga Utredningar, SOU 1994:12, *Suveränitet och demokrati.*

[80] Arts 289 and 238 TFEU; Art 16 TEU.

[81] Art 51 TEU.

[82] PD Marquardt, 'Subsidiarity and Sovereignty in the European Union' (1994) 18 *Fordham International Law Journal* 616.

[83] EPPO Regulation (n 9) Arts 13 and 26–33.

European public goods – that the crimes which the EPPO has been empowered to investigate – the PIF offences – are not of national concern.[84] A careful evaluation of the sovereignty arguments presented by the Member States and national parliaments reveals that they are not mainly related to concerns of loss of national autonomy. The underlying reasons appear related to the Member States' lack of political will to spend resources to protect the Union's financial interests.[85] In addition, protection of those interests is a European public good *par excellence* because the resources that are misappropriated by criminals are ultimately taken from EU citizens, who are the real victims of such crimes. Since the crimes are committed against the EU budget, the Union has an obligation to protect its financial interests and ensure that its financial resources are used in the interests of its citizens as a whole.[86]

In this context, it is difficult to argue that the Member States' claim to sovereignty makes a compelling objection against establishing the EPPO or taking other common measures of criminal justice for the purpose of protecting the Union budget. From the perspective of democratic legitimacy, it would, however, be politically unwise to entirely ignore the will of the Member States in preserving national autonomy. In this regard it should not be forgotten that the establishment of the EPPO, as introduced by the Lisbon Treaty, only involves a *possibility* and not an *obligation* to create such an office.[87] This suggests a more ambivalent perspective of the Member States regarding the creation of a more 'federal' prosecution authority. In this regard it is enlightening to refer to the German Federal Constitutional Court's ruling on the Lisbon Treaty which held that 'the national right of self-determination is affected in an especially sensitive manner when a legal community is prevented from deciding on the punishability of conduct according to their own values'.[88] However, the FCC has accepted the legitimacy of exercising authority over criminal law in cases where the crime has cross-border aspects and the criminals exploit the territorial limitation for states to prosecute such crimes.[89]

It is reasonable to posit that most EU citizens regard themselves as citizens of a Member State rather than of the Union. Even though the traditional notion of sovereignty is not persuasive when limiting the EU's competences, criticism of the Union's democratic deficit should be taken seriously. No international organisation based on democratic principles should believe that true sovereignty can be legitimised entirely without the consent of the people involved.[90] The exercise of

[84] EPPO Regulation (n 9) Art 22.

[85] J Öberg, 'National Parliaments and Political Control of EU Competences – A Sufficient Safeguard of Federalism?' (2018) 24 *European Public Law* 695; SWD (2013) 274 (n 4).

[86] Art 325 TFEU; Wade (n 3).

[87] Art 86 TFEU.

[88] Lisbon Judgment of the German Constitutional Court (n 46) para 363.

[89] ibid paras 358–59.

[90] G Majone, 'Europe's "Democratic Deficit": The Question of Standards' (1998) 4 *European Law Journal* 5; P Craig, 'Democracy and Rule-making Within the EC: An Empirical and Normative Assessment' (1997) 3 *European Law Journal* 105.

criminal law powers at the Union level should therefore not be accepted without ensuring that the EPPO's acts and operations are subject to thorough political and judicial control at EU level and national level.[91]

IV. Is Eurojust a Desirable Alternative to a Centralised European Prosecutor?

Given that we now have established a European Public Prosecutor's Office, the following offers an examination of whether the model of Eurojust could constitute a desirable alternative to such a centralised prosecutor. This section first tracks the legal and political genesis of Eurojust and then offers a more detailed analysis of Eurojust's powers under the Treaties and the Eurojust Regulation.

A. Legal and Political Evolution of Eurojust

Eurojust emerged gradually and incrementally as a direct response to the increasing 'external'[92] threats of organised and transnational crime. A key tool for effectively addressing organised crime on a transnational level is to reinforce pan-European cooperation between prosecutorial authorities of the Member States. Eurojust thus commenced its journey guided by considerations of 'security' or 'safety' to citizens.[93]

External shocks such as 9/11, and the terrorist attacks in the EU, such as in Madrid in 2004 and London in 2005, contributed to make the EU's security agenda more visible and focused on operational cooperation between police authorities and judicial authorities.[94] The Tampere European Council in 1999 laid the foundations for the creation for the European Judicial Cooperation Unit (Eurojust) as an EU agency.[95] The mentioned events of 9/11 accelerated negotiations, with agreement reached at the end of the Belgian presidency in December 2001. Eurojust was formally set up by means of a JHA Council Decision adopted in 2002 with the

[91] V Mitsilegas, 'European prosecution between cooperation and integration: The European Public Prosecutor's Office and the rule of law' (2021) 28 *Maastricht Journal of European and Comparative Law* 245.

[92] See C Harding and J Banach-Gutierrez, 'The Emergent EU Criminal Policy: Identifying the Species' (2012) 37 *European Law Review* 758, 759–62 for the use of 'external' and 'internal' threats when describing EU criminal policy.

[93] Pre-Lisbon Consolidated Version of the Treaty on European Union [2002] OJ C 325/5, Art 29.

[94] JD Occhipinti, 'Still Moving Toward a European FBI? Re-Examining the Politics of EU Police Cooperation, Intelligence and National Security' (2015) 30 *Intelligence and National Security* 234; J Monar, 'Eurojust and the European Public Prosecutor (n 71) 342–43.

[95] Council, 'Presidency Conclusions, Tampere European Council, 15–16 October 1999' (European Parliament, 1999), para 46.

mission of strengthening the fight against serious and organised crime by improving and coordinating cooperation in criminal matters between the competent authorities.[96]

Whilst there have been many actors involved in creating and giving impetus to Eurojust, it appears nonetheless evident that the Member States have been leading players in shaping law and policy in this area. Without the political will of the Member States in Tampere and the Hague, it would have been impractical to create Eurojust. The Tampere European Council in 1999 laid, as mentioned, the foundations for the creation for Eurojust as an EU agency whilst the agency was later set up formally by a JHA Council decision. The Council and Member States equally drove forward the development towards an amended Eurojust Decision,[97] adopted in 2009, as well as the revised Eurojust Regulation of 2018.[98] The evolution of Eurojust has been strongly affected by its intergovernmental design, which means that Member States have been deciding on the identity of Eurojust's members, the powers of national members, their term of office and also the financing of their members.[99]

The Member States' dominant influence in shaping the activities of Eurojust is substantiated by a detailed analysis of the powers of this organisation pre- (and post-) Lisbon. From this review it seems that Member States have jealously guarded their law enforcement powers in this area. Eurojust has not been conferred with any executive powers to take decisions that require national prosecution or police authorities to commence, conduct, coordinate or end criminal investigations. Whilst Eurojust could ask the national authorities to undertake a criminal prosecution on the basis of specific evidence, the latter could decide not to comply with the request.[100] Eurojust's narrow pre-Lisbon Treaty remit was coherent with the overall justification for EU action in criminal justice, which was based on a philosophy of 'cooperation' between national criminal justice systems focused on enhancing synergy without intrusive EU harmonisation.[101] Whilst the Commission advocated an integrated model of EU criminal justice by commissioning the Corpus Juris project and floating ideas about the establishment of a European prosecutor,

[96] V Mitsilegas, *EU Criminal Law*, 2nd edn (Oxford: Hart Publishing, 2022) 395.

[97] Council Decision 2009/426/JHA of 16 December 2008 on the strengthening of Eurojust and amending Decision 2002/187/JHA setting up Eurojust with a view to reinforcing the fight against serious crime [2009] OJ L 138/14.

[98] Regulation (EU) 2018/1727 of the European Parliament and of the Council of 14 November 2018 on the European Union Agency for Criminal Justice Cooperation (Eurojust), and replacing and repealing Council Decision 2002/187/JHA [2018] OJ L 295/138; S Peers, *EU Justice and Home Affairs Law: Volume II: EU Criminal Law, Policing, and Civil Law*, 4th edn (Oxford: Oxford University Press, 2016) 253–57.

[99] See A Mégie, 'Eurojust in Action: An Institutionalisation of European Legal Culture?' in R Colson and S Field (eds), *EU Criminal Justice and the Challenges of Legal Diversity* (Cambridge: Cambridge University Press 2016) 90–94.

[100] Arts 30(2)(b) and 31(2) of the pre-Lisbon Version of the Treaty of European Union; Council Decision 2002/187/JHA of 28 February 2002 setting up Eurojust with a view to reinforcing the fight against serious crime [2002] OJ L63/1, Arts 7 and 8. See also Eurojust Regulation (n 98) Arts 3 and 4.

[101] See Monar, 'Eurojust and the European Public Prosecutor' (n 71) 341–43, 353–55.

Member States appeared reluctant to go that far, stressing the intergovernmental character of the third pillar and putting forward alternatives to harmonisation such as mutual recognition.[102]

The key point here is that the Member States envisioned Eurojust as a 'cooperational' unit having chiefly a 'supportive' role for national authorities. Eurojust was thus never envisaged as a supranational prosecutorial body with executive powers, unlike the European Public Prosecutor's Office.[103] In the absence of more direct powers over national prosecution authorities, it is, however, questionable whether Eurojust in reality is capable of effectively contributing to the fight against serious cross-border crime.[104]

B. Legal Analysis of Eurojust's Powers Post-Lisbon

The Lisbon Treaty suggests nonetheless a significant increase of Eurojust's competencies and a potential qualitative change in its role by giving the agency binding powers to initiate criminal investigations as well as express powers in resolving conflicts of jurisdiction.[105] Article 85 TFEU states Eurojust's mission clearly as being about supporting and strengthening 'coordination and cooperation between national investigating and prosecuting authorities in relation to serious crime affecting two or more Member States or requiring a prosecution on common bases …'. The provision gives the EU legislator competence to adopt regulations through which to determine Eurojust's 'structure, operation, field of action and tasks' including (i) the initiation and coordination of criminal investigations, as well as proposing the initiation and coordination of prosecutions conducted by competent national authorities, particularly those relating to offences against the financial interests of the Union; (ii) the strengthening of judicial cooperation, including by resolution of conflicts of jurisdiction.[106] Importantly, Eurojust's powers come with a substantial limit in that 'formal acts of judicial procedure shall be carried out by the competent national officials'.[107]

The key issue here is to what extent the new wording of Article 85 TFEU opens up a possibility to 'require' national authorities to commence proceedings.[108]

[102] Mitsilegas, *EU Criminal Law* (n 96) 391–92; M Mangenot, 'Jeux Européens et Innovation Institutionnelle: Les Logiques de Création d'Eurojust' (2006) 62 *Cultures et Conflits* 43.

[103] See Art 86 TFEU.

[104] See A Suominen, 'The Past, Present and the Future of Eurojust' (2008) 15 *Maastricht Journal of European and Comparative Law* 217; Monar, 'Eurojust and the European Public Prosecutor' (n 71) 340, 353–55.

[105] See Mitsilegas, *EU Criminal Law* (n 96) 392.

[106] The Eurojust Regulation further specifies that one of the key tasks of Eurojust is to facilitate the execution of requests for, and decisions on, judicial cooperation, including requests and decisions based on instruments that give effect to the principle of mutual recognition, Eurojust Regulation (n 98) Art 2.

[107] See Arts 85(1)–(3) TFEU.

[108] See CONV 426/02 (n 8) 10, 19.

A close reading of Article 85 TFEU suggests the possibility of granting Eurojust a binding power with regard to the initiation of investigations and with regard to the coordination of investigations and prosecutions.[109] Compared to the pre-Lisbon version of the TEU, it is no longer a matter of simply 'facilitating proper coordination'[110] or of 'stimulating and improving coordination between the competent authorities in Member States of investigations and prosecutions in the Member States'[111] but rather a matter of coordinating the investigations and prosecutions, which suggests decision-making power.[112]

Article 85 is more prudent in terms of the initiation of prosecutions than with regard to the initiation of investigations as the wording concerns merely 'proposing' prosecutions to be initiated. It is therefore a matter of allowing Eurojust to set in motion an initiative regarding criminal investigations and Eurojust's binding power ceases when investigations are launched. It does not cover the realisation of investigations and the direction of them – these tasks being covered rather by Article 86 TFEU. Regarding the resolving of conflicts of jurisdiction, it also appears that the expression 'resolution' implies decision-making powers regarding such matters. It is questionable to what extent the Treaty's power could be extended further to imply a power to require one Member State not to prosecute in favour of another. A power to require a national authority to refrain from bringing proceedings should at least be considered to fall within the scope of Eurojust's remit since otherwise its power to 'resolve' conflicts of jurisdiction would be devoid of meaning.[113]

The final important point here is to examine the meaning of 'formal acts of judicial procedure'.[114] The final report of Working Group X stipulated that 'it could be specified that formal acts of judicial procedure in the Member States could be taken by the competent national officials including the national members of Eurojust to the extent that they have received such competence'. It is reasonable to interpret Article 85 in light of this preparatory work. The result appears to be that both investigations and proceedings should be directed by 'competent national officials' including by national members of Eurojust who would be recognised as having such powers, which would imply the strengthening of their powers in this respect. The restriction on giving Eurojust the power to take 'formal acts

[109] See P Craig, *The Lisbon Treaty: Law, Politics, and Treaty Reform* (Oxford: Oxford University Press, 2011) 368.

[110] Pre-Lisbon version of the Treaty of European Union, Art 31, para 2.

[111] Council Eurojust Decision of 2009 (n 104) Art 3, para 1.

[112] It seems clear from Working Group X, CONV 426/02 (n 8) 18–20 that this is an extension of powers. See also Memorandum by Dr Valsamis Mitsilegas, European Union Committee, *The Treaty of Lisbon: an impact assessment* (HL 2007–08, 62-II) E 167–68.

[113] See A Weyembergh, 'The Development of Eurojust: Potential and Limitations of Article 85 of the TFEU' (2011) 2 *New Journal* of *European Criminal Law* 75, 98–99.

[114] See Art 85(2) TFEU. This limitation was particularly underlined in pre-Lisbon Treaty negotiations by several Convention members endeavouring to circumscribe the right to initiate criminal proceedings, Convention, Secretariat of the European Convention, 'Draft sections of Part Three with comments' (CONV 727/03, 27 May 2003) 33.

of judicial procedure' means that it cannot itself bring criminal charges against individuals in whatever form that process takes in the national legal framework.[115]

Whilst it is reasonable to assume that the Commission may be interested in proposing to give Eurojust binding powers given the broad design of Article 85 TFEU, legislative practice has not yet realised those ambitions.[116] Eurojust has indeed been bestowed with various powers pursuant to the 2018 Eurojust Regulation. In carrying out its tasks, Eurojust may ask the competent authorities of the Member States concerned to: (i) undertake an investigation or prosecution of specific acts; (ii) accept that one of them may be in a better position to undertake an investigation or to prosecute specific acts; (iii) coordinate between the competent authorities of the Member States concerned; (iv) set up a joint investigation team and provide it with any information that is necessary for carrying out its tasks; (v) take special investigative measures or any other measure justified for the investigation or prosecution.[117]

However, whilst Eurojust can ask Member State authorities to undertake an investigation or prosecution of specific acts, it cannot compel these authorities to do so. In such instances, Eurojust shall issue a written opinion on recurrent refusals or difficulties concerning the execution of requests for judicial cooperation and send it to the Member State concerned. The Member States may refuse to comply with such requests or to follow the written opinion if doing so would harm essential national security interests, jeopardise the success of an ongoing investigation or jeopardise the safety of an individual.[118] There is a similar regulation on conflicts of jurisdiction where Eurojust can ask national authorities to accept that one of them may be in a better position to undertake an investigation or to prosecute specific acts.[119] Where Member States cannot agree on which of them should undertake an investigation or prosecution after a request from Eurojust, the agency should issue 'a written opinion' on the case which however is not binding on Member States.[120]

The key point here from the legal analysis is that there is nothing in the wording or the aims of the Regulation which suggests that Europol has any binding powers to require Member States to undertake investigations or to settle conflicts

[115] Weyembergh (n 113) 98–99; CONV 426/02 (n 8). Peers has advanced an even more narrow reading suggesting that Art 85 TFEU cannot provides Eurojust with powers to 'require' national authorities to bring proceedings, as such requests would amount to 'formal acts of judicial procedure', S Peers, *EU Justice and Home Affairs Law*, 4th edn (Oxford: Oxford University Press, 2016) 218–19.

[116] See Monar, 'Eurojust and the European Public Prosecutor' (n 71) 347–50; Weyembergh (n 113) 90–98.

[117] Eurojust Regulation (n 98) Art 4(2).

[118] ibid Art 4(6).

[119] Weyembergh also criticises such an extension of jurisdiction on the basis that giving Eurojust too far-reaching powers on forum shopping would be a serious detriment to defendants, suggesting a need to delineate Eurojust's jurisdiction and give the CJEU possibilities for judicial control: Weyembergh (n 113); D Flore, 'D'un réseau judiciaire européen à une juridiction pénale européenne: Eurojust et l'émergence d'un système de justice pénale' in G de Kerchove and A Weyembergh (eds), *L'espace pénal européen: enjeux et perspectives* (Brussels: Brussels University, 2002).

[120] Eurojust Regulation (n 98) recital 14, Arts 4(2), 4(4) and 4(6).

of jurisdiction. This is notwithstanding the fact that Article 85 TFEU offers the powers for the EU legislator to adopt legislation enhancing the agency' s role in that respect. At the present time, Eurojust is thus still just a facilitator without any decision-making powers or binding powers with regard to national authorities. The outcome of Eurojust's interventions is consequently dependent on the power of conviction that it exercises over the authorities concerned.[121]

Given all this, it must be queried to what extent Eurojust fulfils a meaningful role, particularly in the presence of the European Public Prosecutor which is already empowered to order investigations and to prosecute offences before national courts in the field of the EU's financial interests.

There is still, however, an important role for Eurojust to play in the fight against transnational crime. First, the EPPO's powers are at this stage limited to the PIF offences and the ancillary offences.[122] For other serious cross-border offences, the EPPO does not enjoy any binding powers to investigate and prosecute. Furthermore, the EPPO does not enjoy any significant powers in the field of resolution of conflicts of jurisdiction in contrast to Eurojust. There is nonetheless an argument to be made on the basis of the theory of transnational interests and European public goods that Eurojust's powers need to be extended for them to make a real impact. Currently, the Eurojust Regulation does not give Eurojust any binding powers to order an investigation to be commenced or powers to discontinue investigations or prosecutions.[123] As the previous legal analysis stated, there is nothing in the Treaties which hinders Eurojust from being conferred with binding powers over initiation of investigations and with regard to resolution of conflicts of jurisdiction.[124]

Given Eurojust's acquired expertise, resources and unique role as a central mediator between national jurisdictions, it seems that there is a strong normative argument for giving them those powers.[125] Eurojust has demonstrated a strong track record in facilitating and coordinating national authorities' work against organised crime. Eurojust is increasingly included in the day-to-day work of practitioners and authorities across most Member States when it comes to cases with cross-border implications. A case in point is Eurojust's 'coordination meetings' which usually take place at the premises of Eurojust benefitting from the agency's logistical and financial support, gathering both national authorities from different Member States dealing with the same case and national members of Eurojust. These meetings are an ideal platform for all stakeholders to exchange views on

[121] Weyembergh (n 113) 83–84; Flore (n 119); Mitsilegas, *EU Criminal Law* (n 96) 404.

[122] See above section II and EPPO Regulation (n 9) Art 22.

[123] See Eurojust Regulation (n 108) Arts 3 and 4.

[124] See Art 85 TFEU.

[125] Similar relative institutional competence arguments on incentives and comparative efficiency that have been made above in section II with respect to the EPPO apply to Eurojust: COM (2013) 534 final (n 35) 2–3; SWD (2013) 274 (n 4) 6–9, 25–27.

ongoing investigations and their potential coordination, thus becoming aware of the transnational dimension of the crimes under investigation and the links between suspects. As an outcome of the coordination meetings, Eurojust may set up a common strategy and coordinate and facilitate the actions of various national authorities (planning simultaneous arrests, searches, seizures of property) by means of a 'coordination centre' set up at Eurojust.[126]

Another example of Eurojust's strong added value in the work against organised crime is the setting up of Joint Investigation Teams which are considered as essential for an effective approach to cross-border crime. Eurojust is considered as a very valuable facility for bringing together practitioners from prosecution services, police and other investigating bodies from all countries involved to exchange ideas and plans for further actions to be undertaken together on high profile investigations. Eurojust also sits with resources such as translation and access to legal advice which are considered hugely significant, and the agency also facilitates flexibility in doing things in real time working immediately with other Member States.[127] The added value of Eurojust in coordinating complex cases and facilitating the completion of mutual legal assistance in delicate situations has been fully acknowledged by practitioners.[128]

In general, Member States' authorities and Eurojust's own members value Eurojust's informal operational style, which is praised for its efficiency and for not being intrusive into national prosecutorial services.[129] The added value of a binding power for Eurojust to initiate an investigation is that the measure would not depend on the discretion of national authorities and their priorities as they would now be European requests and mandatory to execute.[130] Only Eurojust sits with a sufficient overview to most properly assess when and how a larger criminal investigation should be commenced. For reasons of efficiency and competence, it also seems that Eurojust is much better placed than Member States to resolve conflicts of jurisdiction.

[126] Mitsilegas, *EU Criminal Law* (n 96) 407; S Petit Leclair, 'Justice et Sécurité en Europe: Eurojust ou la Création d'un Parquet Européen' (2012) 20 *Cahiers de la sécurité* 38.

[127] House of Lords' European Union Committee, *Brexit: Future UK-EU Security and Police Cooperation*, 7th Report (London: Stationery Office Limited, 2017) session 2016–17, HL Paper 77, 22–24; House of Lords' European Union Committee, *Brexit: Future UK-EU Security and Policing Co-operation*, 7th Report (London: Stationery Office Limited, 2017) session 2016–17, HL Paper 77, Q 14; House of Lords' European Union Committee, *Brexit: Future UK-EU Security and Policing Co-operation*, 7th Report (London: Stationery Office Limited, 2017) session 2016–17, HL Paper 77, Written evidence from the Crown Office and Procurator Fiscal Service (FSP0003), 3–4.

[128] Final report on the 6th round of mutual evaluations on 'The practical implementation and operation of the Council Decision 2002/187/JHA of 28 February 2002 setting up Eurojust with a view to reinforcing the fight against serious crime and of the Council Decision 2008/976/JHA on the European Judicial Network in criminal matters', Council Doc 14536/2/14 REV 2, 16, 44–45.

[129] P Jeney, 'The Future of Eurojust', Study for the LIBE Committee of the European Parliament (European Parliament, 2012) 93–96, 100.

[130] Report on the Strategic Seminar Eurojust: New Perspectives in Judicial Cooperation Budapest, 15–17 May 2011, Report 14428/11 COPEN 227 CATS 78, 7.

On a final note, it should be emphasised that the power to initiate investigations is not a 'panacea' in the context of strengthening Eurojust or obliging reluctant national authorities to cooperate. Instead, the power would be best used to proactively initiate proceedings based on analysis and to carry out coordinated actions in complex cases. In this vein, the power to initiate an investigation can be regarded as genuinely shifting Eurojust towards a more intelligence-led rationale, whereby it is put in a position of shaping and not only witnessing transnational criminal proceedings.[131]

V. Conclusions

This chapter has centred on analysing the normative foundations for having centralised European public prosecutors which are conferred with powers to initiate and realise criminal investigations and prosecutions. The first section offered a principled analysis of the powers of the recently established European Public Prosecutor. The discussion in the chapter emphasised that the EPPO forms a powerful constitutional challenge to Member States' sovereignty in the area of criminal law.[132] Whilst the EPPO, in exercising its enforcement powers, may be perceived as a threat to national sovereignty, there are strong reasons to accept those constraints on member state sovereignty. Only a European public prosecutor has the correct incentives, competencies and resources to effectively prosecute crime against the Union's financial interests, and ultimately to protect the common financial interests of EU citizens. The theory of European public goods provides a strong justification for a centralised European public prosecutor which can defend markedly strong EU interests, such as the protection of the EU budget. The need to confer the EPPO with effective and binding powers arises from the nature of the crimes at issue, which by affecting the Union's own financial interests intrinsically have a Union dimension.[133]

This point would become even more important if the EPPO's powers were to be extended beyond the EU's financial interests. It is apparent that the drafters of the TFEU probably had in mind a broader jurisdiction for the EPPO, to include other offences. Article 86(4) TFEU specifically enables the European Council to extend the powers of the EPPO. In this respect it is plausible that the Commission, in the near future, might wish to extend the powers of the EPPO to the areas of financial crime – an area in which the EU has already legislated by means of

[131] Jeney (n 129) 114–15.

[132] *Lisbon Judgment* (n 46) Case 2 BvE 2/08, 5/08, 2 BvR 1010/08, 1022/08, 1259/08, 182/09 (2009), paras 252–53, 355–62; L Besselink, 'Sovereignty, Criminal Law and the New European Context' in P Alldridge and C Brants (eds), *Personal Autonomy, the Private Sphere and Criminal Law: A Comparative Study* (Oxford: Hart Publishing, 2001).

[133] See above section III.

harmonisation measures under Article 83(1) and 83(2) TFEU. This could include money laundering,[134] corruption, counterfeiting,[135] and market abuse/insider trade.[136]

The most central (and controversial) extension of remit, however, pertains to terrorism – an area in which the EU has already adopted harmonisation measures.[137] This is furthermore a plausible option for an extension of the EPPO's mandate, as there is already a Commission Communication addressing the issue.[138] At this stage, it is not necessary to discuss whether –and to what extent – this proposal might be realised. It suffices to say that, to ensure the legitimacy of this institution, any extension of the EPPO's remit must be confined to protecting clearly defined transnational ('Union') interests. It is only in such instances that the EPPO can provide significant added value, by pooling expertise, competencies and investigative resources.[139]

This brings us to the second section of the chapter and the discussion on the future of Eurojust. The discussion in the chapter suggested that the Member States to date have envisioned Eurojust as a 'cooperational' unit having chiefly a 'supportive' role for national authorities with no executive powers. In the absence of such powers, it is, however, questionable to what extent Eurojust is capable of effectively contributing to the fight against serious cross-border crime. Whilst Article 85 TFEU offers possibilities to enhance Eurojust by giving it serious operational powers, the most recent Eurojust reform fails to provide for binding powers for Eurojust to compel Member States to undertake investigations or to settle conflicts of jurisdiction.[140]

Despite the presence of the EPPO, there is still an important role for Eurojust to play in the fight against transnational crime. Nonetheless, it is argued that

[134] Directive (EU) 2018/1673 of the European Parliament and of the Council of 23 October 2018 on combating money laundering by criminal law [2018] OJ L 284/22.

[135] Directive (EU) 2019/713 of the European Parliament and of the Council of 17 April 2019 on combating fraud and counterfeiting of non-cash means of payment and replacing Council Framework Decision 2001/413/JHA [2019] OJ L 123/18; Directive 2014/62/EU of the European Parliament and of the Council of 15 May 2014 on the protection of the euro and other currencies against counterfeiting by criminal law and replacing Council Framework Decision 2000/383/JHA [2014] OJ L 151/1.

[136] Directive 2014/57/EU of the European Parliament and of the Council of 16 April 2014 on criminal sanctions for market abuse [2014] OJ L 173/79.

[137] Directive (EU) 2017/541 of the European Parliament of the Council of 15 March 2017 on combating terrorism and replacing Council Framework Decision 2002/475/JHA and amending Council Decision 2005/671/JHA [2017] OJ L 88/6.

[138] Communication from the Commission to the European Parliament and the European Council, 'A Europe that protects: an initiative to extend the competences of the European Public Prosecutor's Office to cross-border terrorist crimes', COM(2018) 641 final.

[139] Wade (n 3) 143–46. There are also an emergent discussion at EU level on extending the EPPO's remit to crimes relating to the violation of EU restrictive measures: see European Parliament, Parliamentary question – O-000022/2023, 'Extension of the mandate of the European Public Prosecutor's Office with regard to the criminal offence of violation of Union restrictive measures', 27 April 2023.

[140] See above section IV (A).

Eurojust's powers need to be extended and made binding for them to make a real difference in practice.[141] Given Eurojust's acquired resources and unique role as a central mediator between national jurisdictions, it seems that there is a strong argument for giving them those powers.[142] Crimes that are facilitated by transnational cooperation and open borders are a legitimate subject for EU action to protect the public good of transnational security. It is in such instances that Eurojust can provide significant added value by protecting those interests, by the pooling of expertise, competencies and investigative resources. If Eurojust could contribute to addressing serious cases of transnational crime, there is a legitimate case for an extension of the mandate of Eurojust in terms of binding powers to initiate criminal investigations and resolve conflicts of jurisdiction.[143]

The analysis above also provides some lessons for the general debate on integration in the area of EU criminal justice. The establishment of the EPPO is a paradigmatic example of a shift from a rationale of 'cooperation' to one of 'integration' of national criminal justice systems based on formal powers exercised by EU criminal justice agencies.[144] Whilst not all Member States take part in this development,[145] it clearly reshapes our current view of EU criminal justice as a Member State-controlled policy field. The creation of an integrated EU prosecution authority with significant and autonomous law enforcement powers is strong evidence that Member States are no longer in the driving seat in the field of criminal policy.[146] The establishment of the EPPO, in conjunction with the adoption of the new PIF Directive, makes a compelling argument for holding that the EU appears to have adopted a 'federal vision' of criminal law to protect its financial interests.[147]

It must be conceded that this 'federalisation' of criminal law is – for the time being – confined to the prosecution and investigation of offences directed against the EU's budget. This development, however, asks more fundamental questions about the scope of EU criminal policy should the EPPO stand as a role model for the future direction of integration in this area. The EPPO indeed, perhaps unintentionally, has created a path towards a European criminal justice system. If the EU has its own prosecutor, there is a pressing need for structures

[141] See Eurojust Regulation (n 108) Arts 3 and 4.

[142] Similar comparative efficiency arguments that have been made above in section II with respect to the EPPO apply to Eurojust: COM (2013) 534 final (n 35) 2–3; Commission, 'Commission Staff Working Document, Impact Assessment, Accompanying the Proposal for a SWD (2013) 274 (n 4), 6–9, 25–27.

[143] See Arts 85 and 88 TFEU.

[144] See CJ Bickerton, D Hodson and U Puetter (eds), *The New Intergovernmentalism: States and Supranational Actors in the Post-Maastricht Era* (Oxford: Oxford University Press, 2015) 1–9.

[145] See EPPO Regulation (n 9) recitals 5–9.

[146] See Monar, 'Eurojust and the European Public Prosecutor Perspective' (n 71); Occhipinti (n 94).

[147] C Díez and E Herlin-Karnell, 'Prosecuting EU Financial Crimes: The European Public Prosecutor's Office in Comparison to the US Federal Regime' (2018) 19 *German Law Journal* 1191.

to hold such a body accountable and to ensure that its actions can be subject to judicial scrutiny. The latter is a crucial point for the overall legitimacy of the EPPO's operations in the near future. If the EPPO acts as a federal prosecutor, then there must consequently be put in place equivalent supranational safeguards to ensure that this prosecutor respects the central tenets of the rule of law.[148]

[148] See Mitsilegas, *EU Criminal Law After Lisbon* (n 1) 113–20.

6

The Normative Justification for Having a European FBI

I. Introduction – The Evolution of Europol as an Emergent Supranational EU Crime-Fighting Agency

Europol is a fascinating agency to study, having developed from a technocratic intergovernmental organisation into a powerful 'intelligence' hub with autonomous powers. Whilst the legal framework within which it operates has evolved and it has transformed into a fully-fledged agency, Member States remain resistant to grant Europol full autonomy, leaving the agency constrained in its law enforcement activities.[1] Despite calls for a more substantial transformation of Europol,[2] it appears that the dream of a more integrated operative European policy agency seems far off.[3]

The initial proposal to develop a European policy agency reminiscent of the US Federal Bureau of Investigation (FBI) was advanced in the 1980s by the then German Chancellor Helmut Kohl.[4] The argument for creating a European FBI has been made on expressive and symbolic grounds with the claim that a political and united Europe, with open borders, requires a true cross-border law enforcement agency adequately equipped to act.[5] It has been contended more recently that the rise of extreme right populism, rise in conspiracy theories, the Covid-19 crisis, the deepening polarisation as well as the digital transformation and rise of new technologies and thus opportunities for serious criminality underscore the

[1] K Lingenfelter and S Miettinen, 'Obstacles to supranational operational police powers in the European union: Europol reform and the construction of trust between national police authorities' (2021) 28 *Maastricht Journal of European and Comparative Law* 182.

[2] See M Monroy, 'Negotiations on the Europol Regulation: Will there be a "European FBI" by the end of the year?' 27/10/2021: https://digit.site36.net/2021/10/27/negotiations-on-the-europol-regulation-will-there-be-a-european-fbi-by-the-end-of-the-year/.

[3] G Vermeulen and A De Moor, 'The Europol Council Decision: Transforming Europol into an Agency of the European Union' (2010) 47 *Common Market Law Review* 1089, 1111–12, 1121.

[4] C Fijnaut, 'The "Communitization" of Police Cooperation in Western Europe' in HG Schermers (ed), *Free Movement of Persons in Europe: Legal Problems and Experiences* (Alphen aan den Rijn: Kluwer Academic Publishers, 1993) 75–92.

[5] Renew Position Paper, 'From Europol Towards a European FBI: Boosting the Union's Law Enforcement Competences', 3 December 2020: www.statewatch.org/media/1583/eu-europol-renew-europe-position-paper-4-12-20.pdf, 5–6.

need for deeper police cooperation.[6] The conclusions of a European Council in 1992 suggested a gradual development of Europol functions from a relay station for exchange of information and experience and then in the second phase as an agency with powers to act also within the Member States.[7] Whilst the ambitious notions have not been brought into fruition (and might never be realised) this chapter examines the normative argument for conferring Europol with stronger and more binding powers over national authorities' investigations of transnational crime.[8]

Prior to examining a potential extension of Europol's powers, there is a need to account for the emergence of this agency and the earlier developments of law and policy in this area. Europol transformed originally out of the intergovernmental and 'secretive' TREVI[9] group set up in 1976 by the then 12 EU Member States to counter terrorism and to coordinate policing in the EU.[10] Despite misgivings about Europol's transparency, by the time Europol came into being it was considered a notable change in the mode of legally establishing international police cooperation.[11] In contrast to TREVI, Europol benefitted from a more transparent legal mandate and supranational framework which made it possible for the agency to be engaged in a more coherent approach to law enforcement cooperation.[12]

[6] In July 2020, French and Dutch law enforcement and judicial authorities, alongside Europol and Eurojust, presented the joint investigation to dismantle EncroChat, an encrypted phone network used by criminal networks involved in violent attacks, corruption, attempted murders and large-scale drug transports: Europol/Eurojust joint press release, 'Dismantling of an encrypted network sends shockwaves through organised crime groups across Europe', 2 July 2020: www.europol.europa.eu/media-press/newsroom/news/dismantling-of-encrypted-network-sends-shock-waves-through-organised-crime-groups-across-europe#:~:text=At%20a%20joint%20press%20conference,widely%20used%20by%20criminal%20networks; Europol, 2017 EU Serious and Organised Threat Assessment, 28 February 2017: www.europol.europa.eu/publications-events/main-reports/european-union-serious-and-organised-crime-threat-assessment-2017#downloads; Europol, 'Pandemic profiteering: how criminals exploit the COVID-19 crisis', 27 March 2020: www.europol.europa.eu/publications-events/publications/pandemic-profiteering-how-criminals-exploit-covid-19-crisis; Europol, 'Beyond the pandemic – How COVID-19 will shape the serious and organised crime landscape in the EU', 30 April 2020: www.europol.europa.eu/publications-events/publications/beyond-pandemic-how-covid-19-will-shape-serious-and-organised-crime-landscape-in-eu.

[7] Annex 1 to the Presidency Conclusions emanating from the Luxembourg European Council of 28 and 29 June 1991: https://ec.europa.eu/commission/presscorner/detail/en/DOC_91_2.

[8] B Tupman, *Policing in Europe, Uniform in Diversity* (Exeter: Intellect, 1999).

[9] The name 'Trevi' has been open to many interpretations but is most likely an acronym for 'terrorism, radicalism, extremism and international violence', T Bunyan, 'Trevi, Europol and the European state', Statewatch: www.statewatch.org/media/documents/news/handbook-trevi.pdf; F König and F Trauner, 'From Trevi to Europol: Germany's role in the integration of EU police cooperation' (2021) 43 *Journal of European Integration* 175.

[10] On TREVI and Europol's roots in its structures, see C Fijnaut, 'Policing Western Europe: Interpol, TREVI and Europol' (1992) 15 *Police Studies* 103. M Den Boer and N Walker, 'European Policing after 1992' (1993) 31 *Journal of Common Market Studies* 3.

[11] N Pandit, 'Policing the EU's External Border: Legitimacy and Accountability under Scrutiny' (2012) 13 *ERA Forum* 403.

[12] J Benyon, 'Policing the European Union: The Changing Basis of Cooperation on Law Enforcement' (1994) 70 *International Affairs* 498. JD Occhipinti, 'Still Moving Toward a European FBI? Re-Examining the Politics of EU Police Cooperation' (2015) 30 *Intelligence and National Security* 234, 245–46.

The 1993 Maastricht Treaty established the grounds for police cooperation among Member States[13] but also set significant limits to the EU's powers in these areas as police cooperation was relegated to the third pillar.[14] The Treaties emphasised the importance of operational cooperation through Europol as an intelligence broker, relating to the collection, storage, processing, analysis and exchange of information. Five years after the entry into force of the Treaty of Amsterdam, Europol was also to be enabled to support the preparation, and to encourage the coordination and carrying out, of specific investigative actions by the Member States' authorities, including operational actions of joint teams comprising representatives of Europol in a support capacity.[15] Europol was subsequently established through a convention[16] requiring ratification by all Member States thus placing it outside of the Community legal framework as a markedly intergovernmental organisation.[17]

It took until 1999 before Europol commenced its activities and then fell into the hands of the Council, reinforcing that Member States were the leading players in shaping law and policy in this area.[18] The Member States as a group were responsible for multiple amendments and protocols to the Europol Convention in the early 2000s.[19] Through the new protocols and amendments, Europol's competences extended to participation in Joint Investigation Teams (JITs) and the right to ask Member States to provide information on ongoing criminal investigations, including obtaining access to the Schengen Information System (SIS) and the Visa Information System (VIS) database.[20]

However, Europol was kept at 'arm's length' from supranational control by the Parliament and the Court of Justice, making it challenging to ensure consistent, Union-wide supranational oversight.[21] As a preparation of the Constitutional Treaty, the Commission proposed to replace Europol's convention with a Council Decision allowing more flexibility in amending Europol's legal basis as well

[13] Consolidated version of the Treaty on European Union [1992] OJ C 191/01, Title VI.

[14] M Den Boer, 'Towards an Accountability Regime for an Emerging European Policing Governance' (2002) 12 *Policing and Society* 288. C Fijnaut, 'International Policing in Europe: Present and Future' (1994) 19 *European Law Review* 613.

[15] Arts 30 (1)–(2) of the Treaty on European Union in its pre-Lisbon Version.

[16] Council Act of 26 July 1995 drawing up the Convention based on Article K.3 of the Treaty on European Union, on the establishment of a European Police Office (Europol Convention) [1995] OJ C 316/1.

[17] W Wagner, 'Guarding the Guards. The European Convention and the communitization of police co-operation' (2006) 13 *Journal of European Public Policy* 1230; Vermeulen and De Moor (n 3) 1092.

[18] M Busuioc and M Groenleer, 'Beyond Design: The Evolution of Europol and Eurojust' (2013) 14 *Perspectives on European Politics and Society* 289.

[19] C Hillebrand, 'Guarding EU-Wide Counter-Terrorism Policing: The Struggle for Sound Parliamentary Scrutiny of Europol' (2011) 7 *Journal of Contemporary European Research* 500; Benyon (n 12) 514–15.

[20] Council Framework Decision of 13 June 2002 on joint investigation teams [2002] OJ L 162/1; Council Act of 28 November 2002 (protocol on joint investigation teams) [2002] OJ C 312/1.

[21] Den Boer and N Walker (n 10); Den Boer (n 14) 278; E Guild and S Carrera, 'No Constitutional Treaty? Implications for the Area of Freedom, Security and Justice' (CEPS, 26 August 2009) 2: www.ceps.eu/ceps-publications/no-constitutional-treaty-implications-area-freedom-security-and-justice/.

as conferring it with full status as an agency.[22] Even though the Constitutional Treaty failed, the Council pushed the decision through despite objections from the European Parliament (EP) which then lacked powers to veto the decision. The Council Decision[23] that transformed Europol from an intergovernmental organisation into a Union agency had implications upon Europol's oversight. Of these implications, among the most important was the EP's enhanced role in the control of Europol's budget, which was now funded by the Union.[24] This important development toward supranationalism was bolstered further by the shift brought about by the Council Decision in regard to future amendments, as in contrast to the Europol Convention, it only demanded a qualified majority which would enable quicker compromises to be found at the Union level.[25]

Following the suggestions by Working Group X,[26] the Lisbon Treaty reinforced the 'supranationalisation' of Europol in significant ways.[27] First, by abolishing the pillar structure, the Treaties brought policing into the remit of the ordinary jurisdiction of the Court of Justice.[28] Secondly, by extending the ordinary legislative procedure to Europol, Article 88 TFEU empowers the Commission to propose modifications to Europol's mandate and powers, both of which had already been reinforced in the Treaty. Europol's decision-making procedure was changed fully to QMV in Council, and the introduction of the ordinary legislative procedure strengthened the EP's role, giving it co-legislative rights to adopt, with the Council, regulations that 'determine Europol's structure, management, operation, field of action and tasks'.[29] The Commission's 2013 proposal to recast Europol under the new post-Lisbon legal basis[30] did not suggest any extension of power but centred instead on seeking to align Europol with the new Treaty requirements by introducing a control mechanism by the EP and national parliaments[31] and therefore enhancing democratic legitimacy and accountability.[32] The Stockholm Programme goals envisioned developing Europol as a hub for information exchange between

[22] M Den Boer and W Bruggeman, 'Shifting gear: Europol in the contemporary policing era' (2007) 23 *Politique européenne* 80–81; Vermeulen and De Moor (n 3) 1094.

[23] Council Decision of 6 April 2009 establishing the European Police Office (Europol) [2009] OJ L 121/37.

[24] ibid, Arts 43(6), (9) and (10).

[25] R Dehousse and J Weiler, 'The legal dimension' in W Wallace (ed), *The Dynamics of European Integration* (London: Pinter, 1990), 248.

[26] CONV 426/02, 'Final report of Working Group X "Freedom, Security and Justice"', Brussels, 2 December 2002, 18.

[27] Vermeulen and De Moor (n 3) 1096; S Peers, *EU Justice and Home Affairs: Volume II: EU Criminal Law, Policing, and Civil Law* (Oxford: Oxford University Press, 2016), 269.

[28] Arts 251–281 TFEU.

[29] Art 88(2) TFEU. See furthermore V Abazi, 'The Future of Europol's Parliamentary Oversight: A Great Leap Forward?' (2014) 15 *German Law Journal* 1134; CONV 426/02 (n 26).

[30] See Commission, Proposal for a Regulation of the European Parliament and of the Council on the European Union Agency for Law Enforcement Cooperation and Training (Europol) and repealing Decisions 2009/371/JHA and 2005/681/JHA, COM(2013) 173 final.

[31] Art 88(2) TFEU.

[32] Lingenfelter and Miettinen (n 1).

the law enforcement authorities of the Member States,[33] including training and exchange schemes for Member State law enforcement personnel.

There are two key reflections which can be extracted from the account on the development of Europol. First, security-oriented rationales are the most potent explanation in accounting for the gradual and incremental rise of Europol as a direct response to the 'external'[34] threats of organised and transnational crime.[35] A key tool for effectively addressing organised crime on a transnational level is to enhance pan-European cooperation between police authorities of the Member States. External shocks such as 9/11, and the terrorist attacks in Madrid in 2004 and London in 2005, contributed to make the EU's security agenda more visible and focused on operational cooperation between police authorities. This also triggered the creation of Europol.[36] The second one relates to the emergent supranationalism in this field which is countenanced by continuing dominant Member State influence in shaping the activities of Europol. Whilst Europol recently has been given more powers, information-related tasks, namely (operational and strategic) analysis and facilitation of exchange of information, still represent the core of Europol' s activities. The latter point is substantiated by the fact that Europol – at least pre-Lisbon – was not envisaged to have any executive powers to take decisions that required national prosecution or police authorities to commence or conduct an investigation.[37] The narrow Treaty remit of Europol[38] was – as the case with Eurojust – coherent with the general justification for EU action in criminal justice, which is based on a philosophy of 'cooperation' between national criminal justice systems, focused on enhancing synergy.[39]

Subsequent to this contextual account of the evolution of Europol, the chapter considers the current Treaty remit and constitutional limitations for developing Europol into a stronger supranational agency (II). Based on these theoretical debates, the chapter analyses critically the scope, limits and nature of Europol's powers in light of Article 88 TFEU and the new Europol Regulation (III). The key argument advanced is that Europol should have powers to protect European public goods such as transnational public security where it can do this more effectively

[33] Council, 'The Stockholm Programme: An Open and Secure Europe Serving and Protecting Citizens' (2010) OJ C115/1, paras 4.2.2 and 4.3.

[34] See C Harding and J Banach-Gutierrez, 'The emergent EU criminal policy: identifying the species' (2012) 37 *European Law Review* 758, 761–62 for the use of 'external' and 'internal' threats when describing EU criminal policy.

[35] Treaty on European Union in its pre-Lisbon Version, Art 29.

[36] Occhipinti (n 12); J Monar, 'Eurojust and the European Public Prosecutor Perspective: From Cooperation to Integration in EU Criminal Justice?' (2013) 14 *Perspectives on European Politics and Society* 339, 342–43.

[37] Arts 30(2)(b) and 31(2) of the pre-Lisbon Version of the Treaty on European Union. See also the recent Europol Regulation (EU) 2016/794 of the European Parliament and of the Council of 11 May 2016 on the European Union Agency for Law Enforcement Cooperation (Europol) and replacing and repealing Council Decisions 2009/371/JHA, 2009/934/JHA, 2009/935/JHA, 2009/936/JHA and 2009/968/JHA [2016] OJ L 135/53, Art 6.

[38] Art 88 TFEU.

[39] See Monar (n 36) 353–55.

than the Member States' police authorities. This makes a case for giving Europol binding powers to coordinate and manage national investigations with respect to crimes infringing core supranational interests and transnational crimes which Member States clearly cannot address themselves.

II. Limitations to a European FBI – A Legal Analysis

It is apposite here to first offer some historical context to the development of Europol's powers. Article 30(2) in the pre-Lisbon version of the Treaty on European Union suggested that Europol's powers were limited to 'facilitate and support the preparation, and to encourage the carrying out, of specific investigative actions by the competent authorities of the Member States, including operational actions of [JITs] comprising representatives of Europol' and measures allowing Europol to ask the Member States' authorities 'to conduct and coordinate their investigations in specific cases'.[40] Article 30 TEU was, however, considered too narrow, and Working Group X discussed a broader legal base giving the legislator a greater margin to develop Europol's powers. It suggested that the legal basis for Europol should state the agency's central role within the framework of European police cooperation, define its general scope of action and also indicate that Europol's tasks may include powers relating to intelligence, coordination as well as to participation in operational actions to be carried out jointly with Member States or in JITs. Finally, the provision should clarify that the power to apply coercive measures would always rest with the Member States.[41] The failed Constitutional Treaty accepted the Working Group's suggestions and devised a legal basis with an extension of Europol's tasks to operational actions carried out with the Member States' competent authorities or in the context of JITs[42] and with the limitation that 'the application of coercive measures shall be the exclusive responsibility of the competent national authorities'.[43] Nearly the identical wording of Article III-276 has been assumed by the Lisbon Treaty wherein the provision now is named Article 88 TFEU.

This provision suggests that Europol's main mission is to 'support and strengthen action by the Member States' police authorities … and their mutual cooperation in preventing and combating serious crime'.[44] The 'intelligence' tasks of Europol include the collection, storage, processing, analysis and exchange of information forwarded by the authorities of the Member States or third countries or bodies.[45] Overall, Europol is no longer assigned a role supporting, facilitating,

[40] Pre-Lisbon Version of the Treaty of European Union, Art 30(2).
[41] CONV 426/02 (n 26) 10–11.
[42] Treaty Establishing a Constitution for Europe [2004] OJ C 310/01, Art III-276(2)(b).
[43] Art III-276(3) CT.
[44] Art 88(1) TFEU.
[45] Art 88(2)(a) TFEU.

and requesting action by national police forces, but an implicit role in partnership with national forces. Nonetheless the partnership is not fully equal since Europol does not have the capacity to apply coercive measures and has to rely on the national units for its 'feeding' of information, thus being unable to claim information from the Member States.[46]

Europol's remit is confined to the coordination and implementation of operational action carried out jointly with the Member States' competent authorities or in the context of JITs.[47] Following the wording of the Constitutional Treaty, there is an express exclusion for Europol from exercising 'coercive measures'[48] and a requirement to act in liaison and agreement with each Member State as regards 'operational action'.[49] It is clear that the exercise of Europol powers cannot encroach upon the exercise of the responsibilities incumbent upon Member States with regard to the maintenance of law and order and the safeguarding of internal security.[50]

Given the importance of Europol having potentially 'operational' powers, this notion will be discussed in some detail. The term 'operational actions' should be read narrowly as not covering the simple processing of information used for operational purposes, for which Europol is already competent. Furthermore, the Treaty drafter's intention is only to reserve the application of coercive measures to national agents.[51] At the very least, 'coercive measures' must refer to authorised violence – ie the use of physical force against individuals or other forms of constraint, including detention, arrest and search.[52] Having regard to Court of Justice case law, it is arguable that the term 'coercion' also extends to seizure, the power to examine books and records, and the interception of telecommunication.[53] In *Roquette Frères* the Court of Justice described as 'coercive' the investigatory measures provided for by Article 20 of Regulation 1/2003, which includes the Commission's power to examine an undertaking's business records. Such measures would also arguably be 'coercive' if effected electronically and without the subject's knowledge, given case law from the European Court of Human Rights.[54] In *Halford v United Kingdom*,[55] the ECtHR held that the interception of telephone calls interferes with the exercise of the right to respect for private life

[46] Vermeulen and De Moor (n 3) 75–76.

[47] Art 88(2)(b) TFEU.

[48] Although Mitsilegas contends that the minimalist legal framework regulating JITs entails that officers from Member States, and Europol officials to some extent, are allowed to operate 'extraterritorially' in the territory of another Member State and assume operational tasks leading to a spatial expansion of the reach of police powers in the EU, V Mitsilegas, *EU Criminal Law*, 2nd edn (Oxford: Hart Publishing, 2022) 367–69.

[49] Art 88(3) TFEU.

[50] Art 72 TFEU.

[51] Art 88(3) TFEU.

[52] Peers (n 28) 269–71; Monar (n 36).

[53] N Grief, 'EU Law and Security' (2007) 32 *European Law Review* 752, 762–63.

[54] Case C-94/00 *Roquette Frères* EU:C:2002:603.

[55] *Halford v United Kingdom* (1997) 24 EHRR 523.

and correspondence.[56] This suggests that 'operational actions' cover the conventional and modern 'coercive' measures in criminal investigations[57] and that those powers still rest with the Member States' officials and not Europol. In sum, as the Treaty stands, Europol has neither autonomous investigative capabilities nor coercive powers, making it markedly distinct from national police forces or from federal enforcement agencies such as the FBI.[58]

III. Justifications for Conferring Binding Powers to Europol

This section examines if there is a compelling justification for extending Europol's powers. This also requires us to analyse what is the legitimate role for Europol and if it should be transformed from a clearing house for information and intelligence broker to a truly European police force empowered to deal with criminal offences to be prosecuted at European level.[59]

A. Transnational Criminality

If we commence with the notion of 'transnational interest' for the discussion, it is apparent that serious 'organised' transnational crime was originally the primary way of defining Europol's mandate in the 1995 Europol Convention.[60] Employing three cumulative criteria it stated that Europol was competent to address forms of serious international crime: (i) where there were factual indications or reasonable grounds for believing that an 'organized criminal structure' was involved; and (ii) 'two or more Member States' were affected in such a way as to require a common approach by the Member States owing to the (iii) 'scale, significance and consequences of the offences' concerned.[61] Practice, however, showed that Europol was unable to support Member States in relation to cross-border criminal investigations where involvement was not demonstrated, and the agency's remit was subsequent extended to a power 'when there are serious grounds to believe that these offences may be related to organised criminal activities'.[62]

[56] See also *Klass v Germany* (1978) 2 EHRR 214.

[57] CONV 727/03, 'Draft sections of Part Three with comments', Brussels, 27 May 2003, 35–36.

[58] CONV 69/02, 'Justice and Home Affairs – Progress report and general problems', Brussels, 31 May 2002, 8.

[59] ibid 14.

[60] F Gregory, 'Policing Transition in Europe: The Role of Europol and the Problem of Organized Crime' (1998) 3 *Innovation* 287; M Den Boer (ed), *Organised crime: A catalyst in the Europeanisation of national police and prosecution agencies* (Maastricht: European Institute of Public Administration, 2002).

[61] Europol Convention (n 16) Art 2.

[62] Vermeulen and De Moor (n 3) 1097–98; Council Doc 10810/2.

Pursuant to the current Europol Regulation, there is no limitation to organised crime structures. Europol is competent to intervene by supporting and strengthening Member State action in preventing and combating serious crime affecting two or more Member States, terrorism and forms of crime which affect a common interest covered by a Union policy and related criminal offences.[63] Annex I includes a far-reaching list[64] of offences including conventional serious crime such as terrorism, organized crime, drug trafficking, money-laundering activities, trafficking in human beings, illicit trade in human organs and tissue, illicit trafficking in arms, sexual exploitation, genocide, crimes against humanity and war crimes.[65] It, however, also includes traditional criminal offences such as robbery and aggravated theft, murder and grievous bodily injury, kidnapping, hostage-taking, racketeering, extortion and conventional economic crimes such as corruption, swindling and fraud, and financial market manipulation including offences of a supranational dimension such as crimes against the EU's financial interests. The key point from this enumeration is that the crimes in the list go well beyond the narrower notion of 'particularly serious crimes' of a 'cross-border nature' enshrined in Article 83(1) TFEU.[66]

Article 3 highlights the key issue which is to what extent this definition of Europol's competence is appropriate. One of the central ideas advanced in the book is that EU action is needed to protect transnational interests (including supranational interests) and European public goods (eg transnational public security).[67] As argued above, the establishment of a European Public Prosecutor to prosecute offences against the EU's financial interest is defensible from this approach. Based on this, it is also legitimate to argue that there should be a European police agency to investigate such offences.[68] Whilst those offences are already included in the list, the argument here is that Europol should have binding powers to direct investigation of those offences or powers to require them to be investigated.[69]

[63] Europol Council Regulation (n 37) Art 3, and Art 88 (1) TFEU. This could mean that two or more Member States are confronted with a criminal phenomenon: A De Moor and G Vermeulen, 'Shaping the competence of Europol. An FBI perspective' in M Cools, B de Ruyver, M Easton (eds), *EU and International Crime Control: Topical Issues* (Uitgevers: Maklu, 2010), 69.

[64] The list is nearly identical to the list in the European Arrest Warrant Framework Decision to ensure coherence between these instruments: Council Framework Decision of 13 June 2002 on the European arrest warrant and the surrender procedures between Member States 2002/584/JHA [2002] OJ L 190/1, Art 2(2).

[65] But also at least in conventional cases less serious offences such as immigrant smuggling, motor vehicle crime, racism and xenophobia, environmental crime, counterfeiting and product piracy, forgery of administrative documents, forgery of money and means of payment, illicit trafficking in endangered animal species and plant species, computer crime, illicit trafficking in hormonal substances and illicit trafficking in cultural goods, including antiquities and works of art.

[66] See above ch 4.

[67] See above ch 2.

[68] See above ch 5.

[69] See Europol Council Regulation (n 37) Annex 1.

Historically there has been some political support for extending the agency's remit in respect of those offences. Prior to the Lisbon Treaty, the Commission made a very ambitious proposal[70] entailing a possibility for a Europol official to be appointed to direct the investigation in those instances where a JIT is set up to deal with cases of counterfeiting of the euro currency. Euro counterfeiting was not a novel idea. With the euro replacing the national currencies in a majority of the Member States, traditional objections of national sovereignty would be less convincing.[71] Furthermore, the protection of the euro as a European currency is a core supranational interest which the EU should have the full powers to protect including police enforcement powers.[72] In light of this, there is a compelling argument for reinforcing the role of Europol in the fight against euro counterfeiting and grant the agency independent (from the Member States) investigative powers following the model of the EPPO with regard to protecting the EU's financial interests.[73] In employing the notion of European public goods as the normative criterion for intervention by Europol, we refer to crimes that due to the transnational scale, effects and harm transcend the national borders thus having a European complexion.[74] These are distinctive from instances of crimes where the trans-European argument is tenuous, but which are a political priority to one or several Member States (eg gender-based violence or hate-based speech).[75] Europol was not established to deal with the latter type of offences. It is arguable that transnational serious crime should be within Europol's mandate given its significance, scope and consequences thus calling for a common approach by the Member States.[76]

[70] Inspired by the Friends of the Presidency Options Paper: Council Doc 9184/1/06, Annex: Options Paper reflecting the outcome of the discussion on the future of Europol held during the Austrian Presidency, May 2006.

[71] Vermeulen and De Moor (n 3) 1109–10; W Bruggeman, 'A vision on future police cooperation with a special focus on Europol' in De Zwaan and Goudappel (eds), *Freedom, Security and Justice in the European Union. Implementation of the Hague Programme* (The Hague: TMC Asser Press, 2006); Commission communication on enhancing police and customs cooperation in the European Union, COM (04) 376.

[72] See above ch 2.

[73] Friends of Presidency Options Paper (n 70) 5–6; J Öberg, 'The European Public Prosecutor: Quintessential Supranational Criminal Law?' (2021) 28 *Maastricht Journal of European and Comparative Law* 164; B Hayes (Statewatch analysis), '"The Future of Europol" – more powers, less regulation, precious little debate', August 2016: www.statewatch.org/media/documents/news/2006/oct/future-of-europol-analysis.pdf; L Van Outrive, 'Report on the setting up of Europol' (PE 202.364/fin. / PE/92/0382), Committee on Civil Liberties and Internal Affairs (ed) (Luxembourg: European Parliament, 1992).

[74] Art 83(1) TFEU: 'terrorism, trafficking in human beings and sexual exploitation of women and children, illicit drug trafficking, illicit arms trafficking, money laundering … and organised crime'; Europol Council Regulation (n 37) Annex 1.

[75] See above ch 2 for a discussion of these criminalisation initiatives.

[76] CONV 69/02 (n 58) 9; Vermeulen and De Moor (n 3) 1090; Europol Council Decision (n 16) Art 3.

B. Collective Action, Relative Institutional Competence and European Added Value

The more general contention for an extension of Europol's mandate is that the existing arrangements of operational collaboration – where operational responsibilities lie primarily with the Member States' police authorities rather than Europol – are not sufficiently effective in the fight against cross-border criminality.[77] One of the key criteria for Europol's mandate is thus structural incapacity on the part of Member States to deal effectively with crimes of an internal dimension.[78] Member State authorities are not well placed – given their limited expertise, incentives and resources – to investigate supranational offences such as crimes against the EU's financial interests or euro counterfeiting. This argument finds support in the notion of a 'federal' criminal law in respect of the EU's budget with a common European prosecutor, European law enforcement agencies and EU harmonisation of substantive and procedural criminal law in this area.[79]

With its more than 1,000 staff, 220 Europol Liaison Officers and100 crime analysts and with a yearly budget of €193 million, Europol is capable of supporting more than 40,000 international investigations each year.[80] It is arguable that Europol has more comprehensive expertise in intelligence analysis than its national counterparts – the latter lacking the capacity to conduct large-scale investigations. There is for example evidence that Europol has developed specific expertise in the crucial areas of cybercrime and counter-terrorism that national investigations increasingly rely on.[81] Overall, Europol's contribution to the fight against

[77] CONV 426/02 (n 26) 15–16.

[78] FE Zimring and G Hawkins, 'Toward a principled basis for federal criminal legislation' (1996) 1 *The Annals of the American Academy of Political and Social Science* 15; Commission, 'Staff Working Document – Impact Assessment Report accompanying the document Regulation of the European Parliament and of the Council amending Regulation (EU) 2016/79, as regards Europol's cooperation with private parties, the processing of personal data by Europol in support of criminal investigations, and Europol's role on research and innovation Part 2/2' SWD(2020) 543 final, 119–20; A Saccone, 'Combating International Crime in an Enlarging European Union: What is the Role of Europol?', Lecture in the International Seminar for Experts 'Combating Terrorism and International Organised Crime in the European Union – The Hague Programme and the Role of Europol and Eurojust', organised by the Cicero Foundation in the series 'Great Debates', Paris, 14 and 15 December 2006.

See M Delmas Marty and JAE Vervaele, *The Implementation of the Corpus Juris in the Member States – Penal Provisions for the Protection of European Finances* (Antwerp/Oxford/Groningen: Intersentia, 2001); CONV 69/02 (n 58) 14–15.

European Parliament, 'Statement of Revenue and Expenditure of the European Agency for Law Enforcement Cooperation for the Financial Year 2022, Amending Budget No 2' (2022): www.europol.europa.eu/sites/default/files/documents/42-EUROPOL-AB2_2022%20%283.%20Preliminary%20for%20Europol%20website%29.pdf; CONV 69/02 (n 58).

[79] See Delmas Marty and Vervaele (n 78); CONV 69/02 (n 58) 14–15.

[80] European Parliament, 'Statement of Revenue' (n 78); CONV 69/02 (n 58) 7.

[81] B Pistorius, 'Europe needs its own FBI', Financial Times, 29 September 2020: www.ft.com/content/4b3b8c25-9828-4c9e-98f0-b6617bda285b.

cross-border crime is increasingly appreciated by national criminal justice authorities, but its effectiveness largely depends upon the willingness of those authorities to share information with the agency as Europol cannot oblige Member States to cooperate.[82] Whilst Europol may require the competent authorities of Member States to initiate, conduct or coordinate investigations (and Member States should without undue delay give reasons for not complying with those requests), they are not ultimately obliged to comply with Europol's requests. Furthermore, Member State authorities are not even bound to give reasons for refusals when providing those reasons would jeopardise the success of an ongoing investigation or the safety of an individual, or would be contrary to the essential interests of the security of the state.[83]

In order to maximise the effect of law enforcement cooperation, Europol cannot, however, merely depend on Member States' willingness to share information or to act.[84] Europol should have a mandatory right of initiative to start new investigations and execute law enforcement activities and to proactively engage in and handle cases on its own.[85] In principle, Europol should be given powers to lead a JIT and powers to require national members of the JIT to perform executive measures in the Member State which they represent since the execution of coercive measures remains the responsibility of the competent national authorities.[86]

In general, Member States are very satisfied with Europol's ability to support their action in preventing and combating serious organised crime.[87] Member State practitioners believe that Europol is able to effectively support Member States due to its intelligence, enhanced capabilities and resources to provide specialised operational support and expertise.[88] Recent experience has demonstrated the benefits of Europol's role in supporting individual Member States' investigations concerning high profile sensitive and resource-demanding cases that drew extensive public, media and political attention across the EU.[89] As action at national level alone does not suffice to

[82] Europol Council Regulation (n 37) Art 7. There is strong evidence that national authorities in the past have been very reluctant to share their data with the agency: V Mitsilegas and N Vavoula, 'Strengthening Europol's mandate. A legal assessment of the Commission's proposal to amend the Europol Regulation', Study Requested by the LIBE Committee, May 2021, 25; S Hufnagel, *Policing Global Regions: The Legal Context of Transnational Law Enforcement Cooperation* (Abingdon: Routledge, 2021); Council Document 5397/21 (19 January 2021).

[83] Europol Council Regulation (n 37) Art 6.

[84] M Busuioc, *European Agencies: Law and Practices of Accountability* (Oxford: Oxford University Press, 2013) 146–50; C Cocq and F Galli, 'The Evolving Role of Europol in the Fight Against Serious Crime: Current Challenges and Future Prospects' in S Hufnagel and C McCartney (eds), *Trust in International Police and Justice Cooperation* (Oxford: Hart Publishing, 2017).

[85] Vermuelen and De Moor, 'Shaping competences' (n 63) 82.

[86] Europol Council Regulation (n 37) recital 6.

[87] Europol, '2019 Consolidated Annual Activity Report', 9.6.2020: www.europol.europa.eu/publications-events/publications/consolidated-annual-activity-reports-caar.

[88] Mitsilegas, *EU Criminal Law* (n 48) 389; Hufnagel (n 82); Busuioc and Groenleer (n 18) 298.

[89] In the December 2019 European Parliament Resolution on the Rule of Law in Malta, European Parliament, (P9_TA(2019)0103) after the revelations around the murder of Daphne Caruana Galizia,

address these transnational security challenges, Member States' law enforcement authorities have increasingly made use of the support and expertise of Europol.[90] This argument also connects the intervention of Europol to the 'compensatory' rationale for EU action, suggesting that enlargement in conjunction with the Schengen free movement area has also made it easier for criminals and opened up new troublesome trafficking routes, pervasive organised crime and public corruption.[91]

The counter-argument is that Europol should not be given binding enforcement powers unless strong added value of Europol action can be demonstrated compared to actions of Member States' police authorities.[92] In respect of cooperation in criminal matters concerning core functions of the Member States,[93] there must be compelling arguments to extend Europol's powers. Further obligation on a Member State to act at the request of Europol might be considered disproportionate because those duties encroach upon national sovereignty.[94] It is questionable to what extent it is appropriate to remove control from judicial authority over the opening of their investigations.[95] It is apparent that action by national police authorities, joint investigative teams or law enforcement authorities acting in the territory of another Member State is a very intrusive measure for a state.[96] This has been made apparent in the recent negotiations of a Commission proposal to extend Europol's power to request the initiation of investigations by national authorities. This proposal has been met with great scepticism by the Member States, to the extent that it does not appear that this reform will take place. Member States have considered that no further obligation to act at the request of Europol should be imposed on the Member States.[97]

There are various ways in which Europol adds value compared to enforcement by the Member States' police authorities. Europol sits with superior information sharing capabilities that Member States rely on in their enforcement, particularly through Europol's Secure Information Exchange Network Application (SIENA)

the EP called for the full and continuous involvement of Europol in all aspects of the murder investigation and all related investigations. Similar calls came from civil society (see the letter by the Committee to Protect Journalists: https://cpj.org/2020/05/malta-attorney-general-europol-murdered-daphne-caruana-galizia/); SWD(2020) 543 (n 78) 119–20, 127–28.

[90] SWD(2020) 543 final (n 78) 5.

[91] Occhipinti (n 12) 253.

[92] See Art 5(3) TEU; J Öberg, 'Subsidiarity as a Limit to the Exercise of EU Competences' (2017) 36 *Yearbook of European Law* 391.

[93] See judgment by German Federal Constitutional Court (Lisbon Treaty), Case 2 BvE 2/08, 5/08, 2 BvR 1010/08, 1022/08, 1259/08, 182/09 (2009), paras 252–53, 355–62.

[94] See Arts 4(2) and 5(4) TEU.

[95] Council, Document no 5527/4/2, 24, 29, 50–51, 97, 115.

[96] CONV 426/02 (n 26) 14.

[97] Commission, 'Proposal for a Regulation of the European Parliament and of the Council amending Regulation (EU) 2016/794, as regards Europol's cooperation with private parties, the processing of personal data by Europol in support of criminal investigations, and Europol's role on research and innovation', COM (2020) 796 final, Art 1(3) of the Commission's proposal for a revised Europol Regulation, new amended wording of Art 6(1) of the Europol Regulation; V Mitsilegas and N Vavoula, 'Strengthening Europol's Mandate: A Legal Assessment of the Commission's Proposal to Amend the Europol Regulation', Study for the LIBE Committee of the European Parliament, 2021.

which connects Europol's liaison officers, experts and law enforcement agencies in all Member States. Europol's involvement in JITs also makes a positive, 'practical impact' on the fight against transnational crime and is likely to be increased in the future because of the agency's well-established liaison network, increased capacity and 'mobile office' technology. Europol also has an extensive central criminal information and intelligence database which is used by Europol officials, seconded national experts and staff in law enforcement authorities in the Member States. Member States also make use of the support Europol offers for operational coordination in large-scale operations involving several countries by means of Europol's Operational Centre. In addition, a mobile office can be deployed for on-the-spot support operations in Member States providing a live connection to Europol's databases and platforms. Europol's specialised centres provide tailor-made operational support. For example, the European Cybercrime Centre strengthens the law enforcement response to cybercrime in the EU by offering its advanced digital forensics tools and platforms to operations in Member States, whereas the European Counter Terrorism Centre provides operational support to Member States in investigations following terrorist attacks, cross-checking operational data against the data Europol already has and analysing all available investigative details to compile a structured picture of the terrorist network.[98]

C. Comparative Federalism and State Sovereignty

If we look at an extension of Europol's mandate, we could envisage – from a comparative federalism perspective – that the agency would also address other offences. In the US federal system, it is common to confer more centralised powers of prosecution and investigation in areas of public corruption, voter and election fraud, benefit fraud, embezzlement, to avoid both actual and perceived conflict.[99] These offences are, however, not necessarily in themselves of a Union-wide ramification. The exception is where these offences – whether corruption, fraud or embezzlement – are committed against the EU's financial interests.[100] The latter clearly belong to the legitimate sphere of a European Public Prosecutor and should in the future also be encompassed within Europol's investigative mandate.

The common features for conferring jurisdiction to central units rather than state law enforcement agencies relate to institutional competence where relevant factors such as efficiency, resources, incentives (conflicts of interests or corruption), expertise and specialisation should be decisive for decisions on

[98] SWD (2020) 543 final (n 78) 6–8. The Intellectual Property Crime Coordinated Coalition should also be mentioned in this regard.

[99] R Barkow, 'Federalism and Criminal Law: What the Feds Can Learn from the States' (2011) 109 *Michigan Law Review* 519, 547–48.

[100] Directive (EU) 2017/1371 of the European Parliament and of the Council of 5 July 2017 on the fight against fraud to the Union's financial interests by means of criminal law [2017] OJ L 198/29, Arts 3 and 4.

centralisation.[101] Centralised law enforcement is also warranted where problems of collective action impel states not to devote sufficient resources to enforcement efforts.[102] Federal legislators thus tend to assume jurisdiction in complex cases, high-tech crimes involving multi-jurisdictional activity where the scope of the offences exceeds the investigative and prosecutorial resources of state law enforcement, and regulatory crimes which cross the jurisdictional boundaries of states (eg environmental crimes, antitrust and securities violations).[103] In addition, centralised law enforcement may provide efficiency benefits by more easily producing the interstate coordination necessary to such an investigation. A centralised system of law enforcement facilitates the more efficient use of highly specialised resources (including advanced technology and experts) that can enhance the successful prosecution of transnational organised crime.[104]

The argument from comparative federalism also lends some support for centralised law enforcement in the EU context. Nonetheless, the analogy has some important limits. First, the EU context differs significantly from the federal US system where there is already a centralised prosecutor and federal police agency. The discussion at EU level is not really at the stage of political maturity where real law enforcement competences would be transferred to a European agency like Europol.[105] Law enforcement and prosecution are thus (with the potential exception of the EPPO) still very much state powers strongly linked to the constitutive features of the sovereign state. Secondly, the argument from comparative federalism does not necessarily entail the transfer of powers from the state to the centralised level. It has been widely argued in the literature that state prosecutors and police agencies are rather in need of resources than centralised agencies assuming the whole investigation.[106] Central governments may thus offer state jurisdictions help

[101] Barkow (n 99) 579–80.

[102] T Stacy and K Dayton, 'The Underfederalization of Crime' (1997) 6 *Cornell Journal of Law & Public Policy* 247, 284, 294; Judicial Conference of the United States, Long Range Plan for the Federal Courts (1995) 21, 24–25; RJ Miner, 'Federal Courts, Federal Crimes, and Federalism (1987) 10 *Harvard Journal of Law and Public Policy* 126; WP Marshall, 'Federalization: A Critical Overview' (1995) 44 *De Paul Law Review* 719, 733–36.

[103] Iowa Department of Justice, Office of the Attorney General, Area Prosecutions Division: www.iowaattorneygeneral.gov/about-us/divisions/area-prosecutions (listing cases requiring specialized legal training as including Medicaid fraud, violence against women, environmental crime, securities fraud, obscenity, correctional institution crime and tax crimes); Barkow (n 99) 555–56; Massachusetts Attorney General: www.mass.gov/orgs/office-of-the-attorney-general; California Office of the Attorney General, About Us: https://oag.ca.gov/office; R Scott Palmer and BM Linthicum, 'The Statewide Prosecutor: A New Weapon Against Organized Crime' (1985) 13 *Florida State University Law Review* 654-63.

[104] Stacy and Dayton (n 102) 286–90.

[105] Vermuelen and De Moor, 'Shaping competences' (n 63).

[106] Stuntz has made a compelling justice argument for decentralisation and funding of state investigations and prosecutors. By giving more state and federal money to urban police forces and increasing the number of criminal cases tried by locally selected juries, this would make criminal law enforcement more locally democratic as powers would be placed in the hands of residents of those neighbourhoods where the most criminals and crime victims live. When high-crime cities have exercised the most control over criminal justice within their borders, punishment levels have been more moderate and

with everything from electronic surveillance to technical support to additional resources, all without taking over criminal prosecutions at the state level (similar to that which Europol and Eurojust offer to Member States).[107]

The argument in the book suggests that Europol should not become involved in fighting crimes that lack a strong transnational dimension. Indeed, given the nature of cross-border crime and terrorism in the EU's area of free movement, it is difficult to make the case that combating these threats is best left to national levels of law enforcement.[108] However, some forms of crime-fighting and counter-terrorism are simply too sensitive for Member States to allow much or any pooling of their sovereignty.[109] These concerns for national sovereignty manifest themselves in the various ways in which the third pillar remains alive under the Lisbon Treaty.[110] For example, concerns for national sovereignty help explain why national vetoes persist for operational police cooperation and the activity of law enforcement on foreign soil.[111]

Moreover, due to concerns for sovereignty, there is little appetite at present to endow Europol with much greater operational powers. We are here referring to powers for Europol to launch its own investigations, powers to require national authorities to execute arrests and commence prosecutions and powers to pull criminal intelligence out of Member States' databases (rather than relying on national authorities to provide these). Whilst sovereignty by itself is not a particularly rational argument against centralisation, it has resonance in the field of law enforcement where the exercise of Europol's powers theoretically would transcend the territorial borders of the state, thus being involved in operational actions.[112] The legitimacy of such far-reaching enforcement powers for Europol could be questioned particularly in light of the potentially far-reaching consequences for individuals' freedoms and rights. In light of the limited accountability and legitimacy of the agency, it is only justified to confer Europol with operational powers for those crimes which are linked to the EU's core interests (eg fraud against the EU's financial interests, counterfeiting of the euro, violation of EU restrictive measures and so forth).[113] There is also a plausible normative argument to extend

discrimination less pervasive than today; WJ Stuntz, 'Unequal Justice' (2008) 121 *Harvard Law Review* 1969, 2025–26, 2040.

[107] Barkow (n 99) 18–23, 52–54; Stuntz (n 106) 2025; S Sun Beale, 'Too Many and Yet Too Few: New Principles to Define the Proper Limits for Federal Criminal Jurisdiction' (1995) 46 *Hastings Law Journal* 979, 1008; DL Shapiro, *Federalism: A Dialogue* (Evanston: Northwestern University Press, 1995) 118–40.

[108] Occhipinti (n 12) 244.

[109] L Besselink, 'Sovereignty, Criminal Law and the New European Context' in P Alldridge and C Brants (eds), *Personal Autonomy, the Private Sphere and Criminal Law: A Comparative Study* (Oxford: Hart Publishing, 2001).

[110] J Öberg, 'The Legal Basis for EU Criminal Law Legislation' (2018) 43 *European Law Review* 366.

[111] Occhipinti (n 12) 245.

[112] V Mitsilegas and F Giuffrida, 'Bodies, Offices and Agencies' in V Mitsilegas, *EU Criminal Law* (Oxford: Hart Publishing, 2022); A Weyembergh, 'The Development of Eurojust: Potential and Limitations of Article 85 of the TFEU' (2011) 2 *New Journal of European Criminal Law* 75, 83–84.

[113] See above ch 5, section III re similar discussion on the EPPO and sovereignty and democracy.

Europol's powers now to the areas of cybercrime and internet-based trafficking of child pornography which lacks a strong territorial basis and where Europol is already playing a leading role.[114] Inter-connectivity and blurring of the boundaries between the physical and digital world permeate borders and entail a need for a centralised law enforcement agency like Europol in such investigations.[115]

In the future, there is an argument for enhancing Europol's operational powers in a few other selected key areas. Such proposals would be to give Europol powers to enable it to participate more proactively in investigations into leading organised crime groups in Member States where there are doubts about the quality of such investigations'[116] and to confer powers on Europol to request the initiation of cross-border investigations in cases of serious attacks against whistle-blowers and investigative journalists.[117] These types of offences are very difficult to resolve at the national level due to the complexity of the investigations.[118] There is also a case for conferring on Europol a stronger role in the fight against serious international crime and terrorism originating from specific regions by giving it powers to coordinate and direct the numerous EU and Member State law enforcement initiatives in the specific region.[119] Given that terrorism is one of the most significant threats to European public security, it is not unreasonable to argue that Europol should have some powers to directly address the common challenges in this regard. These crimes have the potential to affect the Member State where they are committed, as well as other Member States as they transcend boundaries and require a collective response.[120]

IV. Conclusions and Reflections

This chapter has considered the scope and limits of Europol's powers and the normative foundations for extending those powers. Whilst Europol in theory – on the basis of a plausible reading of Article 88 TFEU – could be conferred with a stronger role by requiring Member States to initiate and conduct such a criminal investigation, the current Europol Regulation does not make those powers binding.[121] Europol also lacks binding powers to request information from Member States' law enforcement authorities, making it more difficult for the agency to pursue its intelligence work. Given strong Member State reluctance to

[114] Occhipinti (n 12) 253–56.

[115] Europol, 'Serious and Organised Threat Assessments 2017' (n 6).

[116] EP, 'Resolution of 28 March 2019 on the situation of the rule of law and fight against corruption in the EU, specifically in Malta and Slovakia' (P8_TA(2019)0328).

[117] EP, Resolution of 10 July 2020 on a comprehensive Union policy on preventing money laundering and terrorist financing (2020/2686)RSP)).

[118] SWD(2020) 543 final PART II (n 90) 120.

[119] Öberg, 'The European Public Prosecutor: Quintessential Supranational Criminal Law' (n 73).

[120] Europol Council Regulation (n 37) recital 6.

[121] Europol Council Regulation (n 37) Art 6.

confer such powers to the agency due to state sovereignty concerns, it appears that Europol, despite a reasonably clear Treaty mandate for more operational action, has not yet been equipped with powers with which the agency can make a real difference.

Nonetheless, the case needs to be made why Europol is in need of binding operational powers. It was argued that it is only justified to confer Europol with operational powers for those crimes which are linked to the EU's core supranational interests, such as crimes against the EU's financial interests and counterfeiting of the euro and in the areas of cybercrime and internet-based trafficking of child pornography where Europol is already playing a leading role. The common features for conferring jurisdiction to Europol (as well as other EU criminal justice agencies) relate to institutional competence where relevant factors such as efficiency, incentives and expertise should be decisive for expanding the agency's powers further.[122] The key argument for expanding Europol's powers is thus a collective action problem where EU action is needed to protect the goods of public security by tackling transnational criminal activity which no Member State can tackle alone. Terrorism and other transnational organised crimes could satisfy those criteria by constituting the most significant threats to European public security, having the potential to affect the Member State where they are committed as well as other Member States.[123]

In light of the limited legitimacy of Europol, it is, however, questionable to extend binding Europol powers more generally to address transnational organised crime. On substantive terms, it is also difficult to demonstrate a strong added value of Europol actions compared to Member State actions.[124] A future move towards the formation of a European FBI would require a serious overhaul of the way in which police cooperation is undertaken in Europe, a publicly endorsed mandate by the EP in an oversight role as well as changes in the legal systems of the Union and of Member States. The powers of Europol would need to be significantly expanded, to include, in the first instance, powers of arrest and perhaps also require a European Criminal Court. An appropriate federal political structure would be required, including a central sovereign EU government with direct authority over citizens in the territory and which is not dependent on constituent states.[125] Such a transformation to a European FBI seems to be far-fetched and hardly an appropriate policy to purse.[126] It is also difficult to make a compelling

[122] See above section III (B).
[123] See above section III (A).
[124] See above section III (C).
[125] L Van Outrive, 'Report on the setting up of Europol' (PE 202.364/fin. / PE/92/0382). Committee on Civil Liberties and Internal Affairs (Luxembourg: European Parliament, 1992).
[126] In addition to the traditional law enforcement responsibilities, the FBI also has significant intelligence responsibilities whereas Europol only has investigative powers: JW Koletar, 'Federal Bureau of Investigation' in DM Schulz (ed), *Encyclopedia of law enforcement. 2. Federal law enforcement* (Thousand Oaks: Sage, 2005); TD Poveda, 'Federal Bureau of Investigation' in JR Greene (ed), *The encyclopedia of police science* (New York: Routledge, 2007); F Verbruggen, 'Euro-Cops? Just say maybe. European lessons from the 1993 reshuffle of US drug enforcement' (1995) 3 *European Journal of Crime,*

argument that these reforms are warranted for Europol to be able to sufficiently protect European public goods and transnational interests (with the exception outlined on core supranational interests and certain other special cross-border offences).[127]

Seen from the perspective of a possible path towards genuine supranational police powers, it is clear that formal legal constraints continue to limit Europol's potential to develop into an autonomous and operational police power. At the level of legislative competences, the Treaty exclusions will require national authorities' proactive support in any future operational tasks and the feeding of data, given that 'coercive measures' remain excluded at the level of the Treaty.[128] However, the intergovernmental legal framing of Europol is contrasted in practice with a clear tendency of supranationalism. As seen in this chapter, it is clear that Europol has been endowed with powers that enable it to do more than just collect and analyse information. Since 2007 Europol has been allowed to participate in JITs and to ask national authorities to launch investigations. Whilst Member States cannot be compelled to comply with requests, Europol has used its right of initiative informally to pressure Member States to start a particular investigation without making a formal request. Because they point out unaddressed crimes, such requests may embarrass Member States and, in light of the criminal intelligence already possessed by Europol, can be difficult to refuse. All of this implies a more autonomous role for Europol, indicating a shift in the direction of supranationalism.[129] Coupled with an increasing number of strategic tasks, the enhanced role of Europol suggests that the traditional boundaries between 'operational' and 'non-operational' powers have become rather blurred. Gathering and processing information, as Europol does, generates 'knowledge' and produces 'evidence', which by their very essence are no different from a traditional house search conducted by a police unit using its operational power.[130]

If one looks at Europol through a neo-functionalist lens, it becomes apparent that once one area of law enforcement is integrated then others around it will follow.[131] Indeed, following the most recent Treaty reform in Lisbon, we can now

Criminal Law and Criminal Justice 150; A De Moor, 'The role of Europol in joint investigation teams. A foretaste of an executive European Police Office' in M Cools and others (eds), *Gofs Research Paper Series – Vol II. Readings on Criminal Justice, Criminal Law & Policing* (Antwerp: Maklu, 2009).

[127] Beale (n 107) 994–95; M Den Boer and W Bruggeman, 'Shifting gear: Europol in the contemporary policing era' (2007) 23 *Politique européenne* 77.

[128] Lingenfelter and Miettinen (n 1) 191.

[129] Occhipinti (n 12) 240; Monar, 'Eurojust and the European Public Prosecutor Perspective' (n 36); S Leonard and C Kaunert, 'The Development of Europol's External Relations: Towards Supranationalism?' (2021) 28 *Maastricht Journal of European and Comparative Law* 229; W Bruggeman, 'What are the options for improving democratic control of Europol and for providing it with adequate operational capabilities?' (2006) 1 *Studia Diplomatica* 164; Council Framework Decision of 13 June 2002 on joint investigation teams [2002] OJ L 162/1; Council Act of 28 November 2002 (protocol on joint investigation teams) [2002] OJ C 312/1.

[130] Mitsilegas, *EU Criminal Law* (n 48) 389; Hufnagel (n 82); Mitsilegas and Giuffrida (n 112); Busuioc and Groenleer (n 18) 298.

[131] A Stone Sweet and W Sandholtz, 'European integration and supranational governance' (1997) 4 *Journal of European Public Policy* 297; J Öberg, 'Exit, Voice and Consensus – A Legal and Political

observe the growing trend towards the creation of a common European public prosecutor, the harmonisation of domestic criminal law and the general communitarisation of EU criminal law.[132] It is already taking place with plans to create a single 'European Judicial Space' for all the territory of the EU for the purposes of prosecuting fraud against the EU budget.[133] We can also see a visible trend in the mandate of Europol in the shift from specific crimes towards more general and serious crime which suggests a pattern of incremental growth resembling the rest of the JHA policies.[134] Thus, whilst it is unlikely or desirable that Europol will transform into a European FBI, it is highly likely – given the above – that the agency over time will take on new powers, develop a stronger European mindset and gradually break free from its 'intergovernmental' shackles.

Analysis of the Emergency Brake in EU Criminal Policy' (2021) 46 *European Law Review* 506; J Monar, 'Reflections on the place of criminal law in the European construction' (2021) 27 *European Law Journal* 356.

[132] S Peers, 'Mission Accomplished? EU Justice and Home Affairs Law after the Treaty of Lisbon' (2011) 48 *Common Market Law Review* 661; V Mitsilegas, *EU Criminal Law after Lisbon: Rights, Trust and the Transformation of Justice in Europe* (Oxford: Hart Publishing, 2016).

[133] Occhipinti (n 12).

[134] Den Boer and Bruggeman (n 127) 78.

7

Conclusions and Reflections

I. Key Findings of the Book

This book has endeavoured to contribute to the debate on the normative justifications for EU criminal law. Initially, it offered a descriptive account of the justifications used to date by the EU legislator to legitimate the use of criminal law.

Chapter 1 suggested that it is possible to infer three principal drivers for EU criminal law and policy: 'security' for EU citizens; ensuring the effectiveness of EU policies; and subsequently a 'rights-based approach' to EU criminal policy. 'Effectiveness' and other 'functional'[1] considerations have been the primary justifications for EU action in respect of the development of EU regulatory criminal law and the rise of a European Public Prosecutor. In the area of the eurocrimes in Article 83 TFEU and in respect of the development of EU criminal justice agencies such as Europol and Eurojust, the justification for EU action has instead been driven by 'security'-based rationales.[2] In this instance, criminal law is employed to serve a more 'repressive' agenda of criminal enforcement. Post-Lisbon we could also identify a stronger 'fundamental rights'-based approach to EU criminal law facilitated by a stronger Treaty mandate to enact legislation on procedural standards and individual rights.[3]

All these rationales offer different ways of explaining why the European Union wishes to take action in the area of criminal law and wherefore the EU level might be a better venue than Member State level for undertaking those actions. These are conventionally the key justifications also for a national legislator when considering the use of criminal law as the state has a responsibility and therefore also powers to take actions to protect the central public good of security.[4] However, the arguably excessive use of security and effectiveness-based rationales has led to a repressive EU criminal policy to date which has trumped other important considerations such as justice and freedom.[5] A more compelling justification for a future

[1] See J Monar, 'Reflections on the place of criminal law in the European construction' (2021) 27 *European Law Journal* 356.

[2] V Mitsilegas, *EU Criminal Law After Lisbon* (Oxford: Hart Publishing, 2022) ch 3.

[3] See above ch 1.

[4] See eg Monar (n 1); P Caeiro, 'Constitution and development of the European Union's penal jurisdiction: responsibility, self-reference and attribution' (2021) 27 *European Law Journal* 441.

[5] See Art 67 TFEU.

EU criminal policy is to adopt a stronger rights-based approach which would be helpful in restoring the integrity and legitimacy of this EU polity.[6] Nonetheless, whilst the evolution of EU criminal law partly can be legitimated by a rights-based rationale, a more comprehensive deepening of the integration of the EU criminal justice system requires a more robust justification for accepting such major encroachments into the Member States' criminal justice systems.[7]

In the first part of the book and Chapter 2, an analytical framework was developed for identifying the circumstances which deserve intervention on the part of the EU in the area of criminal law. It first discussed legitimacy in EU criminal law which was analysed from the perspectives of criminal law theory and philosophy proceeding from the premise that the normative justification for EU criminalisation must as a first step be based on a criminal law moral theory of harm or public wrong.[8] It suggested that EU criminalisation at least needs to substantiate serious harm of criminal activity before it can be subjected to EU regulation given the strong endorsement of the harm principle in the official documents of the EU institutions and the Treaties.[9] However, from the particular perspective of the European Union context, it is appropriate to also analyse the question of criminalisation on the basis of the public goods framework which fits into the general EU law constitutional framework.[10]

The book subsequently ventured into an examination of the arguments from competitive federalism, economic and legal theories of market failures, and European public goods to assess the justificatory rationale for EU action in criminal justice. Building on Duff's work on public goods in criminal law, it was claimed that the key justification for supranational action lies in demonstrating the existence of European public goods (eg internal market and the provision of security for EU citizens) and other important transnational interests deserving of protection by means of criminal law. It should also be shown that the Union is better placed (given its resources, expertise and incentives) than Member States to protect those interests.[11] The argument on European public goods was defended on the idea of 'transnational interests' as this has been articulated in political philosophy and transnational legal theory. The underlying premise for this argument is that national democratic processes do not have comprehensive mechanisms to ensure

[6] See eg A Weyembergh and N Franssen, 'From facts and political objectives to legal bases and legal provisions' (2021) 27 *European Law Journal* 368; I Wieczorek, 'The Emerging Role of the EU as a Primary Normative Actor in the Area of Criminal Justice' (2021) 27 *European Law Journal* 378 for this argument.

[7] See C Harding and J Banach-Gutierrez, 'The Emergent EU Criminal Policy: Identifying the Species' (2012) 37 *European Law Review* 758; Commission, 'Communication from the Commission to the European Parliament, the Council, the European Economic and Social Committee and the Committee of the Regions, Towards an EU Criminal Policy: Ensuring the effective implementation of EU policies through criminal law', COM(2011) 573 final.

[8] See above ch 2, section II.

[9] See Art 83(1) TFEU.

[10] See above ch 2, section III; Art 5(3) TEU.

[11] See above ch 2, section III (B).

that foreign interests are sufficiently considered within their decision-making processes. The EU is typically better placed than Member States to protect collective transnational interests in the meaning of European public goods.[12]

On this basis, the EU should prima facie be justified to use criminal law to address transnational market failures,[13] transboundary externalities or collective action problems resulting from serious cross-border criminality where it is unlikely that Member States, because of perverse incentives, are capable of addressing the problem properly, or indeed willing to do so.[14] The notion of European public goods also includes a sub-category of intrinsic supranational interests such as the protection of the EU budget where the protection of the interest at stake is central for the existence of the Union. Furthermore, the nature of this public good, ie the protection of the budget, entails that criminal justice authorities of Member States are systematically predisposed to deprioritise the protection of the Union's financial interests.[15] The EU's power to criminalise fraud and other behaviours targeted against the EU's financial interests[16] could thus be justified on the basis that the EU is better positioned than Member States to protect the public good of the EU budget.[17]

On the basis of the framework developed in the first part of the book, the second part examined the justifications for harmonisation of domestic criminal law. Chapter 3 analysed the scope for EU action in the area of criminal procedure and rejected, from a principled perspective, the 'instrumental' justification for exercising EU competence to enable mutual recognition in Article 82(2) TFEU. On the basis of sociological and legal research on 'trust-building' and an analysis of the EU legislator's account of the 'trust' problem, it was argued that there is a very narrow role for harmonisation in creating mutual trust and thus enhancing

[12] A Somek, 'The Argument From Transnational Effects I: Representing Outsiders Through Freedom of Movement' (2010) 16 *European Law Journal* 315, 323–24; C Joerges and J Neyer, 'From intergovernmental bargaining to deliberative processes: The constitutionalisation of comitology' (1997) 3 *European Law Journal* 273, 294; M Kumm, 'Constitutionalizing Subsidiarity in Integrated Markets: The Case of Tobacco Regulation in the European Union' (2006) 12 *European Law Journal* 503.

[13] See S Collignon (ed), *The Governance of European Public Goods* (Cham: Palgrave Macmillan, 2017); F Zuleeg, 'The rationale for EU action: What are European Public Goods?', paper prepared for the BEPA Workshop on 'The political economy of EU public finances: designing governance for change', 5 February 2009: www.researchgate.net/publication/237445090_The_Rationale_for_EU_Action_What_are_European_Public_Goods; B Coeuré and J Pisani-Ferry, 'The Governance of the European Union's International Economic Relations: How Many Voices?' in A Sapir (ed), *Fragmented Power: Europe and the Global Economy* (Brussels: Bruegel, 2007) for a discussion of market failures and European public goods.

[14] See above chs 2 and 3; S Weatherill, 'Competence creep and competence control' (2004) 23 *Yearbook of European Law* 1, 33–34.

[15] J Öberg, 'National Parliaments and Political Control of EU Competences – A Sufficient Safeguard of Federalism?' (2018) 24 *European Public Law* 695; M Wade, *EuroNEEDs – Evaluating the need for and the needs of a European Criminal Justice System – Preliminary Report* (Freiburg: Max Planck Institute for Foreign and International Criminal Law, 2011).

[16] Directive (EU) 2017/1371 of the European Parliament and of the Council of 5 July 2017 on the fight against fraud to the Union's financial interests by means of criminal law [2017] OJ L 198/29.

[17] See above chs 2 and 5.

mutual recognition. On the basis of the general 'transnational interests' argument, it was suggested that the EU's competence for regulation of national procedural rules should be limited to cross-border cases; ie where the defendant or the victim's suspect is not a citizen in the Member State where they are tried and in cases where the crime is committed abroad. In these instances, EU action is justified to correct the dysfunctional workings of national political processes by giving 'virtual' political rights to foreign victims and defendants. In cross-border situations, there is a clear interest for the EU to intervene to protect the legitimate interests of individual defendants or victims (who exercised their right of free movement) who otherwise would not have a voice in the national democratic procedure. On the basis of this conceptualisation of the cross-border criterion, a general critique was put forward against discretely selected EU proposals in the field of defence rights and victim rights that cover both domestic and cross-border proceedings.[18]

Chapter 4 analysed the justifications for EU legislative activity in substantive criminal law, first discussing harm-based theoretical accounts as rationales for such harmonisation. It noted that the harm criterion in Article 83(1) TFEU does not offer very much guidance in establishing what level of empirical evidence is needed to substantiate that criminalisation of a certain offence is in line with this criterion. It was nonetheless contended that the proposal on violence against women and the proposal on hate crime and hate-based speech satisfied the criterion of constituting 'particularly serious offences' in light of the damage of these offences to the individual and society. The chapter subsequently examined the cross-border justification for harmonisation of substantive criminal law and argued that the EU legislator's general assumption that divergences between Member States' sanctioning regimes lead to distortions in the form of safe havens and a race to the bottom is often misplaced. There is a strong body of literature instead suggesting that differences in sanctioning regimes or differences in criminalisation have limited impact on the choice of location for firms or criminals or on the tendency of Member States to engage in regulatory races. The chapter also offered a critique of the far-reaching Commission proposal on criminalisation of conventional hate crime and the Commission's proposal to criminalise rape and domestic violence against women, as it was not clearly substantiated that these are offences having a cross-border dimension or cross-border implications as required by Article 83(1) TFEU. The final part of the chapter examined mutual recognition as a justification for harmonisation of substantive criminal law and found that there is limited evidence supporting the need for EU harmonisation of substantive criminal law in ensuring effective judicial cooperation.[19]

Thereafter, the third part of the book applied the theory of transnational interests and European public goods to assess the appropriate scope and competences for EU criminal justice agencies such as Europol, Eurojust and the European Public

[18] See above ch 3.
[19] See above ch 4.

Prosecutor's Office (EPPO). Chapter 5 discussed the normative foundations for having a European Public Prosecutor, maintaining that the argument on European public goods provides a strong justification for a centralised European public prosecutor which can defend common and strong EU interests, such as the protection the EU budget. The need to confer the EPPO with effective and binding powers arises from the nature of the crimes in question, which by affecting the EU's own financial interests inevitably have a Union dimension.[20] Only a European Public Prosecutor has the correct incentives, competencies and resources to effectively prosecute crime against the Union's financial interests and protect the common financial interests of EU citizens. Despite the presence of the EPPO, it was argued that Eurojust still has an important role to play in the fight against transnational crime since the EPPO's powers are limited to the PIF offences and it lacks – in contrast to Eurojust – any significant powers in the field of resolution of conflicts of jurisdiction.[21] Nonetheless, it is argued that Eurojust's powers need to be extended and made binding for it to make a real difference in operational law enforcement.[22] Given Eurojust's acquired resources, expertise and unique role as a central mediator between national jurisdictions, it seems that there is a strong argument for extending the mandate of Eurojust in terms of binding powers to initiate criminal investigations and resolving conflicts of jurisdiction in the area of transnational organised crime.[23]

Chapter 6 considered finally the case for giving more substantial and operational powers to Europol, the European agency for law enforcement. It was argued that it is only justified to confer Europol (similarly to the assessment in respect of the EPPO) with operational powers for those crimes which are linked to the EU's core supranational interests (eg crimes against the EU's financial interests and counterfeiting of the euro). There is also a normative argument to extend Europol's powers in the area of typical cross-border offences such as cybercrime and internet-based trafficking of child pornography where Europol is already playing a leading role. The common features for conferring jurisdiction to Europol relate to institutional competence where relevant factors such as efficiency, incentives and expertise speak in favour of expanding the agency's powers further. In light of the limited legitimacy of Europol, it is more questionable to extend binding Europol powers more generally to address serious cross-border crime. It is difficult to make a sustained normative argument that Europol – given the strong linkage between law enforcement and state sovereignty – needs to have such far-reaching and general powers to function effectively.[24]

[20] See above ch 5, section II.

[21] See above ch 5, section III.

[22] See Regulation (EU) 2018/1727 of the European Parliament and of the Council of 14 November 2018 on the European Union Agency for Criminal Justice Cooperation (Eurojust), and replacing and repealing Council Decision 2002/187/JHA [2018] L 295/138, Arts 3 and 4.

[23] See above ch 5, section IV.

[24] See above ch 6, sections II–III.

II. Reflections on Normative Justifications for EU Criminal Law

A. Autonomous and Instrumental Justifications

A useful distinction to reflect on the analysis in this book is to review EU criminal law in light of the notions of autonomous and instrumental justifications. An autonomous justification does not require a linkage to another EU policy or objective. In this respect, it could refer to an autonomous function as regards the fight against crime or other functions, concerning individual rights, free movement and equality of treatment before the law. An instrumental justification can be defined as being concerned with its sustaining role for other aspects covered by the construction of a European criminal area of justice.[25] It primarily sees the legitimate role of the EU in the area of criminal law to adopt acts which further other overarching EU objectives and policies, eg mutual recognition or the functioning of the internal market. Several recent contributions subscribe to the notion that the European Union should go beyond the instrumental role in criminal law to advance a stronger fundamental rights policy[26] or even a more articulated value-based EU criminal law.[27] The previous work of the author has primarily argued for a more limited role for the EU in the area of criminal law and as an actor which should employ criminal law to predominantly and effectively further the EU's objectives.[28] From an internal EU law perspective, it is clearly more orthodox to justify supranational intervention in criminal law to protect the EU's policies and interests (the instrumental role) on the basis of the current Treaty mandate.[29]

The starting position when assessing the merits of these different positions is that the choices of what to accept as normative justifications for policy-making in criminal law have important ramifications for the legitimacy of the Union legal order. If we acknowledge 'autonomous' justifications for EU harmonisation,[30] and its role in establishing a European common sense of justice,[31] this implies

[25] A Weyembergh, 'The Functions of Approximation of Penal Legislation within the European Union' (2005) 12 *Maastricht Journal European & Comparative Law* 149.

[26] I Wieczorek, 'The Emerging Role of the EU as a Primary Normative Actor in the Area of Criminal Justice' (2021) 27 *European Law Journal* 378.

[27] J Monar, 'Reflections on the place of criminal law in the European construction' (2021) 27 *European Law Journal* 356; L Mancano, 'A theory of justice? Securing the normative foundations of EU criminal law through an integrated approach to independence' (2021) 27 *European Law Journal* 477.

[28] J Öberg, *Limits to EU Powers: A Case Study of EU Regulatory Criminal Law* (Oxford: Hart Publishing, 2017) ch 8.

[29] J Turner, 'The Expressive Dimension of EU Criminal Law' (2012) 60 *The American Journal of Comparative Law* 555.

[30] A Weyembergh, 'Approximation of criminal laws, the Constitutional Treaty and the Hague Programme' (2005) 42 *Common Market Law Review* 1567, 1578–82.

[31] See Art 67 TFEU; T Elholm, 'EPPO and a common sense of justice' (2021) 28 *Maastricht Journal of European and Comparative Law* 212.

a comprehensive remit for legislative action. If we conversely only recognise the 'functional'[32] rationales for harmonisation, there will be a narrower scope for EU action, potentially impairing the EU's ability to promote fundamental rights for individuals.[33]

The broader 'autonomous' approach would accept that EU action in criminal law can be justified with reference to the Union's need to reaffirm its core 'common values',[34] and to strengthen its political identity – the expressive dimension of EU criminal law.[35] This dimension includes ideas of communicating a common sense of justice and to express that 'certain forms of conduct are unacceptable'.[36] The autonomous approach suggests that the European Union by reinforcing common moral norms can help build the supranational demos which is seen by many as a prerequisite to genuine legitimacy. Through the conduct that it chooses to criminalise, the EU can distinguish itself from other polities around the world which do not penalise the same conduct, thus cementing its identity. Taking the examples of gender-based violence and hate speech – which lack a clear cross-border dimension and may be adequately addressed at the national level[37] – it appears that the EU legislator chose the criminal label in these instances to reaffirm the Union's core values and to strengthen its polity by expressing the Union's commitment to human rights and equal treatment.[38]

One of the key objections to the autonomous justifications of EU criminal law is the legitimate fear that the EU political institutions use their powers in illegitimate ways thereby usurping national powers ('competence creep').[39] Whilst the 'autonomous' justification model might have a strong political appeal, the argument here wishes to qualify this approach. There are inherent constraints under EU law as to what extent expressive EU criminal law can be pursued. Since the current Treaties provides no clear authorisation for justifying criminal law interventions on expressive grounds, it thus seems that the EU will endanger its legitimacy if

[32] See Monar, 'Reflections on the place of criminal law' (n 27).

[33] Weyembergh, 'The Functions of Approximation of Penal Legislation' (n 25).

[34] See Art 2 TEU; P Pescatore, *Law of Integration* (Leiden: AW Sijthoff, Springer, 1974, English translation); L Azoulai, 'Editorial Comments: EU law between common values and collective feelings' (2018) 55 *Common Market Law Review* 1329.

[35] Turner (n 29) 564–74; T Elholm, 'Does EU Criminal Cooperation Necessarily Mean Increased Repression?' (2009) 17 *European Journal of Crime, Criminal Law and Criminal Justice* 191, 224–25.

[36] Commission, 'Proposal for a Directive of the European Parliament and of the Council on criminal sanctions for insider dealing and market manipulation', COM (2011) 654, recital 7.

[37] See above ch 4 for a discussion of these two prominent examples of EU legislation.

[38] Turner (n 29) 571–72; S Coutts, 'Supranational public wrongs: The limitations and possibilities of European criminal law and a European community' (2017) 54 *Common Market Law Review* 771; European Parliament Recommendation to the Council of 21 June 2007 Concerning the Progress of the Negotiations on the Framework Decision on Action to Combat Racism and Xenophobia [2008] OJ C 146 E/361.

[39] See M Pollack, 'Creeping Competence: The Expanding Agenda of the European Community' (1994) 14 *Journal of Public Policy* 95; European Council, 'Laeken Declaration on the future of the European Union', 14–15 December 2001, 3–5; R Lang, 'The EU's New Victims' Rights Directive: Can Minimum Harmonization Work for a Concept like Vulnerability?' (2013) 22 *Nottingham Law Journal* 90, 95.

it keeps adopting criminal law on this basis. It is therefore argued that the more autonomous rights-based approach to EU criminal law needs to be aligned with the idea of European public goods and transnational interests.[40]

However, it is not convincing to only accept instrumental EU action in criminal law[41] to the extent necessary to promote certain EU objectives. There thus needs to be an open debate about why the nature and impact of the crime is such that it deserves to be addressed at the supranational level.[42] There is also a normative basis in the Treaties for a less 'functional' approach to EU criminal law. This is the fact that one of the objectives of the EU is to create a common area of justice.[43] Whilst the Treaties only mention the combating and repression of crimes and by judicial cooperation through mutual recognition,[44] there is clearly a legitimate role for the EU to more actively pursue a rights-based approach on the basis that it protects European public goods and markedly transnational interests.[45]

This refined middle-way approach sits between instrumental harmonisation and more value-based EU action in criminal law. Whilst this approach goes beyond the objective of enhancing mutual recognition and judicial cooperation[46] and the strengthening of the common market,[47] the departure point for this approach is still that the EU needs to establish the existence of European public goods which are better protected at EU level. This approach will accept EU involvement in matters where Member States – because of their perverse incentives or lack of capabilities – cannot address the problems of cross-border criminality, and instances where the EU intervenes to protect transnational or supranational (eg EU budget and the currency) interests. This approach arguably entails a more legitimate and resilient approach to supranational intervention in this area, which is something to build on when designing a future EU policy in the area of criminal justice.[48]

B. Reactive and Proactive EU Criminal Law

When analysing the normative justifications for EU criminal law, this book has also sought to spark a more comprehensive debate on what kind of policy the

[40] Wieczorek (n 26) makes a similar argument in her article although her approach is more liberal towards employing an autonomous justification.

[41] Coutts, 'Supranational public wrongs' (n 38) 788, n 66 directed this criticism legitimately against my previous work on harmonisation of EU criminal law.

[42] Turner (n 29) 578.

[43] See Art 3(2) TEU; Art 67(1) TFEU.

[44] See Art 67(3) TFEU.

[45] See Arts 82(2) and 83(1) TFEU and the 'reference' to cross-border dimension.

[46] Arts 67(1) and 82(2) TFEU.

[47] E Spaventa, 'Should we "harmonize" fundamental rights in the EU? Some reflections about minimum standards and fundamental rights protection in the EU composite constitutional system' (2018) 55 *Common Market Law Review* 997, 1000–2.

[48] J Vogel, 'Why is the harmonisation of penal law necessary? A comment' in A Klip and H van der Wilt (eds), *Harmonisation and Harmonising Measures in Criminal Law* (Amsterdam: Royal Netherlands Academy of Science, 2002) 55–64.

EU should be pursuing and the Union's legitimate role in this policy field.[49] There is broad agreement in the literature that EU criminal law so far has developed 'haphazardly' as a responding mechanism to different external (security) threats, events or crises.[50] The EU's Treaty mandate to regulate criminal law has been interpreted liberally, leading to criticism against the EU for engaging in expansionist and 'expressionist' law-making marked by signalling politics.[51] In many ways, this more 'reactionary' EU criminal policy has developed as a response to external and internal threats caused by real-life developments around the world. The instance of legislation on terrorism and counter-terrorism is a case in point of such EU criminal policy being strongly connected to events such as 9/11 and the terror bombings in Madrid (2004) and London (2005).[52] It is equally clear that EU criminal legislation on market abuse in 2014, financial crime and fraud against the EU's financial interests (the 2017 PIF Directive), including the creation of the European Public Prosecutor's Office in 2017, has been propelled by the aftermath of the financial crisis that hit the world in 2008.[53] This is no judgment on the legitimacy of the EU to act to address external threats and events and political developments. There is a legitimate role for the EU to act in this area. As suggested by Monar, there is a priori justification for the EU equally as the Member States – and responsibility[54] – to protect fundamental public goods such as public order and thereby combat terrorism and serious organised crime.[55]

Furthermore, criminal law should not be used lightly within the EU context. Criminal law is still regarded as an essential feature of state sovereignty representing a community's fundamental choice to use coercive measures in order to protect core values. It constitutes a fundamental political decision that defines a community and for that reason it is a decision that any sovereign community – as a key rule – should be able to make for itself through a democratic process, unless special features of the crimes make it impossible to respond effectively at the national level. The German Federal Constitutional Court, in its *Lisbon Judgment*, has prominently, due to the sensitive nature of criminal law for state sovereignty,

[49] Harding and Banach-Gutierrez (n 7); A Weyembergh and I Wieczorek, 'Is There an EU Criminal Policy?' in R Colson and S Field (eds), *EU criminal justice and the challenges of diversity: legal cultures in the area of freedom, security and justice* (Cambridge: Cambridge University Press, 2016).

[50] Monar (n 27); N Franssen and A Weyembergh, 'From facts and political objectives to legal bases and legal provisions: Incremental European integration in the criminal law field' (2021) 27 *European Law Journal* 368; C Harding and J Öberg, 'The journey of EU criminal law on the ship of fools – what are the implications for supranational governance of EU criminal justice agencies?' (2021) 28 *Maastricht Journal of European and Comparative Law* 192.

[51] Elholm (n 35); Turner (n 29).

[52] Franssen and Weyembergh (n 50); Monar (n 27).

[53] Franssen and Weyembergh (n 50); J Öberg, 'Is it "Essential" to Imprison Insider Dealers to Enforce Insider Dealing Laws?' (2014) 14 *Journal of Corporate Law Studies* 111; E Herlin-Karnell, 'White-Collar Crime and European Financial Crises: Getting Tough on EU Market Abuse' (2012) 37 *European Law Review* 481.

[54] P Caeiro, 'Constitution and development of the EU's "penal jurisdiction": attribution, self-reference and responsibility' (2021) 27 *European Law Journal* 441.

[55] Monar (n 27).

expressed its reservations in relation to an excessive use of the Union's new criminal law powers.[56] Given that decision-making at the EU level is still less democratic than at the national level, the invocation of state sovereignty helps protect the legitimacy of criminal law.[57]

On a concluding note, the aspiration of this book is that it will contribute to an advanced understanding of the role of normative justifications for EU criminal law. In particular, it is hoped that the discussion here can encourage new fields of research which might trigger original research questions, novel research agendas and refreshing research collaboration. Whilst this book departs from a conventional doctrinal analysis, it also offers more contextual legal analysis building on findings from political theory, sociology, political science and economics to evaluate the past and future developments of EU criminal law.[58] Whilst it is appreciated that the traditional role of academic lawyers in this field has been confined to giving a strict dogmatic account of the legal developments, the author also wishes to encourage scholars to engage in more sustained debates on EU criminal law.[59] Academics and scholars in this field are equipped with substantial knowledge of the potential effects of EU intervention on national criminal justice systems and significant expertise on relevant moral, political, economic and ethical theories which ought to guide a conscientious EU legislator intervening in the field of criminal law.[60] If we as academic lawyers are able to convey this knowledge and expertise more effectively to those policy-makers, there is a bright future prospect for EU criminal law.

[56] See Judgment of German Federal Constitutional Court of 30 June 2009, *Lisbon Judgment*, Case 2 BvE 2/08, 5/08, 2 BvR 1010/08, 1022/08, 1259/08, 182/09 (2009), para 226.

[57] Turner (n 29) 558; J Monar, 'The EU's Role in the Fight Against Racism and Xenophobia: Evaluation and Prospects After Amsterdam and Tampere' (2000) 22 *Liverpool Law Review* 7, 8; L Pech, 'The Law of Holocaust Denial in Europe: Towards a (Qualified) ETJ-wide Criminal Prohibition', Jean Monnet Working Paper 10/09: https://jeanmonnetprogram.org/wp-content/uploads/2014/12/091001.pdf, 7, 9.

[58] C Joerges, 'Taking the Law Seriously: On Political Science and the Role of Law in the Process of European Integration' (1996) 2 *European Law Journal* 10; L Solumn, 'Interdisciplinarity, Multidisciplinarity, and the Future of the Legal Academy' (2008) *Legal Theory Blog*.

[59] See Special Issue (1998) *Law and Contemporary Problems* 61(1): 'Government Lawyering' and the introductory article, PH Schuck, 'Lawyers and Policymakers in Government' (1998) 61 *Law and Contemporary Problems* 7 more generally on the role of lawyers in policy-making.

[60] R Colson and S Field (eds), *EU Criminal Justice and the Challenges of Legal Diversity* (Cambridge University Press, 2016); J Ouwerkerk, J Altena, J Öberg and S Miettinen (eds), *The Future of EU Criminal Justice – Policy and Practice: Legal and Criminological Perspectives* (Brill Publishers, 2019).

REFERENCES

Books

Ambos, K, *European Criminal Law* (Cambridge: Cambridge University Press, 2018)

Ashworth, A, *Principles of Criminal Law* (Oxford: Oxford University Press, 1999)

Asp, P, *The Substantive Criminal Law Competence of the EU – Towards an Area of Freedom, Security & Justice – Part 1* (Stockholm: Jure, 2013)

—— (ed), *The European Public Prosecutor's Office – Legal and Criminal Policy Perspectives* (Stockholm: Jure, 2015)

—— *The Procedural Criminal Law Cooperation of the EU – Towards an area of freedom, security & justice – Part 2* (Stockholm: Jure, 2016)

Barnard, C, *The Substantive Law of the EU: The Four Freedoms* (Oxford: Oxford University Press, 2022)

Bickerton, CJ, Hodson, D and Puetter, U (eds), *The New Intergovernmentalism: States and Supranational Actors in the Post-Maastricht Era* (Oxford: Oxford University Press, 2015)

Black's Law Dictionary (St Pauls: West Publishing, 1990)

Busuioc, M, *European Agencies: Law and Practices of Accountability* (Oxford: Oxford University Press, 2013)

Cappelletti, M, Seccombe, M and Weiler, J, *Integration Through Law: Europe and the American Federal Experience* (Berlin/New York: De Gruyter, 1986)

Child, JJ, Simester, AP, Spencer, JR, Stark, F, Virgo, GJ, *Simester and Sullivan's Criminal Law: Theory and Doctrine*, 9th rev edn (Oxford: Hart Publishing, 2022)

Collignon, S (ed), *The Governance of European Public Goods* (Cham: Palgrave Macmillan, 2017)

Colson, R and Field S (eds), *EU Criminal Justice and the Challenges of Legal Diversity* (Cambridge: Cambridge University Press, 2016)

Corstens, G and Pradel, J, *European Criminal Law* (The Hague: Kluwer Law International, 2002)

Coutts, S, *Citizenship, Crime and Community in the European Union* (Oxford: Hart Publishing, 2019)

Craig, P, *The Lisbon Treaty: Law, Politics, and Treaty Reform* (Oxford: Oxford University Press, 2011)

—— with De Búrca, G, *EU Law – Text, Cases, and Materials* (Oxford: Oxford University Press, 2020)

Delmas Marty, M and Vervaele, JAE, *The Implementation of the Corpus Juris in the Member States – Penal Provisions for the Protection of European Finances* (Antwerp/Oxford/Groningen: Intersentia, 2001)

Den Boer, M (ed), *Organised crime: A catalyst in the Europeanisation of national police and prosecution agencies* (European Institute of Public Administration, 2002)

Duff, A, *Answering for Crime: Responsibility and Liability in the Criminal Law* (Oxford: Hart Publishing, 2007)

Ely, JH, *Democracy and Distrust: A Theory of Judicial Review* (Cambridge: Harvard University Press, 1980)

Feinberg, J, *The Moral Limits of the Criminal Law Volume 1: Harm to Others* (Oxford: Oxford University Press, 1987)

Fletcher, M, Gilmour, B and Lööf, R, *EU Criminal Law and Justice* (Cheltenham: Edward Elgar Publishing, 2008)

Franklin, JH, *Bodin on Sovereignty* (Cambridge: Cambridge University Press, 2012)

Geelhoed, W, Erkelens, LH, Mei AWH (eds), *Shifting Perspectives on the European Public Prosecutor's Office* (The Hague: TMC Asser Press, 2018)

Gibbs, AH, *Constitutional Life and Europe's Area of Freedom, Security and Justice* (Abingdon: Routledge, 2011)
Giddens, A, *The Consequences of Modernity* (Cambridge: Polity Press 1990)
Haas, E, *The uniting of Europe: political, social, and economical forces, 1950-1957* (Stanford: Stanford University Press, 1958)
Hardin, R, *Trust and Trustworthiness* (New York: Russell Sage Foundation, 2002)
Hart, HLA, *Law, Liberty and Morality* (New York: Random House, 1963)
—— *Punishment and Responsibility* (Oxford: Oxford University Press, 1968)
Herlin-Karnell, E, *The Constitutional Dimension of European Criminal Law* (Oxford: Hart Publishing, 2012)
—— *The Constitutional Structure of Europe's Area of 'Freedom, Security and Justice' and the Right to Justification* (Oxford: Hart Publishing, 2019)
Hufnagel, S, *Policing Global Regions: The Legal Context of Transnational Law Enforcement Cooperation* (Abingdon: Routledge, 2021)
Janssens, C, *The Principle of Mutual Recognition in EU Law* (Oxford: Oxford University Press, 2013)
Klip, A, *European Criminal Law. An Integrative Approach*, 2nd edn (Antwerp: Intersentia, 2012)
—— *European Criminal Law: An Integrative Approach*, 4th edn (Antwerp: Intersentia, 2021)
Koutrakos, P, Nic Shuibhne, N and Syrpis, P (eds), *Exceptions from EU Free Movement Law: Derogation, Justification and Proportionality* (Oxford: Hart Publishing, 2016)
Ligeti, K, *Toward a Prosecutor for the European Union: Volume 1* (Oxford: Hart Publishing, 2012)
Lindberg, L, *The political dynamics of European economic integration* (Stanford: Stanford University Press, 1963)
Loader, I and Walker, N, *Civilizing Security* (Cambridge: Cambridge University Press, 2007)
Luhmann, N, *Law as A Social System* (Oxford: Oxford University Press, 2004)
Mill, JS, *On Liberty* (London: JW Parker and Son, 1859)
Mitsilegas, V, *EU Criminal Law* (Oxford: Hart Publishing, 2009)
—— *EU Criminal Law after Lisbon: Rights, Trust and the Transformation of Justice in Europe* (Oxford: Hart Publishing, 2016)
—— *EU Criminal Law*, 2nd edn (Oxford: Hart Publishing, 2022)
Moore, M, *Placing Blame: A Theory of Criminal Law* (Oxford: Clarendon Press, 1997)
Moravcsik, A, *The Choice for Europe: Social Purpose and State Power from Messina to Maastricht* (Ithaca/New York: Cornell University Press, 1998)
Olson, M, *The Logic of Collective Action. Public Goods and the Theory of Groups, With a New Preface and Appendix* (Boston: Harvard University Press, 1971)
Ouwerkerk, J, Altena, J, Öberg, J and Miettinen, S (eds), *The Future of EU Criminal Justice – Policy and Practice: Legal and Criminological Perspectives* (Leiden: Brill Publishers, 2019)
Packer, HL *The Limits of the Criminal Sanction* (Stanford: Stanford University Press, 1969)
Peers, S, *EU Justice and Home Affairs Law* 3rd edn (Oxford: Oxford University Press, 2011)
—— *EU Justice and Home Affairs Law: Volume II: EU Criminal Law, Policing, and Civil Law*, 4th edn (Oxford: Oxford University Press, 2016)
Peinhardt, C and Sandler, T, *Transnational Cooperation: An Issue-Based Approach* (Oxford: Oxford University Press, 2015)
Peršak, N, *Criminalising Harmful Conduct: The Harm Principle, its Limits and Continental Counterparts* (New York, Springer, 2007)
Pescatore, P, *Law of Integration* (Leiden: AW Sijthoff, Springer, 1974, English translation)
Rawls, J, *A Theory of Justice* (Cambridge: Belknap Press of Harvard University Press, 1999, revised edn)
Rescher, N, *Welfare: The Social Issue in Philosophical Perspective* (Pittsburgh: University of Pittsburgh Press, 1972)
Rock, P, *Constructing victims' rights; the Home Office, New Labour, and victims* (Oxford: Oxford University Press, 2004)
Roxin, C, *Strafrecht Allgemeiner Teil*, 3rd edn (Warszawa: CH Beck, 1997)
Sandel, M, *Liberalism and the Limits of Justice* (New York: Cambridge University Press, 1982)

Sandholtz, W and Stone Sweet, A, *European Integration and Supranational Governance* (Oxford: Oxford University Press, 2004)
Satzger, H, *European and International Criminal Law* (Munich/Oxford: Beck/Hart Publishing, 2012)
Schonsheck, J, *On Criminalization: An Essay in the Philosophy of the Criminal Law* (Dordrecht: Kluwer, 1994)
Shapiro, DL, *Federalism: A dialogue* (Evanston: Northwestern University Press, 1995)
Simester, AP and von Hirsch, A, *Crimes, Harms, and Wrongs: On the Principles of Criminalisation* (Oxford: Hart Publishing, 2011)
Sunstein, C, *The Partial Constitution* (Cambridge: Harvard University Press, 1993)
Tupman, B, *Policing in Europe, Uniform in Diversity* (Exeter: Intellect, 1999)
Wade, M, *EuroNEEDs – Evaluating the need for and the needs of a European Criminal Justice System – Preliminary Report* (Freiburg: Max Planck Institute for Foreign and International Criminal Law, 2011)
Waldron, J, *Liberal Rights: Collected Papers 1981–1991* (Cambridge: Cambridge University Press, 1993)
Ward, I, *A Critical Introduction to European Law* (Cambridge: Cambridge University Press, 2009)
Webster's New World Dictionary (New York: Simon & Schuster, 1989, 3rd College edn)
Wieczorek, I, *The Legitimacy of EU Criminal Law* (Oxford: Hart Publishing, 2019)
Öberg, J, *Limits to EU Powers: A Case Study of EU Regulatory Criminal Law* (Oxford: Hart Publishing, 2017)

Chapters

Alexander, L and Moore, M, 'Deontological Ethics' in E N Zalta (ed), *The Stanford Encyclopedia of Philosophy* (Winter 2021 Edition): https://plato.stanford.edu/archives/win2021/entries/ethics-deontological/
Arroyo Zapatero, L and Munoz De Morales Romero, M, 'Droit penal européen et Traité de Lisbonne: le cas de l'harmonisation autonome' (article 83.1 TFEU)' in G Giudicielli-Delage and C Lazerges (eds), *Le Droit Penal de l'Union Européenne au Lendemain du Traité de Lisbonne* (Paris: Societé de Legislation Compareé, 2012)
Arroyo López, C and Moreno López, R 'Hate Speech in the Online Setting' in S Assimakopoulos, FH Baider and S Millar (eds), *Online Hate Speech in the European Union: A Discourse-Analytic Perspective* (Cham: Springer Nature, 2017): https://link.springer.com/content/pdf/10.1007%2F978-3-319-72604-5.pdf
Baker, E, 'The EU as a Penal Actor' in T Daems, S Snacken and D van Zyl Smit (eds), *European Penology?* (Oxford: Hart Publishing, 2013)
Besselink, L, 'Sovereignty, Criminal Law and the New European Context' in P Alldridge and C Brants (eds), *Personal Autonomy, the Private Sphere and Criminal Law: A Comparative Study* (Oxford: Hart Publishing, 2001)
Bigo, D, Bonelli, L, Chi, D and Olsson, C, 'Mapping the field of the EU internal security agencies' in D Bigo (ed), *The field of the EU internal security agencies* (Paris: l'Harmattan, 2007)
Bruggeman, W, 'A vision on future police cooperation with a special focus on Europol' in De Zwaan and Goudappel (eds), *Freedom, Security and Justice in the European Union. Implementation of the Hague Programme* (The Hague: TMC Asser Press, 2006)
Cocq, C and Galli, F, 'The Evolving Role of Europol in the Fight Against Serious Crime: Current Challenges and Future Prospects' in S Hufnagel and C McCartney (eds), *Trust in International Police and Justice Cooperation* (Oxford: Hart Publishing, 2017)
Coeuré, B and Pisani-Ferry, J, 'The Governance of the European Union's International Economic Relations: How Many Voices?' in A Sapir (ed), *Fragmented Power: Europe and the Global Economy* (Brussels: Bruegel, 2007)

Colson, R, 'Domesticating the European Arrest Warrant: European Criminal Law between Fragmentation and Acculturation' in R Colson and S Field (eds), *EU Criminal Justice and the Challenges of Legal Diversity. Towards A Socio-Legal Approach to EU Criminal Policy* (Cambridge: Cambridge University Press, 2016)

Conant, L, 'Compliance and What EU Member States Make of It' in M Cremona (ed), *Compliance and Enforcement of EU Law* (Oxford: Oxford University Press, 2012)

Dehousse, R and Weiler, J, 'The legal dimension' in W Wallace (ed), *The Dynamics of European Integration* (London/New York: Pinter Publishers, 1990)

De Moor, A, 'The role of Europol in joint investigation teams. A foretaste of an executive European Police Office' in M Cools and others (eds), Gofs Research Paper Series – Vol II. *Readings on Criminal Justice, Criminal Law & Policing* (Antwerp: Maklu, 2009)

Dougan, M, 'From the Velvet Glove to the Iron Fist: Criminal Sanctions for the Enforcement of Union Law' in Marise Cremona (ed), *Compliance and the Enforcement of EU Law* (Oxford: Oxford University Press, 2012)

Fijnaut, C, 'The "Communitization" of Police Cooperation in Western Europe' in HG Schermers (ed), *Free Movement of Persons in Europe: Legal Problems and Experiences* (Dordrecht: Martinus Nijhoff Publishers, 1993)

—— 'Police Co-operation and the Area of Freedom, Security and Justice' in N Walker (ed), *Europe's Area of Freedom, Security, and Justice* (Oxford: Oxford University Press, 2004)

Flore, D, 'D'un réseau judiciaire européen à une juridiction pénale européenne: Eurojust et l'émergence d'un système de justice pénale' in G de Kerchove and A Weyembergh (eds), *L'espace pénal européen: enjeux et perspectives* (Brussels: Brussels University, 2002)

Koletar, JW, 'Federal Bureau of Investigation' in DM Schulz (ed), *Encyclopedia of law enforcement. 2. Federal law enforcement* (Thousand Oaks: Sage, 2005)

Mitsilegas, V, 'Normative Foundations of European Criminal Law' in R Schütze (ed), *Globalisation and Governance: International Problems, European Solutions* (Cambridge: Cambridge University Press, 2018)

Lacey, N, 'Contingency, Coherence and Conceptualism: Reflections on the Encounter between "Critique" and "the Philosophy of the Criminal Law"' in RA Duff (ed), *Philosophy and the Criminal Law: Principle and Critique* (Cambridge: Cambridge University Press, 1998)

Lavenex, S, and Wallace, W, 'Justice and Home Affairs – Towards a European Public Order' in H Wallace and others (eds), *Policy-Making in the European Union* (Oxford: Oxford University Press, 2005)

Luhmann, N, 'Familiarity, Confidence, Trust: Problems and Alternatives' in D Gambetta (ed), *Trust: Making and Breaking Cooperative Relations* (Oxford: University of Oxford, 2000, electronic edn)

Mégie, A, 'Eurojust in Action: An Institutionalisation of European Legal Culture?' in R Colson and S Field (eds), *EU Criminal Justice and the Challenges of Legal Diversity* (Cambridge: Cambridge University Press, 2016)

Monar, J, 'Decision-Making in the Area of Freedom, Security and Justice' in A Arnull and D Wincott (eds), *Accountability and Legitimacy in the European Union* (Oxford: Oxford University Press, 2002)

Nieto Martín, A and Muñoz de Morales Romero, M 'The Office of the European Public Prosecutor and Related Offences: Deconstructing the Problem' in P Asp (ed), *The European Public Prosecutor's Office – Legal and Criminal Policy Perspectives* (Stockholm: Jure, 2015)

Nollkaemper, A, 'The Role of National Courts in Inducing Compliance with International and European Law – A Comparison' in M Cremona (ed), *Compliance and Enforcement of EU Law* (Oxford: Oxford University Press, 2012)

Nuotio, K, 'Harmonization of Criminal Sanctions in the European Union – Criminal Law Science Fiction' in A Strandbakken and E Johannes Husabø (eds), *Harmonization of Criminal Law in Europe* (Antwerp/Oxford/Groningen: Intersentia, 2005)

Poveda, TD, 'Federal Bureau of Investigation' in JR Greene (ed), *The encyclopedia of police science* (New York: Routledge, 2007)

Raz, J, 'Autonomy, Toleration, and the Harm Principle' in R Gavison (ed), *Issues in Contemporary Legal Philosophy* (Oxford: Clarendon Press, 1987)

Tadić, FM, 'How harmonious can harmonisation be? A theoretical approach towards harmonisation of (criminal) law' in A Klip and H van der Wilt (eds), *Harmonisation and Harmonising Measures in Criminal Law* (Amsterdam: Royal Netherlands Academy of Science, 2002)

Taylor, C, 'Cross-Purposes: The Liberal-Communitarian Debate' in NL Rosenblum (ed), *Liberalism and the Moral Life* (Cambridge: Harvard University Press, 1989)

Van den Moor, A and Vermeulen, G, 'Shaping the competence of Europol. An FBI perspective' in M Cools, B de Ruyver, M Easton (eds), *EU and International Crime Control: Topical Issues* (Uitgevers: Maklu, 2010)

Van Vooren, B and Wessel, R, *EU External Relations Law: Text, Cases and Materials* (Cambridge: Cambridge University Press, 2014)

Vervaele, JAE, 'The European Public Prosecutor's Office (EPPO): Introductory Remarks' in W Geelhoed, L Erkelens and AWH Meij (eds), *Shifting Perspectives on the European Public Prosecutor's Office* (The Hague: TMC Asser Press, 2018)

Vogel, J, 'Why is the harmonisation of penal law necessary? A comment' in A Klip and H van der Wilt (eds), *Harmonisation and Harmonising Measures in Criminal Law* (Amsterdam: Royal Netherlands Academy of Science, 2002)

Von Hirsch, A, 'Extending the Harm Principle: "Remote" Harms and Fair Imputation' in AP Simester and ATH Smith (eds), *Harm and Culpability*, (Oxford: Oxford University Press, 1996)

Walker, N, 'In Search of the Area of Freedom, Security and Justice: A Constitutional Odyssey' in N Walker (ed), *Europe's Area of Freedom, Security, and Justice* (Oxford: Oxford University Press, 2004)

Weyembergh, A and Wieczorek, I, 'Is There an EU Criminal Policy?' in R Colson and S Field (eds), *EU Criminal Justice and the Challenges of Legal Diversity* (Cambridge: Cambridge University Press, 2016).

Articles

Abazi, V, 'The Future of Europol's Parliamentary Oversight: A Great Leap Forward?' (2014) 15 *German Law Journal* 1134

Alegre, S and Leaf, M, 'Mutual recognition in European judicial cooperation: A step too far too soon? Case study – The European arrest warrant' (2004) 10 *European Law Journal* 200

Asp, P, 'The Importance of the Principles of Subsidiarity and Coherence in the Development of EU Criminal Law' (2011) 1 *European Criminal Law Review* 44

—— with others, 'A Manifesto on European Criminal Policy' (2013) 11 *Zeitschrift für Internationale Strafrechtsdogmatik* 430

Azoulai, L, 'Editorial Comments: EU law between common values and collective feelings' (2018) 55 *Common Market Law Review* 1329

Baker, E, 'Criminal jurisdiction, the public dimension to "effective protection" and the construction of community-citizen relations' (2001) 4 *Cambridge Yearbook of European Legal Studies* 25

—— 'Governing Through Crime – the Case of the European Union' (2010) 17 *European Journal of Criminology* 187

Barkow, R, 'Federalism and Criminal Law: What the Feds Can Learn from the States' (2011) 109 *Michigan Law Review* 519

Bebchuk, LA, 'Federalism and the Corporation: The Desirable Limits on State Competition in Corporate Law' (1992) 105 *Harvard Law Review* 1435

Benyon, J, 'Policing the European Union: The Changing Basis of Cooperation on Law Enforcement' (1994) 70 *International Affairs* 498

Bermann, G, 'Taking Subsidiarity Seriously' (1994) 94 *Columbia Law Review* 332

Besselink, LFM, 'The Parameters of Constitutional Conflict after *Melloni*' (2014) 39 *European Law Review* 531

Börzel, TA and Risse, T, 'From the Euro to the Schengen Crises: European Integration Theories, Politicization, and Identity Politics' (2018) 25 *Journal of European Public Policy* 83
Bruggeman, W, 'What are the options for improving democratic control of Europol and for providing it with adequate operational capabilities?' (2006) 1 *Studia Diplomatica* 164
Busuioc, M and Groenleer, M, 'Beyond Design: The Evolution of Europol and Eurojust' (2013) 14 *Perspectives on European Politics and Society* 289
Caeiro, P, 'Constitution and development of the European Union's penal jurisdiction: responsibility, self-reference and attribution' (2021) 27 *European Law Journal* 441
Cary, WL, 'Federalism and Corporate Law: Reflections upon Delaware' (1974) 83 *Yale Law Journal* 663
Chamon, M, 'Implied exclusive powers in the ECJ's post-Lisbon jurisprudence : the continued development of the ERTA doctrine' (2018) 55 *Common Market Law Review* 1109
Coutts, S, 'Supranational public wrongs: The limitations and possibilities of European criminal law and a European community' (2017) 54 *Common Market Law Review* 771
Craig, P, 'Democracy and Rule-making Within the EC: An Empirical and Normative Assessment' (1997) 3 *European Law Journal* 105
Dailey AC, 'Federalism and Families' (1995) 143 *University of Pennsylvania Law Review* 1787
Davies, G, 'Democracy and Legitimacy in the Shadow of Purposive Competence' (2015) 21 *European Law Journal* 2
Deakin, S, 'Legal Diversity and Regulatory Competition: Which Model for Europe?' (2006) 12 *European Law Journal* 440
De Moor, A and Vermeulen, G, 'The Europol Council Decision: Transforming Europol into an Agency of the European Union' (2010) 47 *Common Market Law Review* 1089
Den Boer, M and Walker, N, 'European Policing after 1992' (1993) 31 *Journal of Common Market Studies* 3
—— 'Towards an Accountability Regime for an Emerging European Policing Governance' (2002) 12 *Policing and Society* 288
—— with Bruggeman, W, 'Shifting gear: Europol in the contemporary policing era' (2007) 23 *Politique européenne* 77
Díez, C and Herlin-Karnell, E, 'Prosecuting EU Financial Crimes: The European Public Prosecutor's Office in Comparison to the US Federal Regime' (2018) 19 *German Law Journal* 1191
Duff, RA, 'Law, Language and Community: Some Preconditions of Criminal Liability' (1998) 18 *Oxford Journal of Legal Studies*
—— 'Theorizing Criminal Law: A 25th Anniversary Essay' (2005) 25 *Oxford Journal of Legal Studies* 353
Dugard, J and Van den Wyngaert, C, 'Reconciling Extradition with Human Rights' (1998) 92 *American Journal of International Law* 187
Elholm, T, 'Does EU Criminal Cooperation Necessarily Mean Increased Repression?' (2009) 17 *European Journal of Crime, Criminal Law and Criminal Justice* 191
—— 'EPPO and a common sense of justice' (2021) 28 *Maastricht Journal of European and Comparative Law* 212
Enriques, L and Gatti, M, 'The Uneasy Case for Top-Down Corporate Law Harmonization in the European Union' (2006) 27 *University of Pennsylvania Journal of International Economic Law* 939
Eser, A, 'The Principle of "Harm" in the Concept of Crime – A Comparative Analysis of the Criminally Protected Legal Interests' (1965–1966) 4 *Duquesne University Law Review* 345
Fijnaut, C, 'Policing Western Europe: Interpol, TREVI and Europol' (1992) 15 *Police Studies* 103
—— 'International Policing in Europe: Present and Future' (1994) 19 *European Law Review* 613
Fletcher, G, 'Domination in Wrongdoing' (1996) 76 *Boston University Law Review* 347
Franssen, N and Weyembergh, A, 'From facts and political objectives to legal bases and legal provisions' (2021) 27 *European Law Journal* 368
Genschel, P and Jachtenfuchs, M, 'More Integration, Less Federation: The European Integration of Core State Powers' (2016) 23 *Journal of European Public Policy* 42
—— 'From market integration to core state powers: the Eurozone crisis, the refugee crisis and integration theory' (2018) 56 *Journal of Common Market Studies* 178

Gregory, F, 'Policing Transition in Europe: The Role of Europol and the Problem of Organized Crime' (1998) 3 *Innovation* 287
Grief, N, 'EU Law and Security' (2007) 32 *European Law Review* 752
Harding, C, 'Review of V Mitsilegas, EU Criminal Law' (2010) 35 *European Law Review* 301
—— with Banach-Gutierrez, J, 'The Emergent EU Criminal Policy: Identifying the Species' (2012) 37 *European Law Review* 758
—— with Öberg, J, 'The journey of EU criminal law on the ship of fools – what are the implications for supranational governance of EU criminal justice agencies?' (2021) 28 *Maastricht Journal of European and Comparative Law* 192
Hart, HLA, 'The House of Lords on Attempting the Impossible' (1981) 1 *Oxford Journal of Legal Studies* 149
Herlin-Karnell, E, 'White-Collar Crime and European Financial Crises: Getting Tough on EU Market Abuse' (2012) 37 *European Law Review* 481
Hillebrand, C, 'Guarding EU-Wide Counter-Terrorism Policing: The Struggle for Sound Parliamentary Scrutiny of Europol' (2011) 7 *Journal of Contemporary European Research* 500
Hoffmann, S, 'Obstinate or Obsolete? The Fate of the Nation State and the Case of Western Europe' (1966) 95 *Daedalus* 862
Horsley, T, 'Subsidiarity and the Court of Justice: Missing Pieces in the Subsidiarity Jigsaw?' (2012) 50 *Journal of Common Market Studies* 267
Hyman, J, *Action, Knowledge, and Will* (Oxford: Oxford University Press, 2015)
Joerges, C, 'Taking the Law Seriously: On Political Science and the Role of Law in the Process of European Integration' (1996) 2 *European Law Journal* 10
—— with Neyer J, 'From intergovernmental bargaining to deliberative processes: The constitutionalisation of comitology' (1997) 3 *European Law Journal* 273
Kaunert, C, '"Without the Power of Purse or Sword": The European Arrest Warrant and the Role of the Commission' (2007) 29 *Journal of European Integration* 387
König, F and Trauner, F, 'From Trevi to Europol: Germany's role in the integration of EU police cooperation' (2021) 43 *Journal of European Integration* 175
Korsell, L and Larsson, P, 'Crime and Justice in Scandinavia' (2011) 40 *Crime and Justice* 519
Kumm, M, 'Constitutionalizing Subsidiarity in Integrated Markets: The Case of Tobacco Regulation in the European Union' (2006) 12 *European Law Journal* 503
Lang, R, 'The EU's New Victims' Rights Directive: Can Minimum Harmonization Work for a Concept like Vulnerability?' (2013) 22 *Nottingham Law Journal* 90
Langbein, JH, 'Controlling Prosecutorial Discretion in Germany' (1973) 41 *University of Chicago Law Review* 453
Lavenex, S, 'Mutual recognition and the monopoly of force: limits of the single market analogy'(2007) 14 *Journal of European Public Policy* 762
Le Boeuf, J, 'The Economics of Federalism and the Proper Scope of the Federal Commerce Power' (1994) 31 *San Diego Law Review* 555
Lee, FJ, 'Global Institutional Choice' (2010) 85 *New York University Law Review* 328
Leonard, S and Kaunert, C, 'The Development of Europol's External Relations: Towards Supranationalism?' (2021) 28 *Maastricht Journal of European and Comparative Law* 229
Lenaerts, K, 'Constitutionalism and the Many Faces of Federalism' (1990) 38 *American Journal of Comparative Law* 205
—— 'The Principle of Subsidiarity and the Environment in the European Union: Keeping the Balance of Federalism' (1994) 17 *Fordham International Law Journal* 846
Lingenfelter, K and Miettinen, S, 'Obstacles to supranational operational police powers in the European union: Europol reform and the construction of trust between national police authorities' (2021) 28 *Maastricht Journal of European and Comparative Law* 182
Lööf, R, 'Shooting from the Hip – Proposed Minimum Rights in Criminal Proceedings' (2006) 12 *European Law Journal* 421
MacCormick, N, 'Law as institutional fact' (1974) 90 *Law Quarterly Review* 102
Maduro, M, 'Reforming the Market or the State? Article 30 and the European Constitution: Economic Freedom and Political Rights' (1997) 3 *European Law Journal*

Majone, G, 'Europe's "Democratic Deficit": The Question of Standards' (1998) 4 *European Law Journal* 5
Mancano, L, 'A Theory of Justice? Securing the Normative Foundations of EU Criminal Law through an Integrated Approach to Independence' (2021) 27 *European Law Journal* 477
Mangenot, M, 'Jeux Européens et Innovation Institutionnelle: Les Logiques de Création d'Eurojust' (2006) 62 *Cultures et Conflits* 43
Marquardt, PD, 'Subsidiarity and Soverignty in the European Union' (1994) 18 *Fordham International Law Journal* 616
Marshall, WP, 'Federalization: A Critical Overview' (1995) 44 *De Paul Law Review* 719
Marshall, SS and Duff, RR, 'Criminalization and sharing wrongs' (1998) 11 *Canadian Journal of Law and Jurisprudence* 7
Melander, S, 'Ultima Ratio in European Criminal Law' (2013) 3 *European Criminal Law Review* 45
Miner, RJ, 'Federal Courts, Federal Crimes, and Federalism (1987) 10 *Harvard Journal of Law and Public Policy* 126
Mitsilegas, V, 'The Constitutional Implications of Mutual Recognition in Criminal Matters in the EU' (2006) 43 *Common Market Law Review* 1277
—— 'The Limits of Mutual Trust in Europe's Area of Freedom, Security and Justice: From Automatic Inter-State Cooperation to the Slow Emergence of the Individual' (2012) 31 *Yearbook of European Law* 319
—— 'The Symbiotic Relationship between Mutual Trust and Fundamental Rights in Europe's Area of Criminal Justice' (2015) 6 *New Journal of European Criminal Law* 457
—— 'Autonomous Concepts, Diversity Management and Mutual Trust in Europe's Area of Criminal Justice' (2020) 57 *Common Market Law Review* 45
—— 'European prosecution between cooperation and integration: The European Public Prosecutor's Office and the rule of law' (2021) 28 *Maastricht Journal of European and Comparative Law* 245
Monar, J, 'The EU's Role in the Fight Against Racism and Xenophobia: Evaluation and Prospects After Amsterdam and Tampere' (2000) 22 *Liverpool Law Review* 7
—— 'Eurojust and the European Public Prosecutor Perspective: From Cooperation to Integration in EU Criminal Justice?' (2013) 14 *Perspectives on European Politics and Society* 339
—— 'Reflections on the place of criminal law in the European construction' (2021) 27 *European Law Journal* 356
Oates, WE, 'An Essay on Fiscal Federalism' (1999) 37 *Journal of Economic Literature* 1120
Occhipinti, JD, 'Still Moving Toward a European FBI? Re-Examining the Politics of EU Police Cooperation' (2015) 30 *Intelligence and National Security* 234
Ogus, A, 'Competition between National Legal Systems: A Contribution of Economic Analysis to Comparative Law' (1999) 48 *The International and Comparative Law Quarterly* 405
Ouwerkerk, J, 'The Potential of Mutual Recognition as Limit to the Exercise of EU Criminalisation Powers' (2017) 7 *European Criminal Law Review* 5
—— 'Old Wine in a New Bottle: Shaping the Foundations of EU Criminal Law Through the Concept of Legal Interests (Rechtsgüter)' (2021) 27 *European Law Journal* 426
Palmer, SR and Linthicum, BM, 'The Statewide Prosecutor: A New Weapon Against Organized Crime' (1985) 13 *Florida State University Law Review* 653
Pandit, N, 'Policing the EU's External Border: Legitimacy and Accountability under Scrutiny' (2012) 13 *ERA Forum* 403
Paternoster, R, 'How Much Do We Really Know about Criminal Deterrence?' (2010) 100 *Journal of Criminal Law and Criminology* 765
Peers, S, 'Mutual Recognition and Criminal Law in the European Union: Has the Council Got it Wrong?' (2004) 41 *Common Market Law Review* 5
—— 'Mission Accomplished? EU Justice and Home Affairs Law after the Treaty of Lisbon' (2011) 48 *Common Market Law Review* 661
Peršak, N, 'Principles of EU criminalisation and their varied normative strength: Harm and effectiveness' (2021) 27 *European Law Journal* 463

Petit Leclair, S, 'Justice et Sécurité en Europe: Eurojust ou la Création d'un Parquet Européen' (2012) 20 *Cahiers de la sécurité* 38
Pollack, M, 'Creeping Competence: The Expanding Agenda of the European Community' (1994) 14 *Journal of Public Policy* 95
Radaelli, CM, 'The Puzzle of Regulatory Competition' (2004) 24 *Journal of Public Policy* 1
Revesz, R, 'Rehabilitating Interstate Competition: Rethinking the "Race to the Bottom" Rationale for Federal Environmental Regulation' (1992) 67 *New York University Law Review* 1210
Rigotti, C and McGlynn, C, 'Towards an EU criminal law on violence against women: The ambitions and limitations of the Commission's proposal to criminalise image-based sexual abuse' (2022) 13 *New Journal of European Criminal Law* 452
Robinson, PH and Darley, JM, 'Does Criminal Law Deter? A Behavioural Science Investigation' (2004) 24 *Oxford Journal of Legal Studies* 173
Romeu, R, 'Law and Politics in the Application of EC Law: Spanish Courts and the ECJ 1986–2000' (2006) 43 *Common Market Law Review* 395
Schimmelfennig, F, 'What's the News in "New Intergovernmentalism"? A Critique of Bickerton, Hodson and Puetter' (2015) 53 *Journal of Common Market Studies* 723
Scholz, JT and Pinney, N, 'Duty, Fear, and Tax Compliance: The Heuristic Basis of Citizenship Behavior' (1995) 39 *American Journal of Political Science* 490
Schuck, PH, 'Lawyers and Policymakers in Government' (1998) 61 *Law and Contemporary Problems* 7
Sevenster, HG, 'Criminal Law and EC Law' (1992) 29 *Common Market Law Review* 29
Shapiro, M, 'The Giving Reasons Requirement' (1992) *University of Chicago Legal Forum* 179
Somek, A, 'The Argument From Transnational Effects I: Representing Outsiders Through Freedom of Movement' (2010) 16 *European Law Journal* 315
Spaventa, E, 'Should we "harmonize" fundamental rights in the EU? Some reflections about minimum standards and fundamental rights protection in the EU composite constitutional system' (2018) 55 *Common Market Law Review* 997
Special Issue (1998) *Law and Contemporary Problems* 61(1): 'Government Lawyering'
Stacy, T and Dayton, K, 'The Underfederalization of Crime' (1997) 6 *Cornell Journal of Law & Public Policy* 247
Stewart, RB, 'Environmental Law in the United States and the European Community: Spillovers, Cooperation, Rivalry, Institutions' (1992) *University of Chicago Legal Forum* 41
Stone Sweet, A and Sandholtz, W, 'European integration and supranational governance' (1997) 4 *Journal of European Public Policy* 297
Suominen, A, 'The Past, Present and the Future of Eurojust' (2008) 15 *Maastricht Journal of European and Comparative Law* 217
Sverdrup, U, 'Compliance and Conflict Management in the European Union: Nordic Exceptionalism' (2004) 27 *Scandinavian Political Studies* 23
Swaine, ET, 'Subsidiarity and Self-Interest: Federalism at the European Court of Justice' (2000) 41 *Harvard International Law Journal* 1
Teichman, D, 'The Market for Criminal Justice: Federalism, Crime Control, and Jurisdictional Competition' (2005) 103 *Michigan Law Review* 1831
—— with T Broude, 'Outsourcing and insourcing crime: The political economy of globalized criminal activity' (2009) 62 *Vanderbilt Law Review* 795
The Federalist Number 10, [22 November] 1787, Founders Online, National Archives: https://founders.archives.gov/documents/Madison/01-10-02-0178
Tiebout, C, 'A Pure Theory of Local Expenditures' (1956) 64 *Journal of Political Economy* 416
Trauner, F and Ripoll Servent, A, 'The Communitarization of the Area of Freedom, Security and Justice: Why Institutional Change does not Translate into Policy Change' (2016) 54 *Journal of Common Market Studies* 1417
Turner, J, 'The Expressive Dimension of EU Criminal Law' (2012) 60 *The American Journal of Comparative Law* 555
Tyler, TR, 'Public Trust and Confidence in Legal Authorities: What Do Majority and Minority Group Members Want from the Law and Legal Institutions?' (2001) 19 *Behavioural Science and Law* 215

Van den Bergh, R, 'The subsidiarity principle in European Community law: some insights from law and economics' (1994) 1 *Maastricht Journal of European and Comparative Law* 337
Verbruggen, F, 'Euro-Cops? Just say maybe. European lessons from the 1993 reshuffle of US drug enforcement' (1995) 3 *European Journal of Crime, Criminal Law and Criminal Justice* 150
Vermeulen, G, 'A European Judicial Network Linked to Europol? In Search of a Model for Structuring Trans-National Criminal Investigations in the EU' (1997) 4 *Maastricht Journal of European and Comparative Law* 359
Vogel, D, 'Trading up and governing across: transnational governance and environmental protection' (1997) 4 *Journal of European Public Policy* 556
Väyrynen, P, 'Normative Explanation And Justification' (2021) 55 *Noûs* 3
Vick, DW, 'Interdisciplinary and the Discipline of Law' (2004) 31 *Journal of Law and Society* 163
Wagner, W, 'Guarding the Guards. The European Convention and the communitization of police co-operation' (2006) 13 *Journal of European Public Policy* 1230
Weatherill, S, 'Competence creep and competence control' (2004) 23 *Yearbook of European Law* 1
Weyembergh, A, 'The Functions of Approximation of Penal Legislation within the European Union' (2005) 12 *Maastricht Journal of European and Comparative Law* 149
—— 'Approximation of criminal laws, the Constitutional Treaty and the Hague Programme' (2005) 42 *Common Market Law Review* 1567
—— 'The Development of Eurojust: Potential and Limitations of Article 85 of the TFEU' (2011) 2 *New Journal of European Criminal Law* 75
Whelan, P, 'A Principled Argument for Personal Criminal Sanctions as Punishment under EC Cartel Law' (2007) *The Competition Law Review* 7
Wieczorek, I, 'A Needed Balance Between Security, Liberty and Justice. Positive Signals Arrive From the Field of Victims' Rights' (2012) 2 *European Criminal Law Review* 141
—— 'The Emerging Role of the EU as a Primary Normative Actor in the EU Area of Criminal Justice' (2021) 27 *European Law Journal* 378
Wischmeyer, T, 'Generating trust through law? Judicial cooperation in the European Union and the "principle of mutual trust"' (2016) 17 *German Law Journal* 339
Wyatt, D, 'Could a "Yellow Card" for National Parliaments Strengthen Judicial as well as Political Policing of Subsidiarity?' (2006) 2 *Croatian Yearbook of European Law & Policy* 1
Xanthoupolou, E, 'Mutual Trust and Rights in the Criminal and Asylum Law: Three Phases of Evolution and the Uncharted Territory Beyond Blind Trust' (2018) 55 *Common Market Law Review* 489
Zimring, FE and Hawkins, G, 'Toward a principled basis for federal criminal legislation' (1996) 543 *The Annals of the American Academy of Political and Social Science* 15
Öberg, J, 'Union Regulatory Criminal Law Competence after Lisbon Treaty' (2011) 19 *European Journal of Crime, Criminal Law and Criminal Justice* 289
—— 'Criminal Sanctions in the Field of EU Environmental Law' 2 (2011) *New Journal of European Criminal Law* 402
—— 'Is it "Essential" to Imprison Insider Dealers to Enforce Insider Dealing Laws?' (2014) 14 *Journal of Corporate Law Studies* 111
—— 'Subsidiarity and EU Procedural Criminal Law' (2015) 5 *European Criminal Law Review* 19
—— 'Subsidiarity as a Limit to the Exercise of EU Competences' (2017) 36 *Yearbook of European Law* 391
—— 'The Legal Basis for EU Criminal Law Legislation – A Question of Federalism?' (2018) 43 *European Law Review* 366
—— 'National Parliaments and Political Control of EU Competences – A Sufficient Safeguard of Federalism?' (2018) 24 *European Public Law* 695
—— 'Trust in the Law? Mutual Recognition as a Justification to Domestic Criminal Procedure' (2020) 16 *European Constitutional Law Review* 33
—— 'Guest Editorial: EU Agencies in Transnational Criminal Enforcement: From a Coordinated Approach to an Integrated EU Criminal Justice' (2021) 28 *Maastricht Journal of European and Comparative Law* 155

—— 'The European Public Prosecutor: Quintessential Supranational Criminal Law?' (2021) 28 *Maastricht Journal of European and Comparative Law* 164
—— 'Exit, Voice and Consensus – A Legal and Political Analysis of the Emergency Brake in EU Criminal Policy' (2021) 46 *European Law Review* 506
—— 'Normative Justifications of EU Criminal Law: European Public Goods and Transnational Interests' (2021) 27 *European Law Journal* 408

Reports and miscellaneous

Albers, P and others, 'Final Report – Towards a common evaluation framework to assess mutual trust in the field of EU judicial cooperation in criminal matters', March 2011: www.government.nl/documents/reports/2013/09/27/final-report-towards-a-common-evaluation-framework-to-assess-mutual-trust-in-the-field-of-eu-judicial-cooperation-in-criminal-m
Amnesty International, 'Toxic Twitter – Triggers of violence and abuse against women on twitter', ch 2: www.amnesty.org/en/latest/news/2018/03/online-violence-against-women-chapter-2-3/#topanchor
Baker, S, Perry, D and Doobay, A, 'A Review of the United Kingdom's Extradition Arrangements', for UK Government, 4 October 2011, evidence by Lord Justice Thomas
Bayer, J and Bard, P, 'Hate speech and hate crime in the EU and the evaluation of online content regulation approaches', Study commissioned by the European Parliament's Policy Department for Citizens' Rights and Constitutional Affairs, July 2020: www.europarl.europa.eu/RegData/etudes/STUD/2020/655135/IPOL_STU(2020)655135_EN.pdf
Bunyan, T, 'Trevi, Europol and the European state', Statewatch: www.statewatch.org/media/documents/news/handbook-trevi.pdf
California Office of the Attorney General, 'About the Office of the Attorney General': https://oag.ca.gov/office#:~:text=The%20Attorney%20General%20and%20Department,safety%20and%20liberty%20for%20everyone
Committee to Protect Journalists, CPJ leads call to Maltese Attorney General asking for Europol support for murdered journalist Daphne Caruana Galizia, 5 May 2020: https://cpj.org/2020/05/malta-attorney-general-europol-murdered-daphne-caruana-galizia/
Council of Europe, European Commission Against Racism and Intolerance, 'Hate speech and violence': www.coe.int/en/web/european-commission-against-racism-and-intolerance/hate-speech-and-violence
Council of Europe, Project Cybercrime @Octopus, 22 April 2019: https://rm.coe.int/summary-of-the-cybercrime-octopus/1680968ab0
Council of Europe, 'Models of Governance of Online Hate Speech', 2020: https://rm.coe.int/models-of-governance-of-online-hate-speech/16809e671d
European Commission, 'Study on Cross Border Legal Aid Project', JLS/2008/E4/009, Final Report
European Commission, 'Media pluralism and democracy – Special Eurobarometer 452', last update 9 March 2021: https://wayback.archive-it.org/12090/20210728081045/https:/digital-strategy.ec.europa.eu/en/library/media-pluralism-and-democracy-special-eurobarometer-452
European Commission, Directorate-General for Justice and Consumers, Ypma, P, Drevon, C, Fulcher, C and others, 'Study to support the preparation of the European Commission's initiative to extend the list of EU crimes in Article 83 of the Treaty on the Functioning of the EU to hate speech and hate crime: final report' (Luxembourg: Publications Office of the European Union, 2021): https://op.europa.eu/en/publication-detail/-/publication/f866de4e-57de-11ec-91ac-01aa75ed71a1/language-en
European Commission, Directorate-General for Justice and Consumers, Ypma, P, Drevon, C, Fulcher, C and others, 'European Commission, Study to support the preparation of the European Commission's initiative to extend the list of EU crimes in Article 83 of the Treaty on the Functioning of the EU to hate speech and hate crime Annex VII – Analysis and synthesis of all the information and quantitative and qualitative data collected: https://op.europa.eu/en/publication-detail/-/publication/8ef232d3-57e4-11ec-91ac-01aa75ed71a1/language-en

European Commission, Directorate-General for Justice and Consumers, Ypma, P, Drevon, C, Fulcher, C and others, 'European Commission, Study to support the preparation of the European Commission's initiative to extend the list of EU crimes in Article 83 of the Treaty on the Functioning of the EU to hate speech and hate crime Annex VI – Synopsis Report of the consultation activities': https://op.europa.eu/en/publication-detail/-/publication/1473b895-57e8-11ec-91ac-01aa75ed71a1/language-en

European Commission, Directorate-General for Justice and Consumers, Ypma, P, Drevon, C, Fulcher, C and others, 'European Commission, Study to support the preparation of the European Commission's initiative to extend the list of EU crimes in Article 83 of the Treaty on the Functioning of the EU to hate speech and hate crime, Annex 1 – Literature List': https://op.europa.eu/en/publication-detail/-/publication/4a18bedb-57dc-11ec-91ac-01aa75ed71a1/language-en

European Commission, Sanctions Map, last updated 15/09/2023: https://sanctionsmap.eu/#/main

European Commission, 'Overview of sanctions and related resources', last update 7 September 2023: https://finance.ec.europa.eu/eu-and-world/sanctions-restrictive-measures/overview-sanctions-and-related-tools_en#what-are-sanctions-restrictives-measures

European Union Agency for Fundamental Rights, 'Equal protection for all victims of hate crime. The case of people with disabilities' 30 March 2015: https://fra.europa.eu/en/publication/2015/equal-protection-all-victims-hate-crime-case-people-disabilities

European Union Agency for Fundamental Rights, 'Violence against women: an EU-wide survey. Main results report', Strasbourg, 3.3.2014: https://fra.europa.eu/en/publication/2014/violence-against-women-eu-wide-survey-main-results-report#

European Union Agency for Fundamental Rights, 'EU-MIDIS II: Second European Union Minorities and Discrimination Survey' (2017: https://fra.europa.eu/sites/default/files/fra_uploads/fra-2017-eu-midis-ii-main-results_en.pdf

European Union Agency for Fundamental Rights, Survey, 'Experiences and perceptions of antisemitism – Second survey on discrimination and hate crime against Jews in the EU', 10 December 2018: https://fra.europa.eu/en/publication/2018/experiences-and-perceptions-antisemitism-second-survey-discrimination-and-hate

European Union Agency for Fundamental Rights, Survey 'Roma and Travellers in Six Countries', 2020: https://fra.europa.eu/sites/default/files/fra_uploads/fra-2020-roma-travellers-six-countries_en.pdf

European Union Agency for Fundamental Rights, 'Crime, Safety and Victims' Rights', 19 February 2021: https://fra.europa.eu/en/publication/2021/fundamental-rights-survey-crime

European Network of Councils for the Judiciary, 'Mutual Confidence 2009-2010 – Report and Recommendations' (2010): www.encj.eu/images/stories/pdf/mutualconfidence/mc2009-2010en.pdf

European Parliament, 'Statement of Revenue and Expenditure of the European Agency for Law Enforcement Cooperation for the Financial Year 2022, Amending Budget No 2' (2022): </a>www.europol.europa.eu/sites/default/files/documents/42-EUROPOL-AB2_2022%20%283.%20Preliminary%20for%20Europol%20website%29.pdf

European Institute for Gender Equality (EIGE), 'The costs of gender-based violence in the EU' (Luxembourg: Publications Office of the European Union, 2021): https://eige.europa.eu/gender-based-violence/costs-of-gender-based-violence?language_content_entity=en

European Parliamentary Research Service, W van Ballegooij and J Moxom, 'Cost of Non-Europe Report – Equality and the Fight against Racism and Xenophobia', Brussels, European Parliament, 2018: www.europarl.europa.eu/RegData/etudes/STUD/2018/615660/EPRS_STU(2018)615660_EN.pdf

European Parliamentary Research Service, N Lomba, C Navarra and M Fernandes, 'Combating Gender-based Violence: Cyber Violence: European added value assessment', Brussels: European Parliament, March 2021: www.europarl.europa.eu/RegData/etudes/STUD/2021/662621/EPRS_STU(2021)662621_EN.pdf, accessed 28 September 2023

European Parliamentary Research Service, N Lomba, C Navarra, M García Muñoz and M Fernandes, 'Gender-based violence as a new area of crime listed in Article 83(1) TFEU, European added value assessment', 14 June 2021, Brussels, European Union: www.europarl.europa.eu/thinktank/en/document/EPRS_STU(2021)662640

Eurojust, Genocide Network, 'Prosecution of sanctions (restrictive measures) violations in national jurisdictions: a comparative analysis', The Hague, December 2021, Annex: www.eurojust.europa.eu/sites/default/files/assets/genocide_network_report_on_prosecution_of_s anctions_restrictive_measures_violations_23_11_2021.pdf

Europol, *2017 EU Serious and Organised Threat Assessment*, 28 February 2017: www.europol.europa.eu/publications-events/main-reports/european-union-serious-and-organised-crime-threat-assessment-2017#downloads

Europol, '2019 Consolidated Annual Activity Report', 9.6.2020: www.europol.europa.eu/publications-events/publications/consolidated-annual-activity-reports-caar

Europol, 'Pandemic profiteering: how criminals exploit the COVID-19 crisis', 27 March 2020: www.europol.europa.eu/publications-events/publications/pandemic-profiteering-how-criminals-exploit-covid-19-crisis

Europol, 'Beyond the pandemic – How COVID-19 will shape the serious and organised crime landscape in the EU', 30 April 2020: www.europol.europa.eu/publications-events/publications/beyond-pandemic-how-covid-19-will-shape-serious-and-organised-crime-landscape-in-eu

Guild, E and Carrera, S, 'No Constitutional Treaty? Implications for the Area of Freedom, Security and Justice' (CEPS, 26 August 2009) 2: www.ceps.eu/ceps-publications/no-constitutional-treaty-implications-area-freedom-security-and-justice/

Hayes, B (Statewatch analysis), 'The Future of Europol – more powers, less regulation, precious little debate', August 2016: www.statewatch.org/media/documents/news/2006/oct/future-of-europol-analysis.pdf

House of Lords, Select Committee on European Union, 23rd Report, *Judicial cooperation in the EU: the role of Eurojust*, HL Paper 139 (London: Stationery Office Limited, 2004)

House of Lords' European Union Committee, *Report on Procedural Rights in Criminal Proceedings – Report with Evidence*, 1st Report of Session 2004–05, HL Paper 28 (London: Stationery Office Limited, 2005)

House of Lords' European Union Committee, *Breaking the Deadlock: What Future for EU Procedural Rights*? 2nd Report of Session 2006–07 (London: Stationery Office Limited, 2007), HL Paper 20

House of Lords' European Union Committee, *The Treaty of Lisbon: an impact assessment*, 10th Report of Session 2007–08, HL Paper 62-II (London: Stationery Office Limited, 2008) Memorandum by Dr Valsamis Mitsilegas

House of Lords' European Union Committee, *The European Union's Policy on Criminal Procedure*, 30th Report of Session 2010–12, HL Paper 288 (London: Stationery Office Limited, 2012)

House of Lords' European Union Committee, *Brexit: Future UK-EU Security and Police Cooperation*, 7th Report (London: Stationery Office Limited, 2017) session 2016–17, HL Paper 77, Written evidence from the Crown Office and Procurator Fiscal Service (FSP0003)

Inter-Parliamentary Union (IPU) and Parliamentary Assembly of the Council of Europe (PACE), 'Sexism, harassment and violence against women in parliaments in Europe', Issues Brief October 2018: www.ipu.org/resources/publications/issue-briefs/2018-10/sexism-harassment-and-violence-against-women-in-parliaments-in-europe

Iowa Department of Justice, Office of the Attorney General, Statewide prosecutions: www.iowaattorneygeneral.gov/about-us/divisions/area-prosecutions

Jeney, P, 'The Future of Eurojust', Study for the LIBE Committee of the European Parliament, 2012

Judicial Conference of the United States, Long Range Plan for the Federal Courts 21 (1995)

JUSTICE, 'European Arrest Warrants – ensuring an effective defence' (2012): https://www.ecba.org/extdocserv/projects/EAW/JUSTICE_EAW.pdf

Massachusetts Attorney General, 'About the Office': www.mass.gov/orgs/office-of-the-attorney-general

Mitsilegas, V and Vavoula, N, 'Strengthening Europol's Mandate: A Legal Assessment of the Commission's Proposal to Amend the Europol Regulation', Study for the LIBE Committee of the European Parliament, May 2021

Peers, S, 'EU foreign policy sanctions: extending and using EU criminal law powers to enforce them', 2 December 2022, *EU Law Analysis:* http://eulawanalysis.blogspot.com/2022/12/eu-foreign-policy-sanctions-extending.html

PRISM, 'Hate Crime and Hate Speech in Europe: Comprehensive Analysis of International Law Principles, EU-wide Study and National Assessments': https://sosracismo.eu/wp-content/uploads/2016/07/Hate-Crime-and-Hate-Speech-in-Europe.-Comprehensive-Analysis-of-International-Law-Principles-EU-wide-Study-and-National-Assessments.pdf

Renew Position Paper, 'From Europol Towards a European FBI: Boosting the Union's Law Enforcement Competences', 3 December 2020: www.statewatch.org/media/1583/eu-europol-renew-europe-position-paper-4-12-20.pdf

Select Committee on the European Union Home Affairs Sub-Committee, Corrected oral evidence: *Brexit: Future UK-EU Security and Policing Co-operation*, Wednesday 12 October 2016: https://committees.parliament.uk/oralevidence/6071/html/

SELMA Hacking Hate, 'Hacking Online Hate: Building an Evidence Base for Educators', 2019: https://hackinghate.eu/assets/documents/hacking-online-hate-research-report-1.pdf

Solumn, L, 'Interdisciplinarity, Multidisciplinarity, and the Future of the Legal Academy' *Legal Theory Blog* (2008)

Statens Offentliga Utredningar, Suveränitet och demokrati SOU 1994:12

United Nations, 'Plan of Action for Religious Leaders and Actors to Prevent Incitement to Violence that Could Lead to Atrocity Crimes': www.un.org/en/genocideprevention/documents/publications-and-resources/Plan_of_Action_Religious-rev5.pdf

Van Outrive, L, 'Report on the setting up of Europol' (PE 202.364/fin. / PE/92/0382), Committee on Civil Liberties and Internal Affairs (ed) (Luxembourg: European Parliament, 1992)

Vernimmen-Van Tiggelen, G and Surano, L, 'Analysis of the Future of Mutual Recognition in Criminal Matters in the European Union', Call for tenders JLS/D3/2007/03 European Commission – 20 November 2008

Wahl, T and others, *Criminal Procedural Laws across the European Union – A Comparative Analysis of Selected Main Differences and the Impact They Have over the Development of EU Legislation, Annex I, Country Report* (August 2018)

Weyembergh, A and Brière, C, 'Towards a European Public Prosecutor', Policy paper for the European Parliament, LIBE Committee, November 2016

World Health Organization, 'Elder Abuse', 2021: www.who.int/news-room/fact-sheets/detail/abuse-of-older-people

World Trade Organization (WTO) Secretariat, 'World Trade Report 2004 – Exploring the linkage between the domestic policy environment and international trade': www.wto.org/english/res_e/booksp_e/anrep_e/wtr04_2c_e.pdf

Zuleeg, F, 'The rationale for EU action: What are European Public Goods?', paper prepared for the BEPA Workshop on 'The political economy of EU public finances: designing governance for change', 5 February 2009: www.researchgate.net/publication/237445090_The_Rationale_for_EU_Action_What_are_European_Public_Goods

Working papers

Pech, L, 'The Law of Holocaust Denial in Europe: Towards a (Qualified) ETJ-wide Criminal Prohibition', Jean Monnet Working Paper 10/09: https://jeanmonnetprogram.org/wp-content/uploads/2014/12/091001.pdf

Walker, N, 'The European Public Good and European Public Goods', 15 October 2020, Edinburgh School of Law Research Paper No 2020/20: https://ssrn.com/abstract=3712265

Newspaper articles

Monroy, M, 'Negotiations on the Europol Regulation: Will there be a "European FBI" by the end of the year?', 27/10/2021: https://digit.site36.net/2021/10/27/negotiations-on-the-europol-regulation-will-there-be-a-european-fbi-by-the-end-of-the-year/

Pistorius, B, 'Europe needs its own FBI', *Financial Times*, 29 September 2020: www.ft.com/content/4b3b8c25-9828-4c9e-98f0-b6617bda285b

Speeches and lectures

Saccone, A, 'Combating International Crime in an Enlarging European Union: What is the Role of Europol?', Lecture in the International Seminar for Experts 'Combating Terrorism and International Organised Crime in the European Union – The Hague Programme and the Role of Europol and Eurojust', organised by the Cicero Foundation in the series 'Great Debates', Paris, 14 and 15 December 2006

von der Leyen, U, 'State of the Union 2020, Letter of Intent', Brussels, 16 September 2020: https://state-of-the-union.ec.europa.eu/state-union-2020_en

Öberg, J, ' Gender-based violence as a crime under Article 83(1) TFEU', Public Exchange of View of the European Parliament LIBE and FEMM committees on a 'Proposal for a Council decision to add gender-based violence in the areas of crime listed in Article 83 TFEU': www.europarl.europa.eu/committees/sv/exchange-of-views-on-adding-gender-based/product-details/20210527EOT05581

INDEX

www.ingramcontent.com/pod-product-compliance
Ingram Content Group UK Ltd.
Pitfield, Milton Keynes, MK11 3LW, UK
UKHW020819290926
15470UKWH00003B/1254

9 781509 962334